Dislodging Multinationals

A volume in the series

Cornell Studies in Political Economy

EDITED BY PETER J. KATZENSTEIN

A full list of titles in the series appears at the end of the book

Dislodging Multinationals

India's Strategy in Comparative Perspective

Dennis J. Encarnation

Cornell University Press

ITHACA AND LONDON

First published 1989 by Cornell University Press.

International Standard Book Number 0-8014-2315-5
Library of Congress Catalog Card Number 89-730
Printed in the United States of America
Librarians: Library of Congress cataloging information
appears on the last page of the book.

The paper in this book is acid-free and meets the guidelines for
permanence and durability of the Committee on Production Guidelines
for Book Longevity of the Council on Library Resources.

To my parents and
to Jeanie

Contents

Figures and Tables

FIGURES

TABLES

Acknowledgments

Why, over time, have some newly industrializing countries been successful at dislodging multinationals from domestic industries while others have not? This question remains central to our understanding of modern political economy. In my search for an answer, I have followed two parallel tracks: one is theoretical, the other largely empirical. Along the way, I incurred many obligations, especially to those observers who had already analyzed relations among multinationals, the state, and local enterprises in industrializing countries. Their work contains much of value; even so, I have come to differ with both the logic *and* the evidence employed in their interpretations. My own dissent, and its complementary formulation of an alternative perspective, began at Duke University, where Ronald Rogowski introduced me to the theory of rational choice—which then belonged in the arsenal of economists but not of political scientists. To me, Ron convincingly demonstrated that, in its pursuit of analytical rigor, rationalist theory need not serve any single ideology. His lasting influence as a mentor shows itself everywhere in this book.

With theory in hand and hypotheses to test, I embarked during 1977 for a year's research in India. Since then, I have returned annually for shorter stays, and each visit has yielded valuable new interviews with managers in both business and government—informants too numerous to name here. In fact, for many Indian and other foreign managers, a guarantee of anonymity represented the necessary consideration to exchange for their time. Always ready to help in arranging these appointments, and in making my visits both enjoyable and productive, was Vijayan Puliampet—resident director of the Berkeley Professional Studies Program in India. The Berkeley Program itself was an early benefactor of my research, as were the Shell Foundation, the Fulbright Program, and the World Bank. In all, this financial help provided me the necessary time to establish working relationships with several Indian social scientists, among whom S. K. Goyal merits special recognition. My thanks go to him for unselfishly sharing with me the best available data on corporate strategy and government policy in India, and for consistently trying to protect me from errors of interpretation. If these pages compose (as I believe they do) a valuable sourcebook on the first forty years of independent India's political economy, "S. K." deserves credit.

Although my early research on India began at Duke (and continued during a postdoctoral fellowship at Stanford University), nearly all of the work represented in this book must be dated after I joined the faculty of the Harvard Business School, where several colleagues have helped to create a supportive environment. Indeed, Louis T. Wells, Jr., should be credited (or blamed) for actively encouraging me to pursue this line of inquiry. Lou has consistently served as both my sternest critic and my most enthusiastic supporter. Additional help came from my colleagues in the Negotiation Roundtable, especially David A. Lax, whose work has provided fresh analytical insights to complement my interest in rational choice. My analysis has become more comparative since I began working closely with an interdisciplinary group of scholars—led by Thomas K. McCraw—interested in how corporate strategies and government policies vary across industries, change over time, and differ among countries.

My own cross-national perspective has been further clarified by the constructive criticisms of numerous scholars elsewhere within the Harvard community. Here, Stephan Haggard merits special note for his eagerness to share work in progress. Outside Harvard, others have also supplied me with material assistance. In particular, Peter Evans provided extensive advice on how to sharpen both the theoretical argument and the Brazilian comparison; Leroy P. Jones generously granted me unlimited access to his extensive files on Korea. Earlier, the editors of *International Organization*—most notably, Peter J. Katzenstein, aided by Roger M. Haydon—had nudged this project along, partly by introducing me to their helpful readers. Now, they have encouraged publication in the series Cornell Studies in Political Economy. Back in Cambridge, Myron Weiner and the MIT–Harvard Faculty Seminar on South and Southeast Asia have also provided key introductions to scholars of India, who always prove willing to give generously of their time and energy. After receiving all of this assistance, I alone should be held responsible for any remaining errors in this book.

At Harvard, the Business School's Division of Research has supplied ample funds to support my forays into India, Brazil, and Korea, as well as my visits to the head offices of American, European, and Japanese multinationals. The School also employed a small army of research assistants, of whom four deserve separate recognition: Willis Emmons, Sanjeev Mehra, Srinivasa Rangan, and Sushil Vachani. The Division of Research has indulged my ambition to make mountains of data more accessible to readers, through the construction of elaborate graphic illustrations. Weaving these graphics into the narrative proved to be a formidable task, one finally completed with the editorial assistance of Earl Harbert (whose ubiquitous green pen has, in the end, failed to expunge this sentence).

At the beginning of this project, on my first trip to India, I met a barefoot doctor, Jean Clare Smith, who later became my wife. Over the intervening decade, she has not—praise God—researched, typed, or edited this book. Instead, she has kept for us a joint life independent of both our careers. For that, and for much else, I owe her more than I can say.

DENNIS J. ENCARNATION

Tokyo, Japan

Dislodging Multinationals

CHAPTER ONE

Multinationals and Development

In the international political economy, the year 1973 marked a watershed. Buffeted by a fourfold increase in oil prices and by an unexpected volatility in post–Bretton Woods foreign exchange rates, those nations still in communion with the capitalist world order reached a crucial turning point in their relations with multinational corporations. In country after country, national governments and local enterprises, following a long history of engagement in extractive and service industries, threatened finally to dislodge multinational manufacturers as the favored purveyors of access to finance, technology, and markets. From Canada to India, from Mexico to South Korea, 1973 brought new government legislation that codified changes in public policies and in corporate strategies.[1] So pervasive were these results, especially in the newly industrializing countries of Asia and Latin America, that multinationals servicing domestic—as distinct from export—markets often found it difficult to return to their privileged pre-1973 positions. They had been dislodged.

In fact, by successfully dislodging multinationals from growing local markets, government policymakers and corporate managers in newly industrializing countries unwittingly precipitated a global intellectual crisis. Simply put, few observers anticipated such success: most so-called modernization theorists simply had not imagined economic

---

1. United Nations, Centre on Transnational Corporations, *Foreign Investment Policies and Screening and Monitoring Procedures in Selected Developing Countries* (New York, n.d.); U.S. Department of Commerce, International Trade Administration, *Investment Climate Statements: Major Trading and Investing Partners* (Washington, D.C., April 1981), and Domestic and International Business Administration, *Incentives and Performance Requirements for Foreign Direct Investments in Selected Countries* (Washington, D.C., January 1978).

growth in the absence of multinationals and other Western influences;[2] whereas a competing school, the early dependency theorists, did not envision poverty-stricken host countries throwing off the shackles of international capitalism in the absence of violent revolutions.[3] As the received paradigms failed to keep pace with changing realities, a new wave of dependency theorists joined with an emergent faction of bargaining theorists to fill the intellectual vacuum.[4] Their consensus (albeit limited) insisted on at least three sets of conditions—local institutional innovations, competition among multinationals, expansion of host markets—all required to explain the behaviors of those national governments and local enterprises that had acted to dislodge multinational corporations from domestic industries.[5]

Yet these necessary conditions still remained insufficient to ensure that multinationals would, in fact, be dislodged. To the contrary: as the new generation of dependency theorists repeatedly reminded us, several additional factors—technological barriers to entry, domestic political alliances, global economic integration—could severely constrain both local enterprises and the state, thus ensuring multinationals a continuing dominion over host markets.[6] Numerous industry studies supported such claims, and Brazil served as the critical test

2. For the early work of economists concerned with the linkage between domestic and international economies, and with the positive implications of that linkage for development, see Charles P. Kindleberger, *Economic Development* (New York: McGraw-Hill, 1958), esp. pp. 19–20, 295–380; Gerald Meyer and Robert E. Baldwin, *Economic Development: Theory, History, Policy* (New York: Wiley, 1957), esp. pp. 204–69, 398–436.

3. Fernando Henrique Cardoso and Enzo Faletto initiated the formal study of dependency with the publication, in Portuguese and Spanish, of *Dependency and Development in Latin America* in 1969. An expanded and amended English-language translation (Berkeley: University of California Press) appeared in 1979.

4. Peter Evans pioneered this new approach to dependency with his *Dependent Development: The Alliance of Multinationals, State, and Local Capital in Brazil* (Princeton: Princeton University Press, 1979). Earlier, Raymond Vernon had ignited interest in bargaining with his *Sovereignty at Bay: The Multinational Spread of U.S. Enterprises* (New York: Basic Books, 1971).

5. For a comparison of these two perspectives on economic performance, see Joseph M. Grieco, "Foreign Investment and Development: Theories and Evidence," in Theodore H. Moran, ed., *Investing in Development: New Roles for Private Capital?* (Washington, D.C.: Overseas Development Council, 1986), pp. 44–52. Also see Richard E. Caves, *Multinational Enterprise and Economic Analysis* (Cambridge: Cambridge University Press, 1982), esp. pp. 261–76; Thomas J. Biersteker, *Distortion or Development? Contending Perspectives on the Multinational Corporation* (Cambridge: MIT Press, 1978).

6. In addition to Evans, *Dependent Development*, see (in the order of their appearance) Richard Newfarmer, *Transnational Conglomerates and the Economics of Dependent Development* (Greenwich, Conn.: JAI Press, 1980); Gary Gereffi, *The Pharmaceutical Industry and Dependence in the Third World* (Princeton: Princeton University Press, 1983); Douglas C. Bennett and Kenneth E. Sharpe, *Transnational Corporations versus the State: The Political Economy of the Mexican Automobile Industry* (Princeton: Princeton University Press, 1985).

case.[7] Faced with this research, bargaining theorists contended that local institutions had already overcome these constraints in such industries as natural resources and—at least for India (a critical case for them)—technology-intensive manufacturing.[8] Despite their obvious differences in theoretical constructs and empirical tests, however, both schools of thought did have something in common. Neither answered a critical theoretical question: Why, over time, have some host countries been successful at dislodging multinationals from local industries while others have not? This question remains central to my investigation.

To provide my answer, I too turn first to the complex Indian case, which requires some analysis of the changing relations among multinationals, the state, and local enterprises over forty years of Indian political independence. These relations are later compared with events in Brazil and elsewhere. As a way of explaining the variations observed over time, across industries, and among countries, I present in Chapter 1 a causal model that determines the sequence of subsequent chapters: by gaining financial independence and managerial autonomy from foreign enterprises (Chapter 2), Indian enterprises also began to secure technology free of foreign capital (Chapter 3); as a result, they acquired control of markets previously dominated by multinationals and other foreigners (Chapter 4). By dislodging these foreigners from domestic industries, local enterprises and the state in India achieved a level of success unknown to their counterparts in Brazil (Chapter 5). But as we shall see, for this success the Indians paid a relatively high price measured in terms of economic performance.

The findings reported in this book, aside from breaking new empirical ground, have far-reaching implications at the level of theory. Briefly, in contrast to that recent generation of dependency theorists who rely primarily on Brazil and other Latin American countries to verify claims,[9] I find in India that local institutions—public and private—managed to increase dramatically both the available range

7. See Gary Gereffi and Donald Wyman, eds., *Manufactured Miracles: Patterns of Industrialization in Latin America and East Asia* (Princeton: Princeton University Press, forthcoming).

8. For natural resources, see Theodore H. Moran, *Multinational Corporations and the Politics of Dependence: Copper in Chile* (Princeton: Princeton University Press, 1974); for the extension from natural resources to manufacturing, see Joseph M. Grieco, *Between Dependency and Autonomy: India's Experience with the International Computer Industry* (Berkeley: University of California Press, 1984).

9. The new generation of dependency analysis is not limited to Latin America, of course. For applications to Africa, see Thomas Biersteker, *Multinationals, the State and*

of plausible outcomes and the probability of securing their preferred outcome. In India, that is, local enterprises and the state greatly improved their bargaining power relative to multinationals, and also secured access to finance, technology, and markets often controlled by foreigners. Although my refinements do support the claims of bargaining theorists, these scholars should not feel too sanguine. For contrary to their theory—and in partial agreement with that of their dependency critics—multinationals still have proved able to secure mutually advantageous agreements in their bargaining with these local institutions, both at the point of market entry and during later operations. Moreover, contrary to the claims of both the bargaining and the dependency schools, the increased bargaining power of local enterprises and the state does not necessarily improve a nation's economic performance, as my later comparison between India and Brazil makes clear.

A similar conclusion summarizes my findings in a second useful comparison, this time between India and South Korea. Here, my choice of nations has been dictated by the increasing body of scholarship amassed to explain multinational investment among newly industrializing countries, in terms of their development phases and their national policies.[10] That literature advances a central proposition: import-substituting industrialization has created a higher level of dependence on foreign direct investment than have export-oriented development strategies. To support this proposition, scholars have mustered comparisons between Brazil and South Korea, but my alternative comparisons between India and Korea do not agree. Instead, as we shall see, local enterprises and the state in India succeeded in both dislodging multinationals from their existing market positions and simultaneously limiting the market access of new entrants—all at the height of a national drive for import substitution. Yet Korea's relative economic success demands further explanation, because, as I show, it derives in part from Korea's ability to enlist a comparatively greater number of multinationals to that country's export drive.

Control of the Nigerian Economy (Princeton: Princeton University Press, 1987). For applications to Asia, see Folker Froebel et al., *The New International Division of Labour: Structural Unemployment in Industrialised Countries and Industrialisation in Developing Countries* (Cambridge: Cambridge University Press, 1981); Martin Landsberg, "Export-Led Industrialization in the Third World: Manufacturing Imperialism," *Review of Radical Political Economics* 11 (November 1979):50–63.

10. Stephan Haggard, "Foreign Direct Investment and the Question of Dependency," chap. 8 in "Pathways from the Periphery" unpublished manuscript, Center for International Affairs, Harvard University, 1988, and "The Newly Industrializing Countries in the International System," *World Politics* 38 (1986):343–70.

Within India itself, South Korea's success has also prompted an ongoing debate over national economic performance. Here again, I offer fresh insights, since much of that debate has dismissed multinationals as "unimportant" to India's economic performance—even while conceding (in the words of one of the principal protagonists) that "the fastest growing business groups," making the greatest contribution to India's industrial growth, "have also been the quickest in taking advantage of the recent easing of restrictions on foreign collaborations and in forging links with transnational corporations."[11] Indeed, my research and its results speak to that same concession. So cavalier a dismissal of multinationals demands explanation of the condition it describes: by the 1980s India had dislodged multinationals from domestic industries they had previously dominated, as the nation achieved an uncommon level of bargaining success.

INDIA AND BRAZIL COMPARED

To measure India's success, let us examine the market shares of multinationals—a key dependent variable—as those shares differ among countries, vary across industries, and change over time. To begin, let us compare the relative industry positions of the three hundred largest companies in Brazil and India at two points in time. Here, at least since the early 1970s (and continuing into the 1980s), we see that multinationals consistently held a smaller share of the local market in India than they did in Brazil.

Consider the early 1970s. By then, multinationals controlled over one-half of the Brazilian market for chemicals, machinery, and transport equipment. Not so in India, where local enterprises in both the public and private sectors controlled more than one-half of the large producers in these industries. Only in rubber did multinationals occupy a slightly larger position in India than in Brazil. Rather, the market shares of multinationals in a wide range of Brazilian industries—paper, cement, textiles, nonelectrical machinery, transport equipment—were at least twice as large as the market shares of multinationals operating in India. Thus, by the early 1970s Indian enterprises had challenged foreign companies in just those industries dominated in Brazil by multinationals, as we see in Figure 1-1.

Over the next decade Indian enterprises continued to dislodge multinationals from domestic industries, and so did local enterprises

11. Pranab Bardhan, *The Political Economy of Development in India* (Oxford: Blackwell, 1984), pp. 42–43.

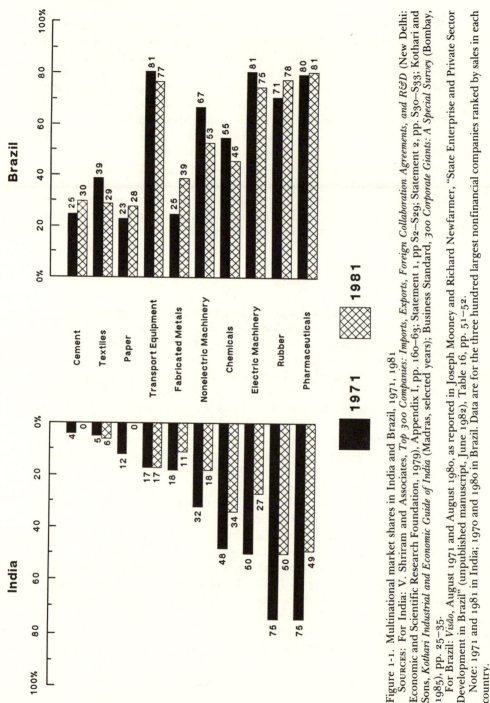

Figure 1-1. Multinational market shares in India and Brazil, 1971, 1981

SOURCES: For India: V. Shriram and Associates, *Top 300 Companies: Imports, Exports, Foreign Collaboration Agreements, and R&D* (New Delhi: Economic and Scientific Research Foundation, 1979). Appendix I, pp. 160–63; Statement 1, pp. S2–S29; Statement 2, pp. S30–S33; Kothari and Sons, *Kothari Industrial and Economic Guide of India* (Madras, selected years); Business Standard, *300 Corporate Giants: A Special Survey* (Bombay, 1985), pp. 25–35.

For Brazil: *Visão*, August 1971 and August 1980, as reported in Joseph Mooney and Richard Newfarmer, "State Enterprise and Private Sector Development in Brazil" (unpublished manuscript, June 1982), Table 16, pp. 51–52.

Note: 1971 and 1981 in India; 1970 and 1980 in Brazil. Data are for the three hundred largest nonfinancial companies ranked by sales in each country.

in Brazil. But only in India did multinationals consistently lose (or barely maintain) their relative position. In fact, in a few industries— cement, paper, fabricated metals, rubber—multinationals lost market share in India as they gained share in Brazil. Even when multinationals lost share in both countries, as in nonelectrical machinery, those losses still proved insufficient in Brazil to dislodge multinationals from their continued control over an industry now firmly in the hands of local enterprises in India. A similar conclusion emerges when, on the other hand, multinationals in the two countries actually retained market shares. In transport equipment, for example, a lack of any change in relative shares left multinationals in control of the Brazilian market but still excluded them from the Indian market. Thus, the 1980s amplified a trend evident a decade earlier, as multinationals continued to hold even smaller market shares in India than they did in Brazil.

Rarely did multinationals suffer greater relative losses in Brazil than they did in India. For one mature industry, textiles, further losses were no longer possible in India, since local enterprises already monopolized the domestic market. During the 1970s Indian enterprises also scored significant gains in more technology-intensive industries—especially in pharmaceuticals, a sector often cited by the new generation of dependency theorists to support their claims.[12] As predicted, multinationals monopolized the Brazilian pharmaceutical market well into the 1980s. Not so in India, however, where by 1980 local enterprises had finally reversed the domination of the pharmaceutical industry by multinationals. In pharmaceuticals, as in textiles, Indian private and public enterprises had gained far greater access to finance, technology, and (then) markets, dislodging multinationals along the way.

FINANCE, TECHNOLOGY, MARKETS

To explain why one country has been able to dislodge multinationals from industry after industry while another has not, both bargaining and dependency theorists typically point to wide variation in the three essential conditions noted above: market expansion, foreign competition, and local institutions. But when we compare India and Brazil along these dimensions, similarities emerge as clearly as do

---

12. Gereffi, *Pharmaceutical Industry and Dependence,* esp. the cross-national comparisons on pp. 167–253.

differences. By the early 1970s the economies of Brazil and India appeared to be roughly comparable in size, and therefore both countries attracted many of the same multinationals that competed globally. Both also spawned comparable institutional innovations, such as private business groups, state enterprises, and regulatory agencies. And both aggressively pursued import-substitution strategies that, according to Stephan Haggard, should have led to comparable patterns of foreign investment.[13] Yet, as we shall see, India actually had as much in common with export-oriented Korea as it did with import-substituting Brazil. To date, research remains inadequate to explain these (and other) important variations.

As a corrective, to account for each country's relative successes and failures in dislodging multinationals, I propose a three-stage causal model. National successes, I argue, result from the sequential steps taken by host-country institutions: stage one mobilizes necessary finance; stage two employs that finance to acquire requisite technologies; and stage three combines that finance and technology to control domestic markets. Following this sequence, local enterprises and the state can overcome a variety of entry barriers as well as other (economic and political) constraints erected by multinationals. In contrast, efforts to reverse the sequence—often, in India and elsewhere, through regulatory actions that initially reserve domestic industries for local enterprises—typically fail to overcome those constraints over a sustained period. That period may, however, be shortened by growth in host markets and competition among multinationals, which together accelerate the sequence of actions whereby local enterprises and the state finally dislodge multinationals. Yet despite such threats, multinationals often remain capable of resisting every effort to dislodge them. Accordingly, multinationals represent one of the most durable institutional innovations operating in the international political economy today.

Multinationals

From the capital markets of more industrialized countries, multinationals have long supplied debt and equity directly to developing economies in the form of fresh inflows from abroad. Multinationals also have reinvested local earnings, whose mobilization and distribution helped to restructure local capital markets. Indeed, local financing of imported raw materials, machinery, other technology—even bricks, mortar, and daily wages—often proved difficult to obtain.

---

13. Haggard, "Foreign Direct Investment and the Question of Dependency."

Substituting for weak capital markets in fledgling economies, multi-nationals became the major conduits for transferring foreign savings. In fact, during the 1960s recorded foreign direct investment by multi-nationals (their debt and equity) accounted for well over one-half of all private capital flows from industrial to developing countries.[14] Multinationals thus emerged—in the view of several economists and political sociologists, at least—as the "engines of growth,"[15] supplying resources and even imparting values that would lead countries from "tradition to modernity."[16]

But in this relationship the economic growth of host developing countries still failed to keep pace with the influx of foreign direct investment. So, during the late 1960s a group of critics—principally from Latin America[17]—imputed causation from correlation.[18] In

14. David J. Goldsbrough, "Investment Trends and Prospects: The Link with Bank Lending," in Moran, *Investing in Development*, p. 174.

15. By the late 1960s many economists viewed foreign private capital as a likely conduit for most of the resources deemed necessary for economic growth. For a summary of this view, see Harry G. Johnson, "The Efficiency and Welfare Implications of the International Corporation," in Charles P. Kindleberger, ed., *The International Corporation* (Cambridge: MIT Press, 1970), pp. 35–56. Indeed, multinationals became one of the "engines of growth," according to Walter W. Rostow, *The Stages of Economic Growth: A Non-Communist Manifesto*, 2d ed. (Cambridge: Cambridge University Press, 1971).

16. Since Max Weber, sociologists have constructed two parallel "ideal types" of social organization and value systems at polar ends of an evolutionary process. At one extreme lie societies that must overcome traditional norms and structures before adopting such radical economic, social, and political transformations as those embodied in modern (capitalist) societies, which lie at the other extreme. See Max Weber, *The Protestant Ethic and the Spirit of Capitalism*, trans. Talcott Parsons (New York: Scribner's, 1958), esp. pp. 39–41, 74–76; and Weber, *Basic Concepts of Sociology*, trans. and ed. H. P. Secher (New York: Philosophical Library, 1962), esp. pp. 59–62. To Weber's ideas, Talcott Parsons added the specialized study of political culture and political socialization, both of which imposed barriers to the transformation from tradition to modernity. See Talcott Parsons, Edward A. Shils et al., *Toward a General Theory of Action* (Cambridge: Harvard University Press, 1951), esp. pp. 76–91, 107–9, 159–67, 176–89. Following both chronologically and conceptually came the work of the first modernization theorists, beginning with Gabriel Almond, "Comparative Political Systems," *Journal of Politics* 18 (January 1956):391–409, and Herbert Hyman, *Political Socialization*, 2d ed. (New York: Free Press, 1969).

17. While modernization theorists looked to Weber and Parsons for intellectual insight, dependency theorists—irrespective of ideological orientation—drew on Marxist and Leninist insights concerning imperialism and the relationship between the state and social classes. To these insights, they often added an analysis of the domestic and international structures that could impede development. This analysis was based on the work of Raul Prebisch and the Economic Commission for Latin America; see his *The Economic Development of Latin America and Its Principal Problems* (New York: United Nations, 1950). Combining these and other intellectual currents, Cardoso and Faletto initiated the formal study of dependency with their *Dependency and Development in Latin America*. The ten-year absence of an English-language edition of this book left to André Gunter Frank the task of introducing dependency theory to U.S. audiences; for his (more Marxist) version, see *Capitalism and Underdevelopment in Latin America: Historical Studies in Chile and Brazil* (New York: Monthly Review Press, 1967).

18. These dependency theorists were not, of course, the only critics; disillusionment

their view, multinationals acted to stunt development in several ways: by monopolizing (rather than supplying) new financial resources; by supplanting (rather than complementing) local enterprise; by displacing (rather than employing) local labor; by aggravating (rather than alleviating) balance-of-payments problems; and by exacerbating (rather than ameliorating) grossly unequal distributions of income in developing countries. Finally, these early dependency theorists concluded that multinationals bargained an unequal exchange in order to perpetuate their advantages by forming political alliances with the state and local enterprises. Nationalists, to overcome these constraints on growth in developing countries, decided to search out alternative sources of foreign capital.

Still, during the 1970s the absolute value of foreign direct investment (FDI) flowing to developing countries continued to grow. And multinationals continued to direct their new investments to those countries with large domestic markets, rich natural resources, or significant export advantages. In fact, during the decade 1973–84, five countries—Brazil, Indonesia, Malaysia, Mexico, and Singapore—collectively accounted for about one-half of all FDI flows to developing countries.[19] Of these, Brazil received the largest share of fresh inflows, and that country showed rapid growth. This increase, for Peter Evans and a new wave of scholars, took the label "dependent development"—economic growth at once aided and constrained by multinationals, which remained possible only so long as "global strategies and local priorities were resolvable through bargaining."[20] Such bargaining intensified during the 1970s, when multinationals, according to Table 1-1, greatly accelerated their Brazilian investments.

---

with the promise of neoclassical and post-Keynesian growth models spread. For the retrospective view of one such critic, see Manning Nash, "Foreword," *Economic Development and Cultural Change* 25, supplement (January 1977):3–19. Outside Latin America, Gunnar Myrdal's account of Indian development since independence emerged as the most eloquent critique of these growth models; see his *Asian Drama: An Introduction to the Poverty of Nations*, vol. I (New York: Pantheon, 1968), pp. 40ff., and his earlier *Economic Theory and Under-Developed Regions* (London: Duckworth, 1957), esp. pp. 100ff. Myrdal argued that social, psychological, and political factors—in addition to economic factors—explained economic growth. See also Everett E. Hagen, "The Process of Economic Development," *Economic Development and Cultural Change* 6 (May 1957):193–215; Bert F. Hoselitz, "Economic Growth and Development," *American Economic Review* 47 (May 1957):28–41.

19. Goldsbrough, "Investment Trends and Prospects," p. 179.

20. Evans, *Dependent Development*, p. 276; also see Peter Evans and Gary Gereffi, "Foreign Investment and Dependent Development: Comparing Brazil and Mexico," in Sylvia Ann Hewlett and Richard S. Weinhert, eds., *Brazil and Mexico: Patterns of Late Development* (Philadelphia: Institute for the Study of Human Issues, 1982).

Table 1-1. Foreign trade and investment in India, Brazil, and South Korea, 1965–1985 (millions U.S. dollars)

	Net direct investment	Net private long-term lending	Net official lending and unrequited transfers	Merchandise trade (f.o.b.)	
				Exports	Imports
India					
1965	33	37	2,164	1,646	−2,683
1970	6	−1	740	1,879	−2,010
1975	−11	−2	1,172	4,666	−4,952
1980	NA*a*	0	1,889	8,303	−13,947
1984	NA	9	1,258	9,465	−15,081
Brazil					
1965	154	132	125	1,596	−941
1970	407	732	245	2,739	−2,507
1975	1,191	1,894	2,059	8,492	−12,042
1980	1,544	2,624	3,687	20,132	−22,955
1985	1,267	501	6,667	25,634	−13,168
Korea					
1965	<1	21	124	175	−416
1970	66	272	296	882	−1,804
1975	53	583	714	5,003	−6,674
1980	−5	−27	2,110	17,214	−21,598
1985	200	−26	1,256	26,442	−26,461

SOURCES: International Monetary Fund, *Balance of Payments Statistics* (Washington, D.C., selected years), and *International Financial Statistics* (Washington, D.C., selected years); World Bank, *World Tables,* 3d ed. (Baltimore: Johns Hopkins University Press for the World Bank, 1984), Economic Data Sheet 2.
*a*Not available.

By contrast with Brazil, India did not host so much foreign direct investment; in fact, during the 1970s India experienced a net *outflow* of capital, as multinationals disinvested. Unlike the foreigners who financed subsidiaries in Brazil, multinationals operating in India relied far more heavily on reinvested earnings and, later, on local capital markets. These local sources alone supported expansion and diversification. In terms of their reliance on multinationals to finance industrialization, then, Brazil and India came to represent extreme opposites.

Lying between these extremes, South Korea began to industrialize by similarly restricting FDI, but later it turned to foreign enterprises (multinationals and especially overseas buyers) to boost Korean export earnings.[21] In Brazil, of course, multinationals also stimulated

21. For the relationship between Korean exports and FDI, see Stephan Haggard and

export earnings and thereby provided another means for transferring foreign savings (in addition to supplying foreign debt and equity).[22] Indeed, for Evans and others, a country's integration into the global production and marketing systems of foreign corporations represented another precondition for dependent development.[23] India, on the other hand, avoided both the costs and the benefits associated with global integration: It neither employed multinationals as major direct investors nor even used them as catalysts to earn foreign exchange as parts of its national drive for industrialization.

India did depend on multinationals to supplement its own limited technological resources, especially by transferring management skills, manufacturing processes, and product innovations to Indian soil. When such technology took the form of machinery and other tangible assets, it could usually be purchased with relative ease. But more intangible technology (ranging from patented processes to know-how shared among employees) proved to be notoriously difficult to buy on open markets, as did established product brands and related marketing skills.[24] Multinationals preferred to limit transfers of these more intangible technological and marketing assets to their several captive affiliates at home and abroad. The more unusual the assets, the more frequently multinationals had to insist that foreign equity ownership and related managerial control be tied to their supply. Indeed, foreign control over intangible technological and marketing assets provided another cause of dependent development. Such control also served as an important constraint on both the state and local enterprises in their bargaining with multinationals.[25]

That constraint grew weaker, however, as technological (and mar-

---

Tun-jen Cheng, "State and Foreign Capital in the East Asian NICs," in Frederic C. Deyo, ed., *The Political Economy of the New Asian Industrialism* (Ithaca: Cornell University Press, 1987), pp. 91–97; Larry Westphal et al., "Foreign Factors in Korea's Industrialization," in Changsoo Lee, ed., *Modernization of Korea and the Impact of the West* (Los Angeles: East Asian Studies Center, University of Southern California, 1981), pp. 217–25.

22. In Brazil, multinationals during 1969 accounted for an estimated two-fifths of a smaller (compared to South Korea) but also growing export volume. See Deepak Nayyar, "Transnational Corporations and Manufactured Exports from Poor Countries," *Economic Journal* 88 (1978):62, 80.

23. Evans, *Dependent Development*, pp. 109, 197–98, 241, 275; Gary Gereffi and Richard S. Newfarmer, "International Oligopoly and Uneven Development: Some Lessons from Industrial Case Studies," in Newfarmer, *Profits, Progress and Poverty*, esp. p. 432.

24. For further discussion, see Caves, *Multinational Enterprise and Economic Analysis*, esp. pp. 3–11, 33, 86, 142.

25. Evans, *Dependent Development*, esp. pp. 178–84.

keting) barriers to entry crumbled. Facing competition from a pro-
liferating number of technology suppliers, multinationals increasingly felt compelled to offer their technology unbundled from foreign
capital, usually on terms favorable to local licensees in India and other
developing countries.[26] Gone were the days when Latin America represented a captive territory of North American firms, or when former
colonies looked only to Britain and France for technology and finance. Now, the state often recognized—indeed, sometimes insti-
gated—international competition among foreign suppliers of technology and finance. Next, it began to exploit that competition.[27] The
host state often challenged long-entrenched multinationals through a
process known as the "obsolescing bargain."[28] Such obsolescence first
appeared in natural resource industries and slowly spread to more
technology-intensive manufacturing, as host governments renegoti-
ated to their better advantage existing contracts with multinationals,
but only after risks had been reduced and project returns had begun
to soar.[29] To assert its prowess, the state actively built local
institutions—regulatory agencies, industrial enterprises, and financial organizations—all of which quickly spread across newly industrializing countries.[30]

The State

Throughout history, the state has played a key role in shaping
economic development, especially in countries that were late to industrialize.[31] Typically, regulation represented the earliest and most per-

---

26. Raymond Vernon and Louis T. Wells, Jr., *Manager in the International Economy*,
4th ed. (Englewood Cliffs, N.J.: Prentice Hall, 1981), pp. 140–42.

27. Grieco, *Between Dependency and Autonomy*, pp. 70–149.

28. For an early discussion of why bargains "obsolesce," see Vernon, *Sovereignty at
Bay*, pp. 45–53.

29. For the evolution of Vernon's thinking regarding the "obsolescing bargain" in
manufacturing (as opposed to natural resource) industries, compare *Sovereignty at Bay*,
p. 256, with *Storm over the Multinationals: The Real Issues* (Cambridge: Harvard University Press, 1977), pp. 171–72. Also see C. Fred Bergsten, Thomas Horst, and Theodore
H. Moran, *American Multinationals and American Interests* (Washington, D.C.: Brookings,
1978), pp. 376–81; Grieco, *Between Dependency and Autonomy*, pp. 151–56.

30. Dennis J. Encarnation and Louis T. Wells, Jr., "Evaluating Foreign Investment,"
in Moran, *Investing in Development*, pp. 61–85.

31. The state's role in economic development has not been confined to former
colonies of industrialized countries. On late-starting European industrial powers, see
Alexander Gerschenkron, *Economic Backwardness in Historical Perspective* (Cambridge:
Belknap Press of Harvard University Press, 1962), esp. pp. 123, 354. Also see Peter
Evans, Dietrich Reuschemeyer, and Theda Skocpol, "On the Road toward a More
Adequate Understanding of the State," in Evans et al., eds., *Bring the State Back In*
(Cambridge: Cambridge University Press, 1985), pp. 347–65.

vasive form of state intervention; it was used especially for controlling international transfers to local markets. Newly independent India joined much of the world in adopting "inward-looking" policies, employing import tariffs and quotas to encourage the local manufacture of goods and services for the domestic market. The hope was that local manufacturing would hold out the promise of making India and other developing countries less dependent on unstable international markets and also on the import policies of more industrialized countries. As a result of these trade restrictions, large underdeveloped domestic markets such as Brazil and India reduced imports as a proportion of ever-growing national production between 1960 and 1970, and they subsequently kept imports flat, despite rapid industrialization and rising petroleum prices (as shown in Table 1-1).

Yet, in Brazil (and most other countries), tariffs and comparable restrictions on import competition proved to be powerful inducements for obtaining foreign investments designed to service local (as opposed to export) markets.[32] Rather than reducing a country's dependence, international trade restrictions actually shifted that dependence from foreign trade to foreign investment.[33] By producing this result, trade restrictions served to complicate the politics of dependence: To retain and expand these and other incentives to invest, multinationals in Brazil and elsewhere formed alliances with local enterprises and the state, whose regulatory and other agencies often appeared to act (in the words of those dependency theorists, citing Karl Marx) "at the behest of, or on behalf of" foreign vested interests.[34]

Not so in India, however. There, regulatory agencies proved far less responsive to foreign pressures. Indeed, in detailing his own view of the state, Pranab Bardhan (offering a different analysis of class relations, but one equally indebted to Marx) concludes that "the autonomy of the Indian state is reflected . . . in its regulatory . . . role."[35] In particular, capital controls in India served to limit the access of multinationals to newly protected domestic markets. Even in South Korea, where the local market enjoyed less import protection,

32. For evidence, see Grant L. Reuber et al., *Foreign Private Investment in Development* (Oxford: Oxford University Press for the OECD, 1973), pp. 120–32, and Stephen Guisinger and Associates, *Investment Incentives and Performance Requirements* (New York: Praeger, 1985), pp. 5–8, 49.
33. This same point has been made by Haggard and others; see n. 10, above.
34. Celso Furtado, *Economic Development of Latin America: Historical Background and Contemporary Problems*, 2d ed. (Cambridge: Cambridge University Press, 1978).
35. Bardhan, *Political Economy of Development in India*, p. 39.

capital controls operated, like those in India, to limit foreign investment. Moreover, for the few multinationals permitted to invest, later expansion and diversification were not guaranteed—in India or elsewhere. In fact, domestic trade restrictions proliferated (capacity licensing in India, for example) largely as a result of a worldwide movement toward economic planning and regulation.

These constraints affected both multinationals and local enterprises, but seldom equally, given the need for domestic institutions to respond to government regulators. For example, multinationals experienced distinct political disadvantages in India, in marked contrast to what they found in Brazil and other developing countries. In Brazil multinationals, the state, and local enterprises cooperated, according to Evans, joining together to form a "triple alliance."[36] By contrast, India's peculiar political economy produced an "uneasy triangle," first analyzed by Michael Kidron, in which "foreign capital could count on being isolated whenever it attempted to retain or create a monopoly position for itself."[37] His observation underscores the atypical role of the Indian state (and of Indian private enterprise) in bargaining with multinationals.

In addition to shaping the entry and subsequent diversification of multinationals, then, the state across developing countries also explored alternative channels for tapping foreign savings, often by employing sovereign guarantees to back up commitments.[38] Typically, the state began by issuing bonds in the private capital markets of more industrialized countries, but succeeding governments squandered this source of foreign exchange. So, during the late 1960s in most developing countries, the state began to shift to new foreign sources, until it became especially effective in attracting medium-term bank loans and suppliers' credits. Initially, these forms of capital were often viewed as a panacea for the chief problem associated with FDI, the "political interference" by "foreign vested interests" which accompanied multinational investments.[39] Such interference did not accom-

---

36. Evans, *Dependent Development*, esp. pp. 11–12, 32–34, 52–56, 236–49, 262, 286, 280–86, 323.

37. Michael Kidron, *Foreign Investments in India* (London: Oxford University Press, 1965), p. 181.

38. For an overview of one important channel, see Barbara Stallings, *Banker to the World: U.S. Portfolio Investment in Latin America, 1900–1986* (Berkeley: University of California Press, 1987).

39. This quotation, from the "Bombay Plan," represented the views of Birla, Tata, and other prominent Indian industrialists; see *Young Indian*, Special Independence Number (1972), para. 82, p. D60.

pany the lending by foreign banks—or so India's industrialists declared as early as 1944.

Not until the 1970s, however, would this opinion of India's industrialists be widely shared in other developing countries. By this time foreign banks had assumed a dominant position almost everywhere outside India. Especially after the 1973–74 escalation of oil prices, cross-border commercial lending to Brazil, South Korea, and other developing countries accelerated (see Table 1-1), as many countries sought financing for their suddenly larger current account deficits. Thereafter, commercial loans and suppliers' credits outpaced direct investments, which during the 1970s declined to one-quarter of a much larger volume of total private flows to developing countries.[40] Brazil, to supplement its accelerated borrowing, soon followed the economic path already successfully charted by South Korea, as both countries boosted export earnings (see Table 1-1), a development encouraged in large part by government policies in these two nations.

In India no such policies emerged. Instead, that nation held itself apart, as one of the last countries to consider "outward-looking" industrialization as a model for future growth. In fact, India has never pursued export promotion with the same vigor that it promoted import substitution, nor has it ever allowed government institutions or local enterprises to participate actively in foreign capital markets. Unlike Indian industrialists, national political leaders did not view foreign borrowing as a harmless replacement for FDI. Rather, they seemed disinclined to allow such foreign participation, a suspicion later shared by all generations of dependency theorists. And again like those theorists, both Indian industrialists and national politicians feared becoming dependent on unstable international markets and on the import policies of the more-industrialized countries. As a result, India has relied not on bank loans but on concessional aid and other official lending to finance its meager imports (see Table 1-1). For access to scarce foreign exchange, Indian enterprises have depended primarily on the state and, to a much lesser extent, on multinationals and foreign banks.

Indians also have relied on the state to mobilize and distribute domestic savings, the largest source of financing for industrialization. Institutions run (or greatly influenced) by government frequently emerged as the most important sources of debt financing, either as intermediaries for foreign loans or as repositories of bank deposits, insurance premiums, tax proceeds, and other domestic savings.

40. Goldsbrough, "Investment Trends and Prospects," p. 174.

These same institutions also increased their equity holdings in private enterprise. In India, as elsewhere, the state gradually emerged as a major—if not the principal—financier of local enterprises, both public and private.[41]

Local Enterprises

Everywhere, state-owned enterprises (SOEs) represented, at least in part, institutional innovations designed to mobilize and distribute resources within the local market. Equally innovative were family-owned conglomerates known as "business houses" in India, as *grupos* throughout most of Latin America, and as *chaebol* in South Korea.[42] To mobilize capital, these home-grown conglomerates pooled funds and reduced the cost of capital below prices prevailing in inefficient financial markets. Then, native hierarchies allocated to favored associates such funds as could not be readily procured locally. Most of these funds represented intercorporate shareholdings and internal savings, occasionally supplemented by investments from affiliated financial institutions. Even after the state had increased its control over the country's capital markets, business groups often remained the preferred customers of state financiers.

Both industrial conglomerates and state enterprises also responded to strong local demand for technologies and skills, which (like capital) could not be readily procured elsewhere. Accordingly, the development of the technology needed to diversify into new markets (and to expand in existing ones) often proved very costly. Of course, collaboration among local enterprises investing in research and development could have reduced these costs, but in developing countries few business groups or state enterprises initially chose to collaborate. Instead, most local enterprises preferred to import know-how from abroad rather than to reinvent it at home, so they tapped published research, hired engineers trained abroad, imported capital goods, and signed contracts licensing less tangible assets. With foreign technology came foreign equity and managerial control, at least to Brazil.

41. For cross-national comparisons, see Douglas C. Bennett and Kenneth E. Sharpe, "The State as Banker and Entrepreneur," *Comparative Politics* 12 (January 1980): esp. 169–70.

42. For a survey of the academic literature on business groups cross-nationally, see Nathaniel H. Leff, "Industrial Organization and Entrepreneurship in the Developing Countries: The Economic Groups," *Economic Development and Cultural Change* 26 (July 1978):661–75, and his "Entrepreneurship and Economic Development: The Problem Revisited," *Journal of Economic Literature* 17 (March 1979):46–64.

There, the unfavorable image of foreign managerial control has led to a common conclusion among researchers: local enterprises remained, at best, a weak third partner in Brazil's triple alliance.[43]

But unlike those in Brazil, business groups and state enterprises in India and a few other developing countries (South Korea, for example), increasingly unbundled technology from foreign equity; then they separately purchased each individual component, including machinery and patents. Such unbundling, as they assumed, would lower the high costs of bundled technology and increase the host's benefits through greater exports, transference of skills, and adaptation of products and processes to local conditions. As expenditures for these adaptations grew, so too did local innovations, which eventually aided the retirement of existing licenses and restricted the need for new ones. To encourage such innovation in India (and in a few other newly industrializing countries), local research and development (R&D) expenditures rose during the 1970s and 1980s.[44] Strong testimony to India's technological progress, for example, appeared suddenly in 1972, when that country became the world's sixth nation to explode a home-made atomic device. Later and less dramatically, India began to generate atomic energy from Indian-designed facilities. As further evidence of development, Indian weather satellites were engineered at home, and India could credit its national R&D to a native body of college-trained technical personnel who, in number, equaled those in the Soviet Union. From its emerging technological base, India also began to export manufacturing technology to Indian joint ventures in Africa and southeast Asia. Overall, by developing local technological alternatives and by exploiting competition among foreign technology suppliers, local Indian enterprises—along with the state—dramatically improved their bargaining position with multinationals.

In exchange for what was required in foreign technological and

43. Evans, *Dependent Development*, p. 280.
44. Expenditures for local R&D, as a percentage of GDP, grew during the 1970s and early 1980s in India and South Korea but fluctuated in Brazil:

Year	Brazil	India	Korea
1974*	0.79%	0.42%	0.39%
1978	0.55	0.53	0.63
1982	0.61	0.71	0.87

*Data for 1975 in Brazil, 1974 in India, and 1970 in South Korea. See UNESCO, *Statistical Yearbook* (Geneva, 1981, 1982, 1983, 1984, 1985).

financial resources, these local enterprises and the state traded access to the domestic market, where they typically erected their own entry barriers. In this process business groups employed interlocking directorates, management pools, and strong social bonds to coordinate buyers, suppliers, and potential competitors in a single conglomerate. State-owned enterprises followed a similar, albeit less extensive, pattern of horizontal diversification and vertical integration, most often in railroads, steel, and other upstream industries requiring large capital outlays and long gestation periods. Downstream, less sizable outlays granted business groups control over local distribution channels, marketing personnel, information regarding consumer preferences, and related ideas for product adaptation and innovation. For these skills there were few substitutes in the domestic market, since governments often limited the number of foreign nationals who could be employed locally.

Everywhere, government regulators created formidable barriers to the entry of competitors. To overcome these barriers, local business groups and state enterprises developed newly powerful organizational and political skills, and they employed them until, finally, even seemingly autonomous government agencies had to respond: "While the state elite from its commanding heights formulated goals and pointed policy directions, neither at the behest of nor on behalf of the property classes," as Bardhan observes, the state nevertheless "could not ignore the serious constraints on the framework of policy actions and certainly on their effective implementation posed by the articulated interests of those classes."[45] In India, especially during policy implementation, local enterprises actively bargained with government regulators for access to markets, just as they bargained with multinationals for access to technology.

Over time, then, local enterprises actually increased their "bargaining power"—a popular concept that has captured the attention of bargaining and dependency theorists alike.[46] Yet, this notion can be problematical, especially since definitions (when offered) have tended to become tautological.[47] As a corrective I offer another version: By

45. Bardhan, *Political Economy of Development in India*, p. 38.
46. See, for example, Grieco, *Between Dependency and Autonomy*, esp. pp. 150–56, and Gereffi, *Pharmaceutical Industry and Dependence*, esp. pp. 73–77.
47. According to both dependency and bargaining theorists, when multinationals exercise power over the state and local enterprises, they can obtain an extremely good deal from bargaining with these institutions; these institutions, in turn, demonstrate power when they can extract an extremely good deal from their bargaining with multinationals. So power appears to be inherent in the bargaining process. Yet, from such analysis, can we tell which party is the more powerful? Theorists of both persuasions

"bargaining power" I mean the ability of multinationals, the state, or local enterprises to improve the range of plausible outcomes available to each, and to improve the probability of securing the outcome that each prefers.[48]

BARGAINING POWER

In a developing country only seldom does any single party— multinationals, the state, or local enterprises—unilaterally control access to finance, technology, and markets. When such unilateral control does prevail, however, there no longer is any need to bargain, since the outcome has been predetermined. More often, each bargaining party exercises only a limited degree of control, and each must therefore bargain aggressively over resources and markets controlled at least in part by others. This interdependence represents an important precondition of real bargaining, and it virtually guarantees a second precondition—the potential for conflict. Without the possibility of conflict during either the initial creation or later distribution of benefits, bargaining will be replaced by instant agreement. The process of creating and distributing these benefits is driven by each party's self-interested maneuvers (and other opportunistic interactions) that link means to ends as efficiently as possible. In all, this constitutes a rational calculus—which, as yet, remains controversial in studies of developing countries.[49] As we see from Figure 1-2, this

---

answer that power is demonstrated when any party obtains a good outcome from another. But defined this way, "bargaining power," as Thomas Schelling reminds us, "mean[s] only that negotiations are won by those who win." See *The Strategy of Conflict* (Cambridge: Harvard University Press, 1960), p. 22. Indeed, as a result of this tautological conception, the differences between power and negotiated outcomes remain unclear.

48. This definition is employed by David A. Lax and James K. Sebenius in *The Manager as Negotiator: Bargaining for Cooperative and Competitive Gain* (New York: Free Press, 1986), p. 250.

49. Many studies of India and other developing countries have contended that rationality represents a value inherent in industrial societies, but it can be acquired only with special effort by individuals from more traditional societies, who habitually behave "irrationally" or "nonrationally." In addition to the modernization theorists cited above, see Alex Inkeles and David H. Smith, *Becoming Modern: Individual Change in Six Developing Countries* (Cambridge: Harvard University Press, 1974), esp. p. 313; Everett E. Hagen, "How Economic Growth Begins: A Theory of Social Change," *Journal of Social Issues* 19 (January 1963):20–34; David McClelland, *The Achieving Society* (Princeton: Van Nostrand, 1961), pp. 1–35. These and similar characterizations have also been applied generously (typically by economists) to bureaucrats and politicians in India and elsewhere. By suggesting that rationality remains constant across societies, I assume

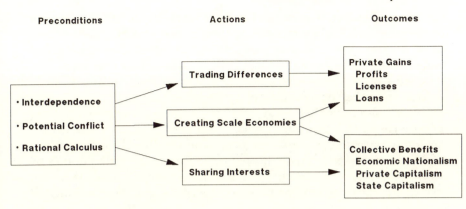

Figure 1-2. The bargaining process
SOURCE: David A. Lax and James K. Sebenius, *The Manager as Negotiator: Bargaining for Cooperation and Competitive Gain* (New York: Free Press, 1986), pp. 6–11, 88–116.

calculus represents the third and final precondition of bargaining.[50]

Such bargaining typically succeeds in splitting up profits, parceling out government permits, allocating state finance, licensing foreign technology—all private gains that one party enjoys while excluding others from the same benefits. To create these private benefits, multinationals, the state, and local enterprises usually trade their different endowments and capabilities. Historically, in India and across developing countries multinationals have supplied technology, and occasionally finance and marketing skills. Local enterprises exchanged their special knowledge of, and access to, domestic buyers—marketing advantages they then mixed with capital from domestic financiers. The state often became the source of such capital, as well as of the

---

instead that, when bargaining, state entrepreneurs, financiers, regulators (even politicians) everywhere pursue a rational calculus not unlike that usually associated with private managers. For the rational calculus of politicians, see Anthony Downs, *An Economic Theory of Democracy* (New York: Harper, 1953). For bureaucrats, see William A. Niskanen, Jr., *Bureaucracy and Representative Government* (Chicago: Aldine-Atherton, 1971). Dependency theorists have also joined (often implicitly) in this assumption. See J. Samuel Valenzuela and Arturo Valenzuela, "Modernization and Dependence: Alternative Perspectives in the Study of Latin American Underdevelopment," in Jose Villamil, ed., *Transnational Capitalism and National Development* (Brighton, Sussex: Harvester, 1979), pp. 37, 45, 52. This article appears in *Comparative Politics* 10 (July 1978):535–57.

50. In effect, Lax and Sebenius have added a fourth precondition—the possibility of agreement—to this list; see *Manager as Negotiator*, p. 11.

necessary permission to expand in local markets. In fact, the trading of different endowments and capabilities for private gain became common practice, and that practice has captured the attention of many writers concerned with relations among multinationals, the state, and local enterprises—not only in India but also in Brazil, South Korea, and other developing countries.[51]

Far less attention has been paid to a second means for securing private gains, the creation of scale economies.[52] Often without ever having to bargain outside of the conglomerate, local business groups and state enterprises have followed the example of multinationals by mobilizing financial and human resources, consolidating their research and development, combining advertising and distribution, and expanding production and operations. These tasks, once accomplished, typically lowered costs below the total for comparable efforts spread over disparate companies. Thus, scale economies within a conglomerate could produce significant gains. Moreover, short of actually merging, oligopolists can also increase profits faster and faster when they agree to collude in a cartel. Aside from economic advantages, such collusion can also generate the political equivalent of economies of scale. For example, companies affiliated in a conglomerate or cartel, by combining lobbying activities, can together secure more government largess from regulators and politicians than can the affiliates acting independently. Whether by combining political action or by exploiting the economics of industrial organization, then, local business groups, state enterprises, and multinationals have available this important second means to create and distribute private gains among affiliated companies.

Although host-country institutions theoretically may share with multinationals a common set of tools for creating and distributing private gains, most dependency theorists remain quite pessimistic about actual prospects for local enterprises and the state to alter fundamentally the bargaining power of multinationals. Given multinationals' control over access to advanced technology in the automobile industry, for example, "the balance of bargaining power," according to Douglas Bennett and Kenneth Sharpe, "may with time shift toward the transnational firms [TNCs] rather than toward the LDC [the de-

51. For a discussion of bargaining in India, see Grieco, *Between Dependency and Autonomy*, pp. 151–70; for Brazil, see Evans, *Dependent Development*, pp. 52–53, 276; for other examples in Latin America, see Gereffi and Newfarmer, "International Oligopoly," p. 434.
52. Lax and Sebenius, *Manager as Negotiator*, pp. 6–11, 88–116.

veloping country]."[53] Indeed, before entry into the host country, multinationals may be at their weakest. But "once established," Gary Gereffi concludes, "manufacturing TNCs begin to acquire domestic political allies and their bargaining position vis-à-vis the government improves."[54] Once these political alliances and technological barriers are in place, moreover, any renegotiation of existing contracts with multinationals becomes much more difficult. That difference may diminish over time in natural resources but seems to persist in manufacturing, according to Gereffi and Richard Newfarmer, for in manufacturing, "the integration of the country's productive resources into the worldwide system of the foreign corporation" increases after the multinational enters and thereby improves its bargaining position with local institutions.[55]

Yet this does not apply to India—or so claims Joseph Grieco, who contends that, at least in the Indian computer industry, the "balance of power" has actually shifted the other way, away "from individual international . . . firms and in favor of [local institutions in] India."[56] In contrast to more pessimistic dependency theorists, Grieco contends that the ability of host countries to secure concessions from multinationals during the renegotiation of contracts in natural-resource industries can be extrapolated to technology-intensive manufacturing. Here, the principal incentive for such renegotiation remains the multinational's profitability: "Projects that succeed take the limelight," according to Raymond Vernon, especially when "what was once a wistful hope" in need of large government concessions to attract foreign investment "becomes a tangible bonanza" that cannot be relocated easily to another country.[57] Governments, seeking to share in this new-found profitability once the risks have been reduced, build new institutions: "Beginning with elementary attempts to tighten the bargaining process," Theodore Moran observes with reference to the copper industry, "the country starts to move up a learning curve that leads from monitoring industry behavior to replicating complicated corporate functions," often through state enterprises.[58] With in-

53. Douglas E. Bennett and Kenneth E. Sharpe, "Agenda Setting and Bargaining Power: The Mexican State versus the International Automobile Industry," *World Politics* 32 (October 1979):86.
54. Gereffi, *Pharmaceutical Industry and Dependence*, pp. 16–61.
55. Gereffi and Newfarmer, "International Oligopoly," p. 432.
56. Grieco, *Between Dependency and Autonomy*, p. 1.
57. Vernon, *Sovereignty at Bay*, p. 48.
58. Moran, *Multinational Corporations and the Politics of Dependence*, p. 160.

23

creased profitability come new foreign competitors, usually few in number, who engage in a follow-the-leader corporate strategy, common not only in natural resources but in manufacturing industries as well.[59] As existing contracts with multinationals thus become obsolescent, Grieco and other bargaining theorists conclude, the balance of power in developing countries swings toward local institutions.

Despite their obvious differences, both bargaining and dependency theorists have combined to predict that the historical shift in bargaining power between host-county institutions and multinationals is unidirectional.[60] In fact, they both contend, the shift in power may yield a zero-sum distribution of benefits, rewarding one party at the expense of another. Their disagreement actually centers on a lesser point: whether multinationals or local institutions represent the principal beneficiaries of that shift. Yet, in a pure form, neither hypothesis finds full support in the Indian case, although the state has probably, on the whole, increased its bargaining power relative to multinationals. But local business groups have done at least as well as the state. (Much research, however, minimizes the importance of such private groups relative to government institutions and foreign enterprises. Or, even worse, it excludes local business groups from the bargaining process entirely, considering instead a "bilateral monopoly" between the state and multinationals.[61]) Challenged in India by both local business groups and the state, multinationals have not been left powerless to respond. In industry after industry, multinationals acted first to reverse the obsolescence of their earlier bargains and then to minimize the possibilities of future obsolescence. Thus, as a result of recent bargaining in India, multinationals, the state, and local enterprises have continued to share the (often positive-sum) outcomes.

Just as bargaining and dependency theorists share the determinative conclusion that power shifts unidirectionally, they also share an uncanny faith in the economic efficacy of bargaining. In Brazil, as Evans maintains, bargaining has led to development with dependence: Otherwise, in the absence of bargaining and the growing power of local institutions, "the global rationality of the multinationals

---

59. Frederick Knickerbocker, *Oligopolistic Reaction and the Multinational Enterprise* (Boston: Graduate School of Business Administration, Harvard University, 1973).

60. See, for example, Grieco, *Between Dependency and Autonomy*, p. 1, and Bennett and Sharpe, "Agenda Setting and Bargaining Power," p. 86.

61. Charles Kindleberger was among the first to conceptualize these relations in terms of a "bilateral monopoly"; see Charles P. Kindleberger and Bruce Herrick, *Economic Development*, 3d ed. (New York: McGraw-Hill, 1977), pp. 320ff.

seriously detracted from their national contribution to local accumulation."[62] Evans's critics agree, and among them, Grieco goes so far as to equate bargaining with the entire process of national development: "As the [host] country attains greater 'bargaining power' relative to multinationals," he argues optimistically, "it forces the balance of benefits to shift in its favor."[63] Although the balance does in fact shift, the total magnitude of all benefits from bargaining may not. Indeed, Bardhan, in his study of the Indian political economy, correctly blames India's slow economic growth on "the process of intense bargaining and hardfought apportionment of benefits among the different partners of the dominant coalition"—itself "a tacit and uneasy alliance."[64] His position I shall later endorse at some length; here, a simple contrast will suffice: Bargaining may have led to development with dependence in Brazil, but in India the outcome proved to be different.

While multinationals, the state, and local enterprises bargained over the creation and apportionment of the private gains associated with economic development, they also sought a second class of benefits. In contrast to private gains, these additional benefits represent common value, shared collectively by all parties, to the exclusion of none.[65] Here, by sharing interests, bargaining yields collective benefits, just as trading differences yields private gains. And the process of creating scale economies, according to Figure 1-1, actually yields both: in politics, for example, enterprises affiliated in conglomerates often lobby government for specific permissions; these individual actions, considered collectively, work to establish broad rules that help to shape all subsequent bargaining. Yet despite their demonstrable importance, these rules (like other collective benefits) have frequently been ignored by bargaining theorists.[66] Nevertheless, in developing

---

62. Evans, *Dependent Development*, p. 276.
63. Grieco, *Between Dependency and Autonomy*, p. 3.
64. Bardhan, *Political Economy of Development in India*, p. 66.
65. Lax and Sebenius, *Manager as Negotiator*, esp. pp. 6–11, 88–94, 106–7, 111–12.
66. The failure of Vernon, Moran, and other bargaining theorists to examine property rights and similar rules emerges in earlier criticism of their work. See, for example, Bennett and Sharpe, "Agenda Setting and Bargaining Power," pp. 58–59; James A. Caporaso, "Introduction: Dependence and Dependency in the Global System," and "Dependence, Dependency, and Power in the Global System: A Structural and Behavioral Analysis," *International Organization* 32 (Winter 1978):1–12, 13–43. Seeking to overcome this deficiency, Caporaso ("Introduction," p. 4) and, later, Gereffi (*Pharmaceutical Industry and Dependence*, pp. 73–74) distinguish the bargaining power to control the outcomes of distinct events from the structural power to govern the broad rules that shape bargaining. Such a distinction becomes unnecessary when we follow the logic I have outlined.

countries such rules typically have centered on the ownership of property, and around such rules have emerged shared interests.

Through their shared interests, then, bargaining parties both shaped the rules governing the creation of property rights and determined which distributions of property were permissible. To illustrate: restrictions on foreign trade and investment satisfied a widely shared and long-standing belief in economic nationalism—the conviction that domestic (as opposed to foreign) ownership of assets, development of technology, and control over markets conveyed both material and psychic benefits—all worth subsidizing at potential public expense (measured in terms of higher prices, lower quality, and scarcity of supply).[67] At the same time, even as economic nationalism extended property rights only to nationals, many such nationals also joined foreigners in a common desire to reduce government interference in agreements privately negotiated, a cornerstone of private capitalism. This private capitalism extended property rights to all individuals, without regard to nationality. Finally, some of these same private owners, including foreign suppliers of technology, joined state entrepreneurs and state financiers in supporting state ownership of assets and state control over markets. In sum, then, state capitalism merged with economic nationalism and private capitalism to become an interest jointly shared by sizable numbers of nationals, and by at least those foreigners who collectively bargained for the creation and distribution of new rights to ownership.

These new rights, like all collective benefits, often prove difficult to create and distribute, in marked contrast to private gains. In fact, the simultaneous pursuit of three sets of property rights itself introduces cross-cutting incentives, and these serve to complicate bargaining among multinationals, the state, and local enterprises. Moreover, since no party can be excluded from the distribution of such rights, potential beneficiaries feel no need to contribute to their creation, especially when other shared interests or prospects for private gain interfere. Instead, these likely beneficiaries become "free riders" whose particular problems—compounded by cross-cutting incentives—severely constrain collective action in pursuit of an interest shared across large, diverse groups.[68]

Nevertheless, despite these constraints, dependency theorists con-

---

67. For a discussion of economic nationalism as a "collective benefit" or "public good," see Harry G. Johnson, "A Theoretical Model of Economic Nationalism in New and Developing States," *Political Science Quarterly* 80 (June 1965):172–77; for a similar treatment, see Robert E. Baldwin, *The Political Economy of U.S. Import Policy* (Cambridge: MIT Press, 1985), esp. pp. 6–32.

68. For the classic formulation of the "free-rider" problem in modern economics, see

tinue to argue that shared interests translate into collective action among multinationals, the state, and local enterprises. That is, shared interests rationally pursued by these interdependent parties can lead to the establishment of a "compradore bourgeoisie" in developing countries,[69] or (more likely) to the establishment of a triple alliance that can overcome differences in interests and endowments. "Over and above the[ir] differences," Evans writes, "is the consensus that all members of the alliance will benefit from the accumulation of indus-trial capital."[70] Yet, during India's first four decades of indepen-dence, internecine conflict among interdependent parties proved a likely (perhaps, the most likely) outcome in their rational pursuit of multiple and, at times, contradictory interests. In India, rather than finding a triple alliance, Kidron observed something quite different: an "uneasy triangle formed by the government and the two wings of the private sector."[71]

INDIA'S UNEASY TRIANGLE

"Be Indian, Buy Indian" nationalists chastised their compatriots at the birth of their nation, in 1947. In the lexicon of the Indian Nation-

---

Paul A. Samuelson, "The Pure Theory of Public Expenditure," *Review of Economics and Statistics* 36 (November 1954):387–90. Our understanding of the problem can actually be traced back to Hume; see William Baumol, *Welfare Economics and the Theory of the State*, 2d ed. (Cambridge: Harvard University Press, 1969), p. 159. The problems caused by such free riders are analyzed by Mancur Olson in *The Logic of Collective Action* (Cambridge: Harvard University Press, 1965), esp. pp. 2, 15. By relaxing several of Olson's restrictive assumptions, other scholars have shown that the probabilities of individual contributions to collective action are often greater than those Olson antici-pated; see, e.g., Terry M. Moe, *The Organization of Interests: Incentives and the Internal Dynamics of Political Interest Groups* (Chicago: University of Chicago Press, 1980), esp. pp. 24–72.

69. Paul A. Baran, *The Political Economy of Growth* (New York: Monthly Review Press, 1957), esp. pp. 205ff. Although Baran substantially revises classical Marxism, he nev-ertheless retains the underlying assumption of Marxist theories of class action, that collective interests translate into collective action. For a critique from a perspective consistent with my own argument, see Olson, *Logic of Collective Action*, pp. 102–10.

70. Evans, *Dependent Development*, p. 11. Put differently, if the members of some group or class have a common interest or objective (in this instance, "the accumulation of industrial capital"), and if they could all be better off after achieving that objective, Evans concludes that the individuals in that group or class would—if they were rational and self-interested—act to achieve their common objective. But, as Olson and other theorists have made clear, such groups face a variety of disincentives—free-rider prob-lems, cross-cutting objectives, etc.—to act collectively, which can be overcome only occasionally by a very few, highly interdependent, large enterprises. See Olson, *Logic of Collective Action*, p. 2; Moe, *Organization of Interests*, esp. pp. 24–72.

71. Kidron, *Foreign Investments in India*, p. 181.

27

al Congress, a single word—*swadeshi*—summarized this concept, and that word became the rallying cry of political movements that organized to rid the subcontinent of both foreign goods and alien customs.[72] Mahatma Gandhi, the most visible Congress leader, invoked the concept often, and he symbolized its meaning. Gandhi himself represented India's national quest for self-reliance. He used only traditional methods to spin and weave the native cloth he wore, and he publicly admonished India's urban elite for their conspicuous consumption of foreign imports. Eventually, Gandhi and other nationalists also demanded that the British actually "Quit India"—the final act in an extended political drama, the end of nearly two centuries of British rule, initially by the East India Company and later by the Crown itself.[73] When the British "Raj" came to its close, Indian political leaders vowed never to repeat their experience of dependence.

Meanwhile, India's industrial leaders echoed nationalist calls for sharp "reductions in the volume of imports," including reductions in expensive foreign technology.[74] By "ultimately reducing our dependence on foreign countries for the plant and equipment required by us," argued G. D. Birla and J. R. D. Tata, the country's two most powerful industrialists, in 1944, the country would need little foreign debt and even less foreign equity—all the better since "political . . . interference from foreign vested interests" inevitably accompanied equity investments by multinationals. According to these industrial-

.

72. The first Swadeshi Movement, 1905–1908, called for a total boycott of foreign, principally imported, goods. Subsequently, the concept of *swadeshi* became synonymous with Indian nationalism. By 1953 a separate Swadeshi League—originally formed to do battle with the dominant producer in the soap industry, the Indian subsidiary of British-owned Unilever—had begun to focus attention on the more general problem of foreign goods produced locally by multinationals. In that same year the Federation of Indian Chambers of Commerce and Industry (FICCI), representing several of the largest Indian industrialists, adopted its famous Swadeshi Resolution, in which the federation reiterated "the importance of Swadeshi in the social and economic regeneration of the country." For details, see Kidron, *Foreign Investments in India*, pp. 25, 108–9, 177, 214; quotation from p. 108. On the first Swadeshi Movement and its immediate aftermath, see Claude Markovits, *Indian Business and Nationalist Politics: 1931–1939* (Cambridge: Cambridge University Press. 1985), esp. pp. 10–11.

73. Gandhi launched the "Quit India" campaign of civil disobedience in May 1942; for details, see Stanley Wolpert, *A New History of India* (New York: Oxford University Press, 1977), pp. 335ff.

74. All quotations in this paragraph are from Sir Purushotamdas Thakurdas et al., *A Plan of Economic Development for India* (Bombay: Commercial Printing Press, 1944), para. 6, 81–82. This plan, later known as the Bombay Plan of 1944, was reprinted in *Young Indian*, Special Independence Number (1972); quotations from pp. D47, D60. In addition to G. D. Birla and J. R. D. Tata, other signers of the Bombay Plan included: Sir Ardeshir Dalal, Kasturbhai Lalbhai, Sir John Matthai, A. D. Shroff, Sir Shri Ram, and Sir Purushotamdas Thakurdas.

ists, domestic production after independence should be geared to meet "the internal demand which we advocate in this plan" (later known as the Bombay Plan). Thus, exports were "likely to diminish in the future." Already a powerful coalition had formed, as prominent industrialists joined political leaders in openly advocating a reduced reliance on foreign finance, technology, and markets.

The new government of independent India shared this concern: Prime Minister Nehru's first Industrial Policy Resolution (in 1948) promised to regulate foreign investment in the "national interest," so that "majority ownership and effective control should always remain in Indian hands."[75] Subsequently, Nehru launched a forty-year Indian experiment with import substitution, a policy carefully guided by the state. By concentrating domestic production to meet the internal demand that Birla and Tata had identified, Nehru hoped to reduce India's dependence on both unstable international markets and the import policies of the more industrialized countries. In pursuing this program, India proved to be unusual; although nationalist leaders and industrialists in other developing countries also paid lip-service to the principle of self-reliance, the Indians' pragmatic commitment to making do with their native resources and markets actually had few imitators.

Nor was India's overall success in reducing the country's dependence on foreign finance, technology, and markets often rivaled abroad. Yet this success appeared only gradually. Compared to the 1940s, for example, the 1960s brought a massive infusion of foreign technology, as India rapidly industrialized in the wake of its first foreign exchange crisis (in 1957). Stunned by that event, Indian industrialists and political leaders increasingly turned toward foreign suppliers to finance technology licenses and machinery imports. Then, encouraged by Nehru's government, multinationals began to enter India without assistance from local partners; as a result, multinationals' shares of the Indian market grew throughout the 1960s. For those few joint ventures that multinationals did form, Tata emerged as a likely partner. Birla, by contrast, more often licensed and imported technology without the use of foreign equity, relying instead on state financial institutions for the requisite foreign exchange.

During the 1970s and 1980s the trend established by Birla con-

---

75. India (Republic), "Industrial Policy Resolution" (April 6, 1948), para. 10, as reprinted in United Kingdom (Government), Board of Trade, *India: Economic and Commercial Relations, 1949* (London: HMSO, 1949), p. 222.

tinued, as did a parallel trend, this one initiated by Tata—toward greater reliance on local R&D. Now, state-owned industrial enterprises actively supported both trends, which allowed them to grow large enough to threaten the existing market shares of both multinationals and the business houses established by (and typically named after) Birla, Tata, and other Indian industrialists. Meanwhile, multinationals suffered a further setback when the Indian state seriously threatened foreign shareholdings, by erecting additional regulatory barriers to multinational expansion there. Faced with relentless encroachment by both Indian business houses and the state, multinationals retaliated by creatively reversing the obsolescence of earlier bargains and by taking steps to minimize future obsolescence. Yet, even in the 1980s, Kidron's "uneasy triangle" remains appropriate as a metaphor: Aside from usefully distinguishing those institutions that have dominated India's political economy since independence, the metaphor accurately characterizes the existing relationship among the bargaining parties, as all three seek access to finance, technology, and markets.

Of course, like any metaphor, Kidron's triangle inevitably distorts some parts of reality. Finance and technology, for example, figure prominently in what finally must be recognized as a much longer list of those resources essential to the production of goods and services. And those services and goods must themselves find markets—again through bargaining—at home and abroad.[76] As for the institutions essential to industrialization, multinationals, the state, and local enterprises do not each behave monolithically, nor are the boundaries between them stricter than semi-permeable. Multinationals, for example, consist of parents and their several subsidiaries, each with its own set of (at least occasionally conflicting) objectives, and multinationals also differ in other important ways. Indeed, former colonial enterprises and modern international corporations often seem to have very little in common except their foreignness. Yet both types of organizations can conveniently be labeled multinationals. Moreover, apparent distinctions between foreign subsidiaries and local enterprises begin to blur when such units join together to form joint ventures—or when local enterprises establish their own subsidiaries abroad, in other developing countries.

76. For a similar conclusion, see Vernon and Wells, *Manager in the International Economy*, pp. 138–43. Of course, natural and human resources may also figure prominently in bargaining among multinationals, the state, and local enterprises. In India, however, questions of access to finance, technology, and markets dominated most such negotiations.

Again, distinctions within the triangle fade when state entrepreneurs managing industrial enterprises establish joint ventures with private entrepreneurs, both local and multinational, or when state financiers invest in private enterprise. Often these investments follow the directives of government regulators and the dictates of local politicians—but not always, since the state is even less centralized and often less coordinated in its use of power than is the modern corporation. Indeed, in India, the diffusion of political authority reached extremes. Elected politicians drawn from the national (British-style) Parliament and from several State[77] assemblies actively engaged in economic policymaking—absolutely free of the centralized authority represented in Brazil, South Korea, and other developing countries by military commanders. Thus, over time, each leg of the India's uneasy triangle has further divided its original share of control over access, first, to finance and, then, to technology—those resources necessary to dislodge multinationals from the domestic Indian market.

77. Throughout this book, following Indian usage, "State" denotes provincial government only, while "state" denotes the national government apparatus.

CHAPTER TWO

Finance

Long after the British had left India, their financial legacy remained.[1] That legacy began with the arrival of the British East India Company in the seventeenth century, which introduced into India the then-revolutionary concept of a joint-stock company. No longer dependent solely on internal savings or outside debt to grow, these new industrial organizations could entice investors to trade capital for the greater risk and potential reward of company ownership. In each of the "presidencies" later ruled by the East India Company—Bombay, Calcutta, and Madras—local stock exchanges supplemented the larger bourses in London and Liverpool. Eventually, Bombay emerged as India's financial capital, even as New Delhi became the political capital. While privately held companies did continue to thrive in India (as elsewhere), they could not mobilize sufficient capital to undertake the larger investments that industrialization demanded. These needs typically had to be met by joint-stock companies.

Later, commercial banking and insurance underwriting also served to mobilize and distribute capital on a scale larger than that familiar to more traditional Indian financiers. By the nineteenth century, British financial institutions had achieved preeminence in the world, and they routinely undertook sizable investments in overseas branches. In India one such institution, the Imperial Bank, superseded three semi-official presidency banks to become (until well after independence) the country's largest repository of time and savings deposits. These,

1. For British influences on the financial development of India, see Raymond W. Goldsmith, *The Financial Development of India, 1860–1977* (New Haven: Yale University Press, 1983), pp. 1–137. This source informs the next four paragraphs.

Imperial then disbursed in the form of loans or credits. British insurance companies soon followed Imperial and other British commercial banks to mobilize local savings, this time through premiums paid by subscribers. As late as independence, British insurers continued to write nearly one-half of all non–life insurance policies in India.[2] Insurers subsequently invested the premiums from these policies in the equity of joint-stock companies, including emergent joint-stock banks. Also, during the early twentieth century and continuing thereafter, a few British manufacturers joined these financial institutions in India, where they invested their plant and equipment directly in on-shore facilities. Overall, then, the British may be credited with introducing into India modern industrial and financial institutions. Naturally, they often retained equity ownership and managerial control.

Though manufacturing corporations and financial institutions did invest directly in Indian branches and subsidiaries, nonetheless most British investors preferred to hold equity in Indian portfolios, over which they exercised much less direct control. To manage such portfolios at the other end of a long and erratic line of communication, investors in London and Liverpool signed contracts with resident British agents in India. The resultant managing agency—a unique Anglo-Indian institution—combined the functions of an investment bank and a holding company.[3] After mobilizing British and (later) Indian capital, this agency allocated investments among joint-stock companies in a diversified portfolio, tied together through interlocking directorships and management contracts. Since long-term contracts (rather than the proportion of equity holdings) determined an agency's corporate directorships and management fees, the agency had every incentive to accumulate companies in its portfolio, as well as to shift investments from established to new ventures. Such portfolio diversification typically followed a pattern of horizontal and vertical integration, designed to establish internal markets among affiliated companies. These business houses, as they came to be known, outlasted the inflow of British capital, and they remained the preeminent industrial organizations in the Indian private sector long after independence. Indeed, as nationals gained control over operations, these Indian business houses served to dislodge foreigners as favored pur-

2. Michael Kidron, *Foreign Investments in India* (London: Oxford University Press, 1965), pp. 4–5.
3. For an early review of the literature on the managing agency, see ibid., pp. 5–11, 59–61, 323–34; for a more recent review, see Goldsmith, *Financial Development of India*, pp. 53–56, 120–22.

veyors of industrial finance—the first step toward eventually dislodging multinationals from the domestic market.

Compared to the private sector, the new government of independent India relied far less on British legacies. However, such legacies were not totally absent: in the East India Company, for example, the British had combined political authority with entrepreneurial activities. But that combination began to disappear after the British Crown replaced the company, in the mid-nineteenth century, and assumed the title of an Indian princely state. Until the outbreak of World War II, the British Raj followed a policy—in finance and other policy arenas—of the least possible interference with the forces of the market.[4] In fact, only two financial institutions were created by the Raj (following British precedent): the postal savings system (in the 1890s) and a central bank (in 1935). The Raj did eventually take over ownership of major railways from British managing agencies, and later it floated government bonds in London and Liverpool to help defray the substantial costs of additional construction and rolling stock. Yet, private former owners, and not the state, continued to manage a few large rail lines. Even during two world wars the scope and intensity of the colonial government's involvement in the mobilization and distribution of capital through either state financial institutions or state industrial enterprises remained moderate. Over the first forty years of Indian independence, however, this British legacy of limited state financial and entrepreneurial activity would be dramatically reversed. But that would not happen immediately.

THE STATE

One of the main characteristics of the Indian economy before independence, and a chief reason for its slow growth after, was the low level of capital formation, especially in the public sector.[5] At independence in 1947, India's central government inherited few investments: public administration, transportation, communications, defense, and some additional infrastructures. Within the several States, a limited

---

4. For further details and a comparison of state intervention in the market before and after World War II, see B. R. Tomlinson, *The Political Economy of the Raj, 1914–1947: The Economics of Decolonization in India* (London: Cambridge University Press, 1979).

5. Goldsmith, *Financial Development of India*, pp. 138–47, and his *The Financial Development of India, Japan, and the United States: A Trilateral Institutional, Statistical, and Analytic Comparison* (New Haven: Yale University Press, 1983), pp. 23–27.

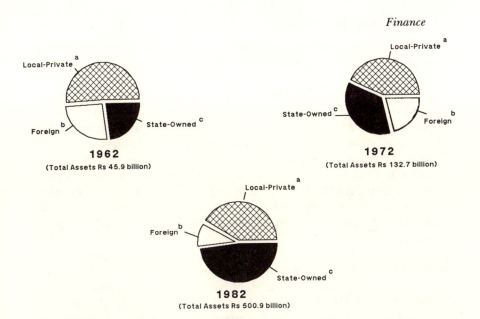

Figure 2-1. Assets owned by state and private enterprises, 1962, 1972, 1982

SOURCES: Reserve Bank of India, *Reserve Bank of India Bulletin* (Bombay, selected years).

Note: Estimates for 1962 interpolated from surveys from 1959 and 1964; estimates for 1982 extrapolated from surveys for 1979.

[a]Includes surveys of large, medium, and small joint-stock and privately held nonfinancial companies minus assets held by foreign enterprises.

[b]Includes surveys of joint-stock and privately held nonfinancial companies with foreign equity greater than 40 percent.

[c]Comprehensive for all departmental and nondepartmental central and State government nonfinancial enterprises.

number of public enterprises also concentrated their investments in a few industries—notably, electricity generation and coal mining. Elsewhere in the Indian economy, state-owned enterprises (SOEs) seemed most remarkable for their absence. Independence brought little appreciable change; in fact, as late as 1962, the state's entrepreneurial activities remained severely limited, according to Figure 2-1.

After 1962, however, state investment grew dramatically, far outpacing investment in the private sector, until by 1972 SOEs held well over one-third of all corporate assets in India (see Figure 2-1). Soon thereafter, the Indian government directly owned—for the first time—a greater share of the industrial economy than did private enterprise. Government also directly controlled those investments through industry ministries, which often dispatched their own officials to oversee daily management or (at the very least) to plan corporate strategy. This direct state control over Indian industrial enterprises continued through the 1980s, as central economic planning propelled the state into becoming a major entrepreneur in national development.

The state also extended its control over the financing of enterprises that ostensibly remained in the private sector. Notably absent from Figure 2-1 are the shareholdings of state financial institutions in private Indian enterprises and (to a lesser extent) multinationals. Yet, during the 1960s those equity holdings became large enough to rival in value government ownership of state enterprises. As state financiers assumed directorships in these private enterprises in proportion to their equity, they opened new prospects for influencing private management directly. Then, as state financiers assumed the privileged position of lead bankers, that influence increased. Indeed, the state accelerated its control over the financing of private enterprise—by means of regulation and institution building—when it eliminated alternative, private suppliers of debt both at home and abroad. Thus, by nationalizing the country's financial markets, the Indian government became the preeminent financier of both state and private enterprise.

In India the preeminence of the state as both financier and entrepreneur held important implications for subsequent bargaining over access to finance. On the one hand, the state's newly won position increased the interdependence of the state and private enterprise, as each sought to influence national industrialization. On the other hand, its preeminence gave the state autonomy to implement its own plans for development independently of private initiative. But before this could happen, the state had to devise a strategy that guaranteed to its own enterprises a central role in India's industrialization.

Central Planning

The state moved to control the financing of national development shortly after independence, when the Cabinet established a planning commission chaired by Prime Minister Nehru. While preparing each plan, the commission mapped the government's financial strategy for the next five years. That strategy, according to leading analysts, had to answer two basic questions: "(1) what was to be the size of [national] investment, and (2) how was th[at] investment to be allocated among alternative uses?"[6] Since over the plan period the available financial

6. Jagdish Bhagwati and Padma Desai, *India, Planning for Industrialization: Industrialization and Trade Policies since 1951* (London: Oxford University Press for the OECD, 1970), p. 114.

resources remained limited, this allocation procedure displayed many characteristics of a zero-sum game; that is, any gain for one class of enterprise or one branch of industry diminished the resources available to another.

From this planning process, government enterprises eventually emerged as principal beneficiaries. But their success was not immediate. Just after independence, widespread political instability following partition and war with Pakistan hampered the work of the planning commission. Consequently, the First Plan (1951–56) largely represented a collection of ongoing projects.[7] As a result, new investment in the public sector remained small throughout the period. Once hostilities had ceased, however, India entered its initial period of sustained industrial growth.[8] During each of the Second (1956–61) and Third (1961–66) plans, total targeted investments nearly doubled and the share directed toward public enterprise climbed steadily, as we can see in Figure 2-2.

As investments in state enterprises grew, the private sector's contribution declined as a proportion of national investment, reflecting the zero-sum nature of the planning process. Initially, small-scale and cottage industries absorbed most of this reduction.[9] Beginning in the late 1960s and continuing into the 1980s, however, the corporate private sector took the brunt of such reductions. Over these years, in fact, contributions by private corporations to India's total capital formation declined from one-fifth to one-tenth, while the public sector continued to account for at least two-fifths (see Figure 2-2). Thus, economic planning established the preeminence of the state as entrepreneur, often at the expense of private enterprise.

Early on, the state concentrated on industrial infrastructure. In fact, during the first two plans the lion's share of government investment went into the national railroads,[10] where in 1948 government granted itself a monopoly in its first Industrial Policy Resolution. In railroads and other state monopolies, government ministries directly

7. A. H. Hanson, *The Process of Planning: A Study of India's Five–Year Plans, 1950–1964* (London: Oxford University Press, 1966), pp. 454–84.

8. This period was later known as India's "golden era of industrial development"; see Lawrence Veit, *India's Second Revolution* (New York: McGraw-Hill for the Council on Foreign Relations, 1976), p. 262.

9. Reserve Bank of India, *Capital Formation and Savings in India: 1950–80*, the Report of the Working Group on Savings (Bombay, 1982), Statistical Annexure 21, p. 164, and Statistical Annexure 25, p. 168.

10. Isher Judge Ahluwalia, *Industrial Growth in India: Stagnation since the Mid-Sixties* (Delhi: Oxford University Press, 1985), Tables 5.2 and 5.3, pp. 77–78; V. K. R. V. Rao, *India's National Income, 1950–80* (New Delhi: Sage Publications, 1980), Table 10.7, p. 157.

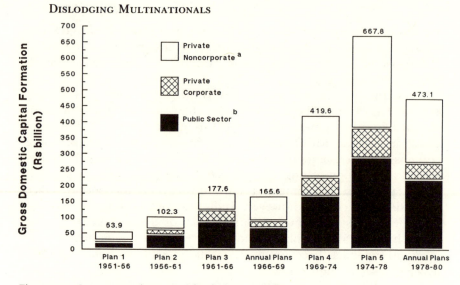

Figure 2-2. Investments in state and private enterprises, 1951–1980

SOURCE: Reserve Bank of India, *Capital Formation and Savings in India: 1950–80, Report of the Working Group on Savings* (Bombay, 1982), pp. 167–68.

[a]Principally small-scale and cottage industries and individual households.

[b]Includes administrative departments, departmental enterprises (principally railroads and electric power networks), and nondepartmental enterprises.

managed wholly state-owned enterprises. These so-called departmental enterprises were not limited to state monopolies, however. During the Third Plan, for example, departmentally operated power companies rivaled (and later surpassed) the railroads as recipients of planned investment.[11] Their growth was aided by the government's second Industrial Policy Resolution, which in 1956 added the generation and distribution of the electricity to a dozen other industries whose future development became the exclusive responsibility of the public sector. Through investments in electricity, railroads, and other departmental enterprises, the central government consolidated its direct ownership of those infrastructures essential for industrial development, while it maintained direct control over their management.

The 1956 resolution also encouraged India's central planners to enter industries previously devoid of state investment. By the middle of the Third Plan (1961–66) one such industry—steel—accounted for nearly one-half of all capital channeled to a new class of public enterprise established to manage state expansion. By 1973 one re-

11. Ahluwalia, *Industrial Growth in India*, pp. 76–83; Rao, *National Income*, pp. 157–58.

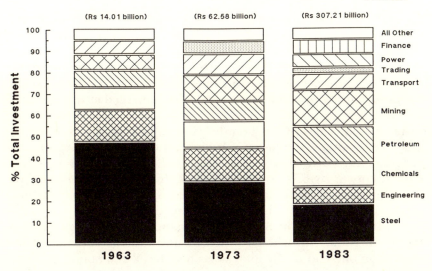

Figure 2-3. Investments in Indian industries by state enterprises, 1963, 1973, 1983
  Sources: India (Republic), Ministry of Industries, Bureau of Public Enterprises,
Report on the Working of Industrial and Commercial Undertakings of the Central Government
(New Delhi: Manager of Publications, 1963–64, 1973–74, 1982–83).
  Note: Includes paid-up capital, reserves, other surpluses, long-term loans, and de-
ferred credits for nondepartmental enterprises operated by the central government.

cently organized holding company for all government investment in
this industry, the Steel Authority of India (SAIL), became the largest
corporation in the country. SAIL and other so-called nondepartmental enterprises, though still controlled by central ministries, enjoyed
slightly greater autonomy than did the railroads or other departmentally operated undertakings. And they also became the recipients
of ever-growing government investments (see Figure 2-3).

Over time, the state's nondepartmental enterprises entered a broad
range of industries until, by 1983, government investments in mining
and petroleum matched those in steel, and they complemented sizable investments in chemicals (see Figure 2-3). In these industries,
previously left to the·private sector, nondepartmental enterprises in-
vaded markets through new start-ups or (less frequently) through the
nationalization of existing private enterprise. So rapid was their expansion that the number of nondepartmental enterprises doubled
every ten years: from 48 in 1961, to 97 in 1971, to 202 in 1981.[12] By

12. Commerce Research Bureau, *Commerce Yearbook of the Public Sector: 1984* (Bombay: Commerce Publications, 1985), p. 12.

the mid-1960s new investments in these enterprises finally exceeded the government's investments in railroads and other departmental undertakings.[13] And during the mid-1970s additional investments finally pushed industrial (nondepartmental) SOEs past the corporate private sector in net capital formation.[14] Indeed, in India's system of financial allocation, nondepartmental SOEs emerged as the principal beneficiaries.

As a result, a few SOEs soon dwarfed all of Indian private enterprise. For example, the roster of India's hundred largest corporations included thirty-five state-owned industrial enterprises in 1980, up from twenty in 1970.[15] Collectively, these thirty-five controlled nearly three-quarters of all the assets employed by the top hundred companies, up from two-thirds in 1970. These few SOEs also dwarfed the rest of the public sector. By 1983, for example, the ten largest corporations in India—all wholly owned by government—accounted for more than one-half of the total assets held by all 209 nondepartmental SOEs operating that year.[16] By concentrating its investments in a small number of large firms, the state sought to exploit economies of scale in its use of scarce capital.

With these scale economies, the state could more readily forgo financial collaboration with multinationals and with other local enterprises. In 1983, for example, multinationals and local private parties each accounted for less than two-tenths of 1 percent of the total equity invested in state-owned industrial enterprises.[17] And each supplied less than one-seventh of the total credit advanced to these same enterprises. All other equity and debt were held by central government ministries, followed far behind by State (that is, provincial) governments and public financial institutions. Within the central government the finance ministry controlled the allocation of capital among industry ministries and their SOEs. Competition within government for these funds was intense, all the more so since the finance ministry

13. Ram N. Lal, *Capital Formation and Its Financing in India*, Delhi School of Economics, Monograph in Economics, No. 3 (Bombay: Allied Publishers, 1976), Table 6.2, p. 109, and Appendix 6.1, pp. 120–21; Commerce Research Bureau, *Commerce Yearbook of the Public Sector: 1971* (Bombay: Commerce Publications, 1972), Table 3, p. 18.

14. Reserve Bank, *Capital Formation and Savings*, Statistical Annexure 22, 23, 24, pp. 165–67.

15. Commerce Research Bureau, *Yearbook of the Public Sector: 1984*, p. 12.

16. India (Republic), Ministry of Finance, Bureau of Public Enterprises, *Annual Report of Industrial and Commercial Undertakings of the Central Government: 1985–86*, 2 vols. (New Delhi: Controller of Publications, 1977), 1: 4, 7.

17. India (Republic), Ministry of Industries, Bureau of Public Enterprises, *Report of the Working of Commercial Undertakings of the Central Government* (New Delhi: Manager of Publications, 1984), pp. 32–33.

severely restricted alternative sources of debt and equity. Thus, the state remained the preeminent financier of its own enterprises.

While the state preferred to finance SOEs internally, foreigners nevertheless owned equity in 18 of the 202 industrial (nondepartmental) SOEs operating in 1983. And private Indian institutions owned equity in 30.[18] The state's acquisition of a controlling share of private equity in existing corporations explained much of this financial collaboration, especially collaboration with private Indian enterprises. In addition, minority foreign-owned joint ventures guaranteed imports of raw materials (as in the case of Madras Refineries), facilitated imports of foreign technology (as in Maruti Udyog's production of automobiles), or improved access to foreign markets (as in Pardip Phosphates).[19] With these few notable exceptions, however, the state has remained throughout the history of independent India the sole financier of its own entrepreneurship.

Nationalizing Financial Markets

Eventually, the state also emerged as a major shareholder in, as well as the principal lender to, private enterprise—through the control it exercised over the country's several financial institutions.[20] Initially, however, the state shared that control with commercial banks, insurance companies, and other private intermediaries. Indeed, in 1948, soon after independence, government investment in the banking network began modestly with a single institution that remained wholly state owned (the Industrial Finance Corporation of India). Only after nearly ten years, in 1955, did the government establish a second development bank (the Industrial Credit and Investment Corporation of India), which combined funds from the World Bank and private Indian sources. Also during the 1950s, the several States added their own financial corporations and development banks to the government-run financial network. Still, public control over India's financial markets remained limited throughout the first decade of independence.

18. India (Republic), Ministry of Industries, Bureau of Public Enterprises, *Annual Report of the Working of Commercial Undertakings of the Central Government* (New Delhi: Manager of Publications, 1984), pp. 19–20.

19. Aurobindo Ghose, "Joint Sector and 'Control' of Indian Monopoly," *Economic and Political Weekly* (Bombay), June 8, 1974, p. 906.

20. Goldsmith, *Financial Development of India*, pp. 163–68, 171–78, 186–90, 200–9; also see, L. C. Gupta, *The Changing Structure of Industrial Finance in India* (London: Oxford University Press, 1969), esp. pp. 103–6.

At the outset of the Second Plan (1956–61), Nehru's government announced its intention to play an even greater role in the allocation of capital for private enterprise: "The state will continue to foster institutions to provide financial aid to the private sector," according to the Industrial Policy Resolution of 1956: "Such assistance, especially when the amount involved is substantial, will preferably be in formal participation in equity capital."[21] With this mandate, the government embarked on its first wave of financial takeovers, a move that greatly expanded the state's role in India's private capital markets. As debate over the resolution continued, the country's largest commercial bank, the British-owned Imperial Bank of India, was nationalized (1955) and merged with banks owned by the former princely States, to create the State Bank of India. And once the resolution was finally adopted in 1956, all life insurance companies were nationalized and merged into the Life Insurance Corporation of India (LIC). With these acquisitions, the government revealed its intention to control not only the allocation of financial resources (through debt and equity) to private enterprise, but also the actual mobilization of those domestic savings (in the forms of insurance premiums and bank deposits) previously controlled by private financial institutions.

Through nationalizations and its own institution building, the government became a major investor in the country's private equity markets. In 1955, prior to the takeover of LIC and the establishment of a series of development banks, government financial institutions owned just two-tenths of 1 percent of the total equity in nongovernment companies. Yet, as we can see from Figure 2-4, this proportion of shareholdings had risen to nearly 20 percent ten years later, after the government had completed its first wave of nationalizations and established its last development bank (the Industrial Development Bank of India). Government shareholdings continued to increase with the establishment (1964) of a small mutual fund (the Unit Trust of India) and with the hostile takeover (1971) of all property insurance companies (reorganized as the General Insurance Corporation of India), since trust funds and insurance premiums had been invested in joint-stock companies. Thus, through nationalizations and new investments, the central government established itself as an important shareholder in ostensibly private enterprise.

By 1970 the central government also had established itself as a

21. India (Republic), "Industrial Policy Resolution" (April 30, 1956), para. 10, as reprinted in India (Republic), Planning Commission, *Programmes of Industrial Development: 1956–61* (Delhi: Manager of Publications, 1956), p. 436.

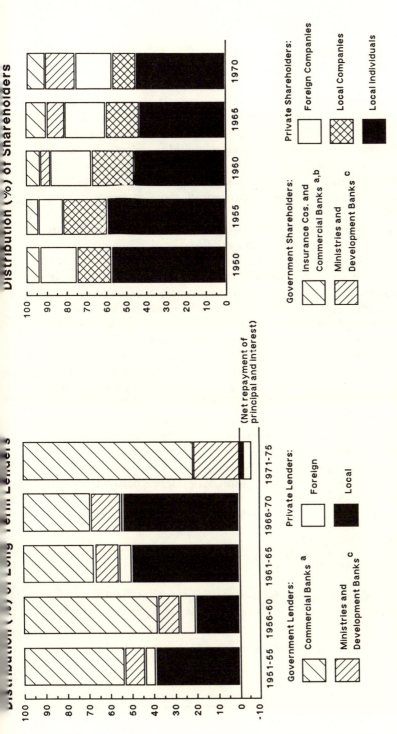

Distribution (%) of Shareholders

100
90
80
70
60
50
40
30
20
10
0

1950   1955   1960   1965   1970

Government Shareholders:

▨ Insurance Cos. and
   Commercial Banks a,b

▧ Ministries and
   Development Banks c

Private Shareholders:

☐ Foreign Companies

▨ Local Companies

■ Local Individuals

Distribution (%) of Long Term Lenders

100
90
80
70
60
50
40
30
20
10
0
-10

1951-55 1956-60 1961-65 1966-70 1971-75

(Net repayment of
principal and interest)

Government Lenders: Private Lenders:

▧ Commercial Banks a   ☐ Foreign

▧ Ministries and   ■ Local
   Development Banks c

Figure 2-4. Sources of debt and equity in private enterprise, 1950–1975
SOURCE: Raymond W. Goldsmith, *The Financial Development of India, 1860–1977* (New Haven: Yale University Press, 1983), pp. 204 and 208,
Tables 3-46 and 3-49.
aIncludes the State Bank of India, formed after the nationalization of the Imperial Bank in 1954, and the fourteen largest privately owned
commercial banks nationalized in 1969. For years prior to 1971, loans from these fourteen banks are included in the totals for local private
lenders.
bIncludes all life insurance companies nationalized in 1956 and merged into the Life Insurance Corporation of India (LIC). For years prior to
1956, LIC shareholdings are included in the totals for local private companies.
cIncludes central government ministries, the Industrial Development Bank of India, the Industrial Credit and Investment Corporation of India,
the Industrial Finance Corporation of India, and the several State finance and industrial development corporations.

major lender to private enterprise, when (the previous year) it nationalized the country's fourteen largest commercial banks. This move increased state control over long-term loans to private enterprise from 55 percent of all such disbursements to 79 percent (see Figure 2-4). During the 1980s that share continued to increase, with the nationalization of most remaining commercial banks. Some sixty other banks remained in private hands (including fifteen owned by foreigners), but they held only 5 percent of the total assets in the financial sector.[22] In comparison with these last private sources, even central government ministries represented more important long-term lenders to private enterprise.

Yet despite their control over financial resources, these several government institutions seldom converted their equity ownership into managerial control; even less frequently did they convert debt into equity, despite policy prescriptions allowing such conversions. Instead, state financiers preferred to influence private management less directly through the directorships they held in proportion to their equity, and through their privileged position as lead bankers. So long as private management generated adequate returns and invested in industries accorded priority by government—two of the many functions government shareholders and lenders were charged to perform by their overseers in the finance ministry and Parliament—state financiers intervened little in corporate planning and even less in daily management. But when private enterprise proved too reluctant to assist public agencies in achieving their several objectives, government financiers moved on rare occasion to convert debt into equity,[23] and ownership into control.[24] Certainly, the credible threat of state control served to heighten the existing interdependence between government financiers and private enterprise, especially the country's largest industrial conglomerates.

INDIAN BUSINESS HOUSES

Before the ascendancy of state-owned enterprises, private industrial conglomerates, known locally as business houses, represented the

22. Goldsmith, *Financial Development of India*, p. 175; this estimate applies to the late 1970s.

23. For data through the mid-1970s, when debt-to-equity conversions reached their modest peak, see D. K. Rangnekar, "Industrial Policy," *The Economic Times Annual: 1975* (Bombay: Economic Times, 1976), p. 33.

24. In one of the most publicized efforts to convert equity ownership into managerial

preeminent industrial organizations in the Indian economy. In fact, a decade after independence the twenty largest Indian business houses controlled over one-third of all corporate assets in India.[25] Another decade later, in 1969, these twenty houses still owned more than one-quarter of the country's corporate assets.[26] Through 1969 several of these houses also dominated India's largest financial institutions. Even after bank nationalization in 1969 and the government's own institution building, Indian business houses enjoyed considerable freedom from state shareholders and lenders in allocating internally generated resources—the second largest reservoir of funds available for private sector growth, following debt.[27] And in the country's equity markets private parties—including industrialists and affiliated companies—still retained a majority of all shareholdings in the private sector (see Figure 2-4).

To mobilize and distribute these financial resources, as well as managerial skills and entrepreneurial talent, India's budding industrialists adopted, even before independence, the same form of industrial organization that had long characterized the colonial British economy—the managing agency system. In theory, each company under the managing agency remained legally independent. In practice, however, equity ownership among companies became linked, and sophisticated systems of interlocking directorates maintained operational control over a large number of companies. Tata, for example, controlled upwards of eighty companies when the government formally abolished managing agencies in 1969; its chief rival, Birla, controlled more than two hundred.[28] In each of these houses, strong social ties of family, caste, religion, language, ethnicity, and region reinforced financial and organizational linkages among affiliated enterprises.[29]

---

control, LIC moved to change all nine directors of Escorts, one of the country's hundred largest companies. See "Comment: Robbing Peter," *Economic Scene* (Bombay), February 1984, pp. 5, 7.

25. R. K. Hazari, *The Structure of the Corporate Private Sector: A Study of Concentration, Ownership and Control* (Bombay: Asia Publishing House for the Planning Commission of the Government of India, 1966), Table 2.2, pp. 36–37.

26. Rakesh Khurana, *Growth of Large Business: Impact of Monopolies Legislation* (New Delhi: Wiley Eastern, 1981), Table 8.12.

27. Goldsmith, *Financial Development of India*, p. 204.

28. These numbers are an average for the period 1956–66; see India (Republic), Ministry of Industrial Development, Internal Trade and Company Affairs, *Report of the Industrial Licensing Policy Inquiry Committee*, P. Dutt, Chairman (New Delhi: Manager of Publications, 1969): *Main Report*, p. 18, and *Appendices: Volume II*, pp. 1–47. Hereinafter cited: Licensing Policy Inquiry, *Main Report*, or Licensing Policy Inquiry, *Appendices* and volume number.

29. B. B. Misra, *The Indian Middle Classes: Their Growth in Modern Times* (London:

Even after SOEs began to challenge their preeminence in the national economy, a few business houses still continued to dominate the private sector. Indeed, one government commission estimated that business houses controlled 47 percent of all assets in the corporate private sector during 1963;[30] ten years later that figure had not changed appreciably (44 percent[31]) despite several government policies introduced in 1969: the abolition of managing agencies, the nationalization of banks often controlled by large houses, and the passage of monopolies legislation designed (in the language of the bill) "to curb the concentration of economic power in private hands." In fact, between 1963 and 1973 the top two houses—Tata and Birla—doubled their share of total private assets (from one-tenth to one-fifth).[32] Subsequently, into the 1980s Indian business houses, aided by government financing, retained control over the corporate private sector.

Central Government Financing

The continued dominance of Indian business houses and the emergence of state financing both held important implications for subsequent bargaining over access to finance: As the state nationalized India's financial markets, growth-minded business houses had to turn to government financial institutions for most long-term debt and for new infusions of equity. Yet these business houses were not left powerless in their dealing with the state. To the contrary, state financial institutions—if they hoped to satisfy their own objectives—had little choice except to invest in enterprises controlled by private industrial conglomerates. As a result, state financial institutions and Indian business houses became increasingly interdependent.

Debt. In the allocation of government loans, that interdependence became evident long before the government gained preeminence by nationalizing the country's largest commercial banks. Between 1956 and 1966, for example, state financial institutions controlled barely 10

Oxford University Press, 1961); Thomas A. Timberg, *Industrial Entrepreneurship among the Trading Communities of India: How the Pattern Differs* (Cambridge: Harvard University Press, 1969); Helen B. Lamb, "Business Organization and Leadership in India Today," in Richard L. Park and Irene Tinker, eds., *Leadership and Political Institutions in India* (Princeton: Princeton University Press, 1959), pp. 251–57.

30. India (Republic), Ministry of Finance, *Report of the Monopolies Inquiry Commission*, vol. 1 (New Delhi: Manager of Publications, 1965), pp. 119–22.

31. Khurana, *Growth of Large Business*, Table 8.12.

32. Ibid.; cf. tables 8.9 and 8.12.

percent of all long-term lending to private enterprise in India (see Figure 2-4). According to data gathered by official parliamentary committees and summarized in Figure 2-5, however, state financial institutions had already begun to concentrate much of their lending in India's largest business houses.

Now, while looking at that figure, consider the government's distribution of foreign currency loans. After India experienced its first foreign exchange crisis, in 1957, tight capital controls proscribed business houses (and everyone else) from tapping foreign capital markets; this severely limited loans from foreign collaborators or cross-border lenders. Instead, the finance ministry allocated the country's scarce foreign exchange among a myriad of potential uses.[33] For example, the ministry automatically set aside sums for foreign debt repayments, embassies abroad, defense, and imports of food, fertilizers, and petroleum. It then channeled the remaining foreign exchange to a few government-run development banks, which controlled the distribution of these funds to private enterprise. On its part, the ministry insisted that, in their lending, these banks distinguish "essential" imports of capital goods and other technology (the most favored) from raw materials, spares, components, and consumer goods (the latter became the least favored). This allocation procedure, like central planning itself, also displayed many characteristics of a zero-sum game, since a gain for one enterprise or sector of the economy reduced the resources available to all others.

Within the private sector India's business houses clearly emerged as the principal beneficiaries of government lending: during the decade ending in 1966 they received over one-half of all foreign currency loans sanctioned by state financial institutions (see Figure 2-5). Indeed, four houses—Birla, Tata, Mafatlal, and Scindia—together accounted for more than 10 percent of all foreign-currency loans. For Mafatlal, the recipient of the largest total amount of government loans (foreign currency and all others), such borrowing contributed to phenomenal growth: With total assets ranked fifteenth among India's business houses in 1964, Mafatlal moved up to third place five years later, a position it subsequently maintained through the 1970s.[34] As growing debt-to-equity ratios also suggested(see Figure 2-4), Mafatlal and the rest of the private sector increasingly relied on government lending to grow.

33. Bhagwati and Desai, *Planning for Industrialization*, pp. 281–334; also see P. J. Eldridge, *The Politics of Foreign Aid in India* (London: Shocken Books for the London School of Economics and Political Science, 1969), esp. Table 49, p. 155.
34. Khurana, *Growth of Large Business*, tables 8.7 and 8.10.

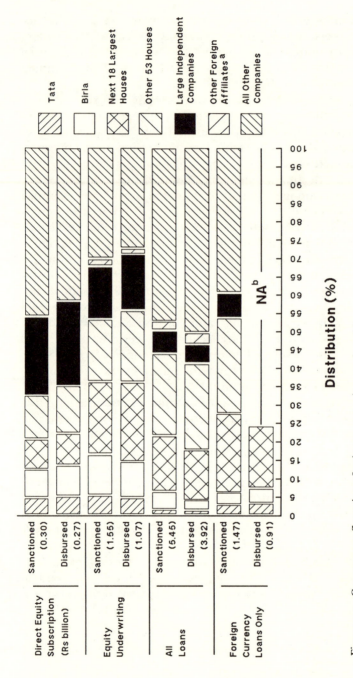

Figure 2-5. Government financing of private enterprise, 1956–1966

SOURCE: India (Republic), Ministry of Industrial Development, Internal Trade and Company Affairs, *Report of the Industrial Licensing Policy Inquiry Committee*, P. Dutt, Chairman (New Delhi: Manager of Publications, 1969), *Main Report*, p. 155, and *Appendices: Volume IV*, pp. 12, 32, 161–80.

[a]Excludes foreign companies also included either under business houses (e.g., ICI) or under large independent companies (e.g., Hindustan Lever).

[b]Not available.

Birla became the second-largest borrower from the government. Indeed, government investigators charged that Birla's ranking resulted from its reservation of loan commitments for investments it did not intend to make.[35] Such "financial preemption" (as investigators termed it) reduced the capital available to other potential borrowers, creating an additional barrier of entry to Birla's competitors. Preemption alone, according to investigators, accounted for much of the difference (noted in Figure 2-5) between debt sanctioned and loans disbursed by financial institutions.

Even in the face of such public criticism, state financial institutions did not alter their preference for servicing loan applications from large business houses. For example, between 1964 and 1978 the government's lead development bank (the Industrial Development Bank of India) awarded them more than 70 percent of the debt (and equity) it invested in private enterprise, although these houses accounted for less than 40 percent of all private corporate assets.[36] In fact, the interdependence of the central government and Indian business houses remained unimpaired, while the houses themselves did not experience any serious dilution of the managerial control traditionally exercised by private conglomerates. Again, a limited conversion of government debt into equity did little to diminish such managerial control, and the role of state bankers remained largely passive.

Equity. Even before the state achieved control over most long-term lending in India, its financial institutions participated actively in the country's equity market. By the mid-1960s private enterprise had become dependent on government institutions for 20 percent of all equity, up sharply from the 1 percent (or less) of ten years earlier (see Figure 2-4). Of course, not all private enterprise shared equally in this growth of government shareholding. Indeed, during the decade ending in 1966, state financial institutions evidenced a strong preference for the shares of Indian business houses.

35. This was a principal finding of the so-called Sarkar Commission. For a review and expansion of these findings, see "Public Monies for Private Empires," *Economic and Political Weekly* (Bombay), January 12, 1974, pp. 15–16; "Pre-emption of Institutional Finance: Procedural Red Herrings," *Economic and Political Weekly* (Bombay), February 2, 1974, pp. 101–2.

36. Data on these loans recomputed from Industrial Development Bank of India, *Operational Statistics: 1964/65–1975/76* (Bombay, 1976), Table 13, p. 37, and Table 15, p. 38. Scattered evidence on disbursements from other financial institutions showed similar trends during the 1970s; for the best compilation of data on disbursements during 1971–74, see the government's response to "starred" questions raised by members of Parliament, in India (Republic), Parliament, House of the People, *Debates*, 4th Lok Sabha (December 20, 1974), esp. pp. 100–2. For data on the ownership of private corporate assets, see Khurana, *Growth of Large Business*, Table 8.12.

Consider the underwriting of new capital issues. Typically in India's thin capital market, such underwriting was undertaken almost exclusively by the government's development banks and insurance companies. Data gathered by an official parliamentary committee indicates that over one-half of all stock offerings underwritten by these state institutions between 1956 and 1966 involved issuances by seventy-three large business houses; the largest twenty houses accounted for more than one-third of all underwritten offerings (see Figure 2-5). Birla alone received roughly one-tenth of all that underwriting assistance. Since stock underwriting during this period became tantamount to stock purchasing (given the "bearish" nature of India's fledgling equity market), public financial institutions—either by choice or by default—eventually became frequent subscribers to the shares underwritten,[37] as we can see from Figure 2-6.

Subsequently, those government subscriptions increased as the number of joint-stock companies multiplied. In fact, between 1965 and 1978 the proportion of equity held by state financial institutions grew even faster than the asset value of those companies surveyed in Figure 2-6. Thus, by 1978 the state had invested in all but a few private companies. Part of this growth in government shareholdings reflected the nationalization of commercial banks and general insurance companies between 1965 and 1978. Far more growth, however, can be traced to increased shareholdings by such existing government institutions as LIC. Though the holdings of such state financial institutions remained widely varied, virtually all government financiers preferred to hold shares in the largest joint-stock companies—which, over time, amounted to a growing proportion of the government's total equity holdings in the Indian economy.[38]

When tallied across state institutions, government shareholdings came to represent a significant proportion of the total ownership in many private enterprises. For example, in 1980 public financial institutions owned at least two-fifths of all outstanding shares in the country's largest private-sector company, Tata Engineering (TELCO, ranked twelfth among all Indian industrial enterprises), and one-fourth of all shareholdings in the country's second-largest private enterprise, Tata Steel (TISCO, ranked sixteenth).[39] Then, since TELCO and TISCO

37. For the wider implications of stock underwriting, see Licensing Policy Inquiry, *Main Report*, pp. 158–59.

38. This was the same conclusion reached by the Dutt Committee earlier, in 1969; see ibid., pp. 140–80.

39. Ghose, "Joint Sector," pp. 906, 916. In other Tata companies, government shareholdings were even larger; see K. Balakrishnan et al., *A Comparative Study of the Growth*

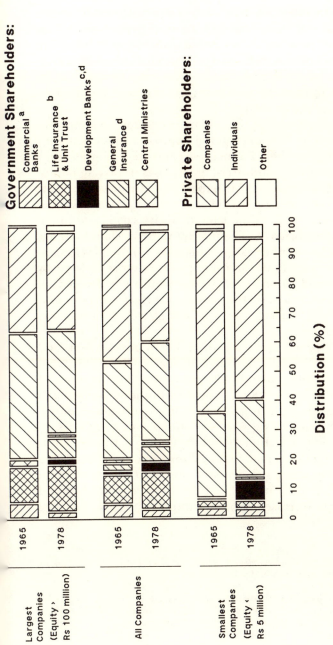

Government Shareholders:

- Commercial [a] Banks
- Life Insurance [b] & Unit Trust
- Development Banks [c,d]
- General Insurance [d]
- Central Ministries

Private Shareholders:

- Companies
- Individuals
- Other

Distribution (%)

Largest Companies (Equity > Rs 100 million)
- 1965
- 1978

All Companies
- 1965
- 1978

Smallest Companies (Equity < Rs 5 million)
- 1965
- 1978

Figure 2-6. Owners of equity in private enterprises, 1965, 1978

SOURCE: Reserve Bank of India, "Survey of Ownership of Shares in Joint-Stock Companies, as at the End of December 1978," *Reserve Bank of India Bulletin*, February 1983, pp. 75, 78, 80–82, 88.

[a] Includes the State Bank of India, plus the fourteen largest privately owned commercial banks nationalized in 1969.

[b] Includes the Life Insurance Corporation of India and the Unit Trust of India.

[c] Includes the Industrial Development Bank of India, the Industrial Credit and Investment Corporation of India, the Industrial Finance Corporation of India, and the several State finance and industrial development corporations.

[d] The 1965 survey did not collect separate data for any of the development banks, or for the property insurance companies that were nationalized in 1971 and merged into the General Insurance Corporation of India (GIC). Instead, that survey aggregated all their holdings with a few other private financial institutions. Therefore, the 1965 shareholdings of the development banks and the GIC represent a rough estimate based on the ratio of development bank to GIC shareholdings for 1978, multiplied by the sum given for "other financial institutions" in the 1965 survey.

together accounted for over one-half of the equity controlled by one business house (Tata), state financial institutions collectively owned approximately one-third of all the shares in that giant house. Similarly, in Birla and several other private industrial conglomerates, public institutions owned as much as one-quarter of all outstanding equity.[40] Thus, for Birla, Tata, and other business houses, government financial institutions actually financed growth.

Yet, as we have already noted, these same institutions seldom converted equity ownership into managerial control, even when they owned majority shares, as they did in a few companies. Rather, they left the management of large industrial enterprises in private hands. What state financial institutions did expect in return were sizable returns on their investments, especially as India's capital market became more robust, beginning in the late 1970s. By 1978 state financiers had achieved this objective: The market value of shareholdings in TELCO, TISCO, and other large joint-stock companies consistently exceeded their face value, according to surveys completed by India's central bank and summarized in the Figure 2-7. Indeed, in most cases, as the stock prices of India's largest private corporations rapidly appreciated, the market value of these shareholdings nearly doubled their face value.

By contrast, as we see in Figure 2-7, the value of government (and private) shareholdings actually declined in nearly all smaller companies surveyed; in several, shareholdings lost one-half or more of their face value. In fact, when state financial institutions did invest in these smaller companies—which generated, in turn, inadequate returns relative to the market as a whole—commissions of official inquiry and the financial press often took them to task.[41] In this investment climate, managers of public financial institutions behaved in a fashion consistent with other risk-averse financiers concerned about optimizing the return to their portfolio of investments—they invested in large, profitable enterprises, typically those owned by business houses.

---

and Strategy of Two Large Indian Business Houses: Birlas and Tatas (Ahmedabad: Indian Institute of Management, March 1980), Table 7.4, p. 126.

40. Ghose, "Joint Sector," pp. 906, 916.

41. A fear of running afoul of Parliament or the press was expressed repeatedly during my interviews with state financiers in Bombay and their overseers in the finance ministry in New Delhi. For an insightful review of such fears by a distinguished public servant, see H. K. Paranjape, "Industrial Growth with Justice—India's Strategy," in Charan D. Wadhva, ed., *Some Problems of India's Economic Policy* (New Delhi: Tata McGraw-Hill, 1977), pp. 331–32; also see Bhagwati and Desai, *Planning for Industrialization*, esp. pp. 148–49, 165–67.

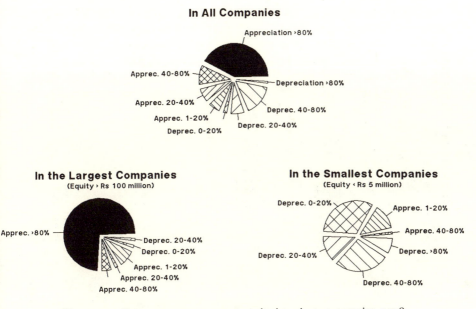

Figure 2-7. Returns on government equity in private enterprise, 1978
SOURCE: Same as for Figure 2-6.

Managers of state financial institutions could not, however, invest with impunity in large companies owned by business houses, no matter how profitable. Indeed, these investments often invoked the wrath of official inquiries concerned with "the concentration of economic power in private hands."[42] To stifle that criticism, state financiers had to demonstrate that their investments also served a larger public interest, such as the development of industries accorded high priority by government. Investments in TELCO and TISCO, for example, satisfied this second objective, since heavy engineering and steel were two of the priority industries in which state-owned industrial enterprises similarly concentrated their investments. So, according to data gathered by India's central bank and reported in Figure 2-8, state financiers invested much more of their equity in private enterprises that operated in nonelectrical machinery and foundaries than they did in the economy as a whole.

In addition to heavy engineering and steel, the Industrial Policy Resolution of 1956 identified industrial chemicals and shipping as priority industries. Again, private enterprises operating in these sec-

42. For example, see Licensing Policy Inquiry, *Main Report*, pp. 141–80.

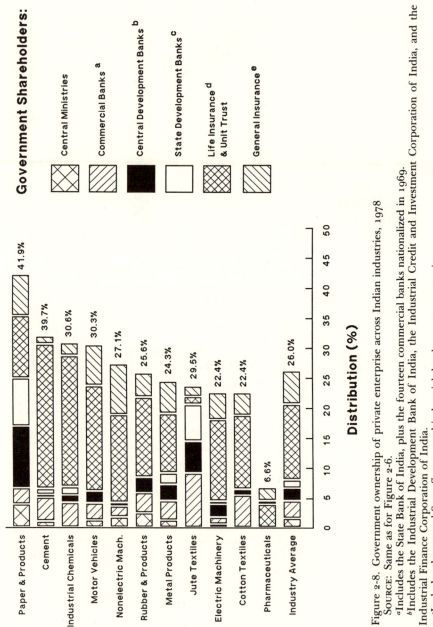

Figure 2-8. Government ownership of private enterprise across Indian industries, 1978
SOURCE: Same as for Figure 2-6.
[a]Includes the State Bank of India, plus the fourteen commercial banks nationalized in 1969.
[b]Includes the Industrial Development Bank of India, the Industrial Credit and Investment Corporation of India, and the Industrial Finance Corporation of India.
[c]Includes the several State finance and industrial development corporations.
[d]Includes the Life Insurance Corporation of India and the Unit Trust of India.
[e]Includes the General Insurance Corporation of India.

tors attracted sizable government shareholdings (see Figure 2-8). Cement and paper later joined the list of targeted industries, and accordingly they also gained favor from state financial institutions. But not all priority industries received government investments. Pharmaceuticals and agricultural chemicals, for example, attracted little attention from government shareholders, even though both ranked among priority industries in the 1956 resolution. (As we shall see later in this chapter, and again in Chapter 4, both industries became heavily populated by multinationals, which sought and received far less state capital than did local enterprise.)

By comparison with development banks and insurance companies controlled by the central government, State (that is, provincial) development banks and nationalized commercial banks remained more decentralized in their lending practices, as they responded to regional concerns. For example, these institutions invested more heavily in jute and cotton textiles, consumer goods industries spread widely over the country (see Figure 2-8). Such industries exercised a direct influence on local employment and therefore on the health of the several State governments.

State Government Financing

To complement their loans, the State development banks and industrial finance corporations also invested directly in India's equity markets, where they typically remained passive investors, like their counterparts at the center. At the same time, several State financial institutions also took a lead role in promoting projects in which the State government owned a sizable proportion—typically 26 percent—of the total equity. Among the earliest provincial investors, the State of Maharashtra promoted six of these so-called joint-sector projects during its Third Plan (1961–66). Later, in the 1970s, nearly all other Indian States imitated that model.[43]

In their selection of partners for joint-sector projects, State banks and development corporations followed the lead of central institutions by strongly preferring Indian business houses. In Maharashtra, for example, business houses headquartered in that State, including two of India's twenty largest houses, became partners in at least four of the six original joint-sector enterprises.[44] In neighboring Gujarat,

43. Ghose, "Joint Sector," p. 907 and n. 13, p. 916; P. K. Ghosh, *Government and Industry: Studies in Regulatory Policy and Practices* (Calcutta: Orion, 1977), pp. 82–83.
44. Ghose, "Joint Sector," pp. 908–10.

India's largest joint-sector enterprise—the Gujarat State Fertilizers Corporation (GSFC), with assets ranked among the country's hundred largest corporations—listed among its shareholders a "who's who" of Gujarati industrialists, including directors from India's third-, ninth-, and twentieth-largest business houses.[45] Thus, government financing again aided the growth of business houses, but now this aid arrived through a different banking network, controlled by the several States.

Partnerships in State-promoted projects were not limited to the largest business houses, however; smaller, regional houses did become involved. For example, India's second-largest joint-sector enterprise—Southern Petro-Chemical Industries Corporation (SPIC), also ranked during 1980 among the country's hundred largest companies—brought together one south Indian business house (Chidambaram) with the government of Tamil Nadu.[46] Other States—notably, Andra Pradesh and Karnataka in the south, and Punjab, Haryana, and Rajastan in the north—established similar partnerships.[47] Through joint-sector projects, State financial institutions thus offered smaller business houses access to capital at a time when such a resource was not always available from those financial institutions controlled by the central government.

In return, State financial institutions, like their counterparts in the central government, seldom converted equity ownership into managerial control. Rather, they sought to marry private management with public finance. To ensure that management remained private, State institutions sought only minority shareholdings, which (according to Indian company law) exempted companies from both audit by government ministries and scrutiny by the State assembly. Minority State shareholdings also meant that GSFC, SPIC, and four of the original projects established in Maharashtra had to register with the central government as private "monopoly" concerns under Indian law (beginning in 1969), even though the governments of Gujarat, Tamil Nadu, and Maharashtra remained the largest (albeit minority) shareholders in each case. The central government therefore treated these joint-sector enterprises no differently than it did TELCO, TISCO, and other companies that mixed government and private equity capital, but not managerial control.[48]

45. Howard L. Erdman, *Politics and Economic Development in India: The Gujarat State Fertilizer Company as a Joint Sector Enterprise* (Delhi: D. K. Publishing House, 1973), p. 43.
46. Ibid., p. 126; Industrial Development Bank, *Operational Statistics*, p. 120.
47. Ghose, "Joint Sector," p. 910.
48. J. R. D. Tata promoted this outcome during the early 1970s, in the so-called Tata

Joint-sector projects did differ, however, from other private enterprise in the degree to which they attracted foreign enterprises as
partners. TELCO, for example, originated as a joint venture between
Tata and Daimler-Benz of West Germany. By contrast, GSFC and
SPIC entailed no foreign equity, despite (as we shall see in Chapter 4)
the large production of fertilizers and other chemicals by majority
foreign-owned subsidiaries and minority affiliates operating in
India.[49]

Foreign Financing

GSFC and SPIC also typified a larger process at work in the Indian
economy: the use of government debt and equity as alternatives to
foreign investment. Indeed, the growing reliance of local enterprises
on government financing greatly reduced the interdependence between Indian business houses and multinationals. TELCO's partnership with Daimler-Benz, for example, ceased in 1962, leaving Tata
and state financial institutions to acquire all outstanding foreign
shares. In TELCO and other enterprises, Indian business houses
proved able to exert their financial independence, bolstered by their
own internal resources and by state funds. But before India's business
houses could exert that independence, they had to complete their
long-awaited takeover of the assets controlled by colonial British managing agencies.

The Indianization of Colonial Enterprises. A gradual acquisition of
British shareholdings began before 1947 and accelerated during and
after both world wars.[50] With their London and Liverpool headquar-
ters unable to invest overseas, British agencies needed to mobilize
local capital as an alternative means of financing wartime expansion
in India and of continuing repatriations to Britain. Here, Indian business houses exploited their opportunities. So massive was the influx
of local capital by mid-1948, in fact, that Indian business held, on
average, more than 85 percent of the equity in colonial managing

Memorandum to Prime Minister Indira Gandhi; for a discussion of the memorandum,
see *Economic Times* (Bombay), August 29, 1972, p. 1.

49. A few joint-sector projects, however, did involve foreign shareholdings. Pepsi-
Cola, for example, in 1986 proposed a joint venture in which it would own 39.9 percent
of the equity, Tata would own 24 percent, and the remaining 36.1 percent would be
owned by Punjab Agro (65 percent owned by the Punjab State government and 35
percent owned by the central government). See "India and Pepsi Gird for Another Cola
War," *Wall Street Journal*, August 26, 1986, p. 28.

50. For a history of this process, see Kidron, *Foreign Investments in India*, pp. 40–61.

agencies, with the remainder owned by foreigners.[51] Thus, only one year after political independence, the financial dependence of colonial British enterprises on Indian shareholders had become nearly complete.

Yet the conversion of equity ownership into managerial control was not immediate, as British managers used several complex methods to ensure continued operational control. Early on, the intermingling of Indian and British capital often resembled a simple form of partnership. In such an arrangement, Tata became associated with MacNeil and Barry; Bangur, with Bird and Gillanders Arbuthnot; Mookerjee and Bannerjee, with Martin Burn.[52] But eventually, the potent insistence of Indian shareholders that ownership in British agencies be converted into control could not be denied. During the 1950s Indian-managed business houses began to replace British firms as the dominant enterprises in the economy. And by 1957 the process of takeover through encroachment had run its course. Already, some of these takeover campaigns had proved both enormous in scope and disastrous for British agencies. Dalmia-Jain, shortly after independence, became one of the top four Indian-owned business houses by means of such wholesale takeover. And Bangur, ranked among the ten largest houses throughout the 1960s and 1970s, emerged from relative obscurity at the end of World War II simply by gobbling up several small British agencies.[53] Overall, this growth through mergers and acquisitions established the early preeminence of Indian industrial conglomerates.

But the Indianization of colonial enterprises left unscathed the few multinationals that had begun to enter India before political independence. Unlike managing agencies, multinationals claimed easier access to foreign financing; they offered to supply fresh equity in the form of cash and capitalized plant and equipment in exchange for access to the Indian market. In most cases, joint ventures married these different assets.

Joint Ventures with Multinationals. For a decade of independence, Indian public policy remained ambivalent concerning joint ventures as a new source of finance. On the one hand, the government expressly prohibited foreign takeovers of existing local enterprises and proscribed foreign-owned portfolio investments. On the other hand,

---

51. Ibid., p. 11.
52. Ibid., pp. 57–58.
53. Hazari, *Corporate Private Sector*, pp. 63–69, 143–48; Kidron, *Foreign Investments in India*, pp. 44, 57.

policy pronouncements talked of foreign investment as an important supplement to domestic savings, especially when these investments bundled foreign equity with foreign technology. With the government ambivalent about joint ventures—and the country traumatized, first by partition and then by the resultant war in 1948 with Pakistan—foreign investment in India plummeted. In fact, between 1950 and 1955 the foreign share of all equity in the Indian private sector declined, from one-fifth to one-eighth (see Figure 2-4). The Indianization of colonial enterprises accounted for much of this decline, which the paucity of new foreign investors entering India failed to offset, as we can see from Figure 2-9.

Between 1948 and 1957, according to that figure, India averaged fewer than forty new foreign collaborations annually. According to sketchy data, only a few of these entailed joint ventures with Indian enterprises.[54] Typically the Indian partner was a business house; Bangur, for example, established five joint ventures with multinationals while completing its takeover of British agencies. Even more active was Tata; by 1958, one-half of its 120 affiliated companies became joint ventures with foreign partners, who typically held minority shares. Only Mahindra evidenced a similar ratio, albeit on a smaller scale, with its ten affiliated companies. Among the remaining top twenty houses, however, such joint ventures proved to be quite rare. During the first decade of political independence financial collaboration with multinationals figured much less prominently in the investment decisions of Indian business houses than did the final acquisition of British managing agencies.

When the takeover of British agencies had run its course, a foreign exchange crisis beset India, just at the outset (1957) of the ambitious Second Plan. With this crisis came a reversal of public policy: Government regulators now began to encourage Indian firms to seek foreign equity as a way of financing new investments and of procuring imports of machinery and raw materials. Local enterprises that secured foreign tie-ups also improved their prospects for receiving licenses to expand.[55] Indeed, this changed policy and the crisis that precipitated it have been credited as the principal incentives for the growth in joint ventures: "Foreign minority partners played a significant role in these [joint] ventures" according to R. K. Hazari, writing in the midst of the

---

54. Hazari, *Corporate Private Sector*, Table 8.3, pp. 336–37.
55. All-India Association of Industries, *Report of the Working of Foreign Collaboration Undertakings in India* (Bombay, February 1968), pp. 1–15; Licensing Policy Inquiry, *Main Report*, pp. 137–38.

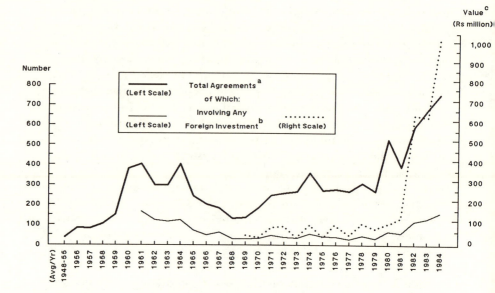

Figure 2-9. Foreign financial and technological agreements, 1948–1984
SOURCE: V. Shriram and Associates, *Top 300 Companies: Imports, Exports, Foreign Collaboration Agreements, and R&D* (New Delhi: Economic and Research Foundation, 1979), pp. 34–35; Indian Investment Centre, *Foreign Investment in India* (New Delhi, selected years).
[a]Includes all annual government-approved foreign tie-ups (technology only, finance only, finance and technology combined).
[b]Includes agreement for finance only, and for finance and technology combined.
[c]Includes foreign debt and equity inflows.

crisis, "because foreign participation in share capital became a necessity only after 1958 due to the foreign exchange crisis."[56] Indeed, Hazari concludes, "most Thapar, Mahindra, and Kirloskar joint ventures appear to owe their origin to the shortage of liquid resources in the group." If these shortages were to be overcome, cooperation was required; accordingly, financial interdependence between Indian and foreign enterprises reached its high point during the early to mid-1960s, as foreign equity flowed into nearly one-third of all tie-ups between Indian enterprises and multinationals (see Figure 2-9). As a result, by 1965 the share of all equity in the Indian private sector owned by multinationals reached 20 percent, having doubled over the previous decade (see Figure 2-4).

During the late 1960s, however, new financial collaboration with multinationals fell off precipitously (see Figure 2-9). As a result, by

56. Hazari, *Corporate Private Sector*, p. 307.

the end of the decade, stocks of existing foreign equity invested in the private sector began to shrink (see Figure 2-4). And by 1973 foreign financial collaboration in Indian industry reached its lowest point in more than a decade (see Figure 2-9). In that year the government again reversed its policy: Amendments to the Foreign Exchange Regulation Act (FERA) now restricted foreign financing, as India experienced another foreign exchange crisis. Between this new crisis and the earlier one in 1957, multinationals and Indian enterprise had entered into no fewer than five hundred financial collaboration agreements—typically bundled with technology—that still remained operational when government policy reversed. (Of course, as in the case of TELCO and Dailmer-Benz, noted above, many other collaboration agreements had been retired during the interim.) As we can also see from Figure 2-10, the vast majority of these still-operational financial collaborations involved Indian enterprises unaffiliated with business houses.

Not all business houses rejected foreign financing, however; Tata was among the most active collaborators, following a pattern evidenced as early as 1958. By 1973 Tata had been joined by Mafatlal, Thapar, and Sarabhai, among the ten largest houses, and by a few others in the next tier—all of which typically combined foreign capital with the supply of foreign technology.[57] Yet most large houses entered into few if any foreign financial agreements. Among the top ten houses, for example, Shri Ram and Scindia became conspicuous for their independence from foreign financing. Several others, like Birla, sought foreign financing only when it was coupled with foreign technology. Even Bangur, noted for its reliance on foreign financing in 1958, had by 1974 significantly diminished capital infusions from multinationals.

When they sought foreign exchange, these business houses became quite successful, as noted earlier, in securing the lion's share of government-dispersed foreign currency loans (see Figure 2-5). Outside of state financial institutions, however, foreign lending remained rare. Local enterprises with foreign technology tie-ups (but no foreign equity) had fewer foreign currency loans outstanding in 1973, for example, than they did just five years earlier (and by 1981, these loans were negligible).[58] Even the number of foreign loans typically

57. In the second tier of business houses, foreign financing was especially prevalent in Goenka (three of five collaboration agreements), Khatau (eight of nine), Kilachand (four of five), Mahindra (six of ten), and TVS (five of six). For the source of these data, see Figure 2-10.

58. Reserve Bank of India, *Foreign Collaboration in Indian Industry: Second Survey*

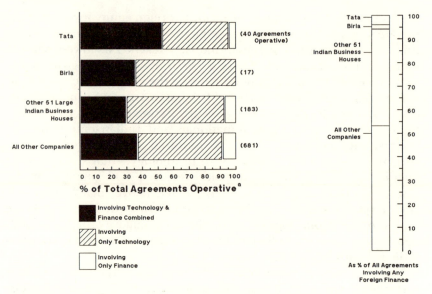

Figure 2-10. Foreign financing of private enterprise, 1973

SOURCES: Same as for Figure 2-5, at *Appendices: Volume II*, pp. 3–93; plus, India (Republic), Directorate General of Technical Development, *Handbook of Foreign Collaboration: 1973* (New Delhi: Manager of Publications, 1974).

[a]Includes all government-approved foreign tie-ups (technology only, finance only, finance and technology combined) still operative in 1973, under the purview of the Directorate General of Technical Development.

remained rather small. For instance, among the country's three hundred largest enterprises in 1971, only twenty-three sought any foreign currency loans to finance their growth.[59] And between 1971 and 1975, payments of principal on these and other foreign loans actually exceeded new borrowings, as we saw in Chapter 1. Throughout the 1970s, in fact, India experienced a net outflow of foreign exchange (see Table 1-1).

For India, independence from foreign financing became a fact of life between the amendment of FERA (1973) and the next relaxation

Report, 1974 (Bombay, 1974), pp. 72–74; and *Foreign Collaboration in Indian Industry: Fourth Survey Report, 1985* (Bombay, 1985), pp. 19, 133–34, 190–92.

59. V. Shriram and Associates, *Top 300 Companies: Imports, Exports, Foreign Collaboration Agreements, and R&D* (New Delhi: Economic and Scientific Research Foundation, 1979), p. 41.

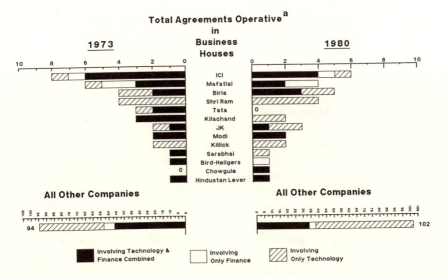

Figure 2-11. Foreign financing and technology licensing in the chemical industry, 1973, 1980

SOURCES: Same as for Figures 2-5 and 2-10; plus, India (Republic), Directorate General of Technical Development, *Handbook of Foreign Collaboration: 1980* (New Delhi: Manager of Publications, 1980), pp. 94–103; and India (Republic), Department of Company Affairs, "List of Companies Considered to Belong to the Twenty Largest Industrial Houses, up to 31 December 1980" (New Delhi, mimeographed, 1981).

Note: Includes industrial chemicals and related products but excludes pharmaceuticals and fertilizers.

[a]Includes all government-approved foreign tie-ups (technology only, finance only, technology and finance combined) still operative in either 1973 or 1980, and under the purview of the Directorate General for Technical Development.

of government restrictions on foreign investment (1980). To illustrate, let us again consider chemicals—a broadly defined industry that, along with industrial machinery, consistently accounted for the most foreign collaborations in India.[60] Between 1974 and 1980, as we see from the Figure 2-11, foreign financial tie-ups declined for Indian business houses, from two-thirds of all collaboration agreements in 1974 to two-fifths in 1980. Among large houses, only Birla actually increased its reliance on foreign financing, always coupled with technology. Conversely, houses like Tata and Sarabhai, long known for their proclivity to seek out foreign financing, by 1980 evidenced no

60. For the number of agreements operative in several industries during 1973 and 1980, see Figure 3-4.

such preference. As for enterprises unaffiliated with business houses, foreign financial agreements declined even more rapidly between 1973 and 1980, although an accelerated liberalization of government policies during the 1980s (discussed below) partially reversed this decline. Yet, before that policy reversal took effect, in 1980, Indian business houses and other local enterprises already had established their financial independence from foreign enterprises.

Still, a few foreign investors survived and even prospered in the Indian chemical industry, including at least two transformed British agencies (see Figure 2-11). In fact, as late as 1973 Killick and Bird-Heilgers combined foreign technological licenses with preexisting financial and managerial assets to rank among the country's twenty largest industrial conglomerates.[61] In this ranking, they were joined by Larsen & Tubro, Parry, and (until 1969) Martin Burn. That year, third-ranked Martin Burn finally fell victim to the process of Indianization, which long before had eliminated most other British managing agencies, as state financial institutions converted their 50-percent shareholdings into managerial control, in a rare case of nationalization.[62] During the 1970s a more gradual process of Indianization claimed most remaining (transformed) British agencies. So, by the early 1980s, only Parry among the large foreign houses in the chemical industry retained foreign directors on its board.

MULTINATIONALS

Earlier, during the heyday of British managing agencies, Imperial Chemical, Unilever, and other British multinationals quietly entered India. Unlike colonial agencies, these multinationals made use at home and abroad of their unique technological and marketing assets. So successful were Imperial Chemical and Unilever in exploiting these assets, in the chemical industry (see Figure 2-11) and elsewhere, that government regulators eventually classified both of them as business houses. Indeed, by 1965 ICI (the Indian subsidiary of Imperial Chemicals) ranked among India's ten largest houses, a position it subsequently has held.[63] And during the 1970s Hindustan Lever (the

61. For the size of each of these houses, see Khurana, *Growth of Large Business*, Table 8.9.
62. For the size of Martin Burn's assets, see Ministry of Finance, *Report of the Monopolies Inquiry Commission*, pp. 81–82, 119. For the size of government shareholdings in Martin Burn, see Licensing Policy Inquiry, *Appendices: Volume IV*, Appendix VI–E(12); and Ghose, "Joint Sector," pp. 906, 916.
63. Ministry of Finance, *Report of the Monopolies Inquiry Commission*, pp. 59–60, 119–20.

Indian affiliate of Unilever) also moved into the ranks of India's twenty largest houses. In the top twenty, ICI and Hindustan Lever were joined by a third multinational, British-American Tobacco (later renamed Indian Tobacco and finally ITC), which also had expanded and diversified its Indian operations. Like transformed British agencies before them, multinationals such as Unilever, Imperial Chemicals, and British-American entered India directly, without any assistance from a joint-venture partner.

The continued dominance of a few transformed British agencies and several multinational enterprises, operating without the assistance of local partners, importantly influenced all subsequent bargaining over access to finance, as we shall see. In particular, these foreign enterprises established a financial independence from Indian business houses, state-owned industrial enterprises, and government financial institutions. With that financial independence came considerable managerial autonomy—freedom from Indian shareholders and Indian lenders in the allocation of internally generated resources and, after 1973, in the determination of foreign equity dilution. Even after equity dilution, multinationals remained the largest shareholders, and they retained managerial control over their Indian operations. As a result, through the late 1970s multinationals remained the preeminent financiers of their own affiliates in India. Not until the 1980s did that change, but even then with no appreciable impact on foreign managerial control.

Foreign Financing

Multinationals established their financial independence and managerial autonomy by channeling most of their equity into majority foreign-owned subsidiaries. This preference for majority shareholdings became evident when foreign financial collaborations peaked, during the early 1960s (see Figure 2-9). In 1961, as we can see from Figure 2-12, multinationals concentrated nearly three-quarters of their foreign equity in majority subsidiaries. In these affiliates, multinational parents owned 80 percent of the total equity. Over the remainder of the decade and into the 1970s the concentration of foreign equity in majority subsidiaries fell off. Still, in 1973 subsidiaries in which foreigners owned, on average, 75 percent of total shares accounted for more than three-fifths of all foreign equity invested in India.

In these subsidiaries, minority local shareholders exercised little financial or managerial control. By 1973, however, amendments to the government's foreign exchange regulations (FERA) threatened to

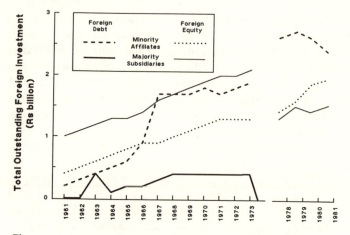

Figure 2-12. Foreign financing of majority subsidiaries and minority affiliates, 1961–1981

SOURCES: Reserve Bank of India, *Foreign Collaboration in Indian Industry: Survey Report, 1968* (Bombay, 1968), pp. 14–16, 44–45, 49, 71; *Second Survey Report, 1974* (Bombay, 1974), pp. 9, 16, 41, 60; *Fourth Survey Report, 1985* (Bombay, 1985), pp. 16, 69, 78, 102, 106, and Appendix I, pp. 183, 187, 191. Data for 1974–77 not available.

Note: Includes year-end stocks of foreign equity or foreign debt; the latter represents long-term loans, typically borrowed from multinational parents or other foreign affiliates.

reduce the shareholdings of multinationals in these and other subsidiaries with more than 40 percent foreign equity. Yet, exemptions outlined in the law allowed Imperial Chemical, Unilever, and several other multinationals to retain, on average, nearly 60 percent of the equity in their affiliates. Indeed, as late as 1978 these majority foreign-owned subsidiaries still accounted for roughly one-half of all foreign stock invested in India (see Figure 2-12). By contrast, the same figure shows that multinationals less frequently sought out local partners to form minority foreign-owned affiliates. While these joint ventures grew in importance during the 1960s and thereafter, by 1973 they continued to represent less than two-fifths of all foreign stock invested in India. That foreign equity typically equaled 30 percent of the total stock invested by all parties in joint ventures—foreign shareholdings which did not always translate into foreign managerial control. Frequently, to bolster such control, multinationals supplemented foreign equity in minority affiliates with foreign debt.

Indeed, in the financing of minority foreign-owned affiliates, foreign debt eventually superseded foreign equity. During 1966 and subsequently, outstanding foreign loans supplied by multinational parents and other overseas affiliates exceeded all foreign stock in these affiliates (see Figure 2-12). And in 1973 foreign debt was one-and-a-half times as large as foreign equity. Although debt-to-equity ratios in all foreign investments fell off in the 1980s, outstanding foreign debt specifically in minority foreign affiliates nevertheless continued to exceed foreign stock.

For multinational partners, the supply of debt to such minority ventures accomplished several objectives. Debt servicing guaranteed some capital repatriation, even when the foreign partner (as a minority shareholder) exercised less influence over payments of dividends and other remittances. Also, by controlling the supply of these loans, multinationals could exercise additional influence over the management of their joint ventures, since few other sources of foreign capital existed. As noted earlier, India remained chronically short of foreign exchange, and the government maintained a stranglehold on the distribution of the limited exchange available. With few alternative sources of foreign finance, minority foreign-owned affiliates had little choice except to turn for long-term debt to their multinational partners.

For these multinational partners, controlling access to foreign exchange through debt financing became, after the amendment of FERA (1973), an even more important source of managerial control. During the late 1970s foreign debt in minority ventures peaked; in 1978, for example, such debt was nearly twice as large as foreign equity (see Figure 2-12). Subsequently, debt-to-equity ratios fell off, as foreigners channeled most of their equity into minority affiliates. By 1978 these minority ventures had become—for the first time in Indian history—the largest repositories of foreign investment. To those multinationals which had originally entered India as minority shareholders were now added foreigners who had been forced by FERA to dilute their equity in existing subsidiaries to 40 percent or less. By means of these changes in policy, the government sought to reduce the outflow of foreign exchange (through dividends and other foreign remittances); instead, it engineered an immediate reduction in the number of new foreign equity investments (see Figure 2-12). Indeed, during the 1970s independent India experienced—again, for the first time in its history—a net outflow of foreign direct investment (according to data examined in Chapter 1). With new foreign sources of capital drying up, multinationals operating in India turned to local sources.

Local Financing

FERA forced multinationals in unprecedented numbers to rely on the Indian equity market for new financing, since—according to a survey completed by India's central bank and reported in Figure 2-13—the government exempted few firms from equity dilution. In fact, between 1973 and 1981 fewer than one-third of all multinationals with more than 40 percent foreign equity did not sell existing foreign shares or issue new equity to Indians. As we shall see in later chapters, these privileged subsidiaries operated in "high-priority industries," typically ones that employed "sophisticated technology" or exported a "significant proportion" of output. According to exemptions outlined in FERA, foreigners could retain up to 74 percent of the equity in such subsidiaries, and up to 100 percent when they exported all of their output. Other multinationals subject to FERA were forced to dilute their foreign holdings.

As we can see in Figure 2-13, most multinationals reduced their foreign shareholdings to 40 percent or less. Often, they simply sold existing foreign equity to Indian nationals. Imperial Computers (ICL), for example, followed this scheme to dilute the shareholdings in its previously wholly owned subsidiary to 40 percent. ICL overcame an initial reluctance to reduce foreign shareholdings when its principal foreign competitor in India, IBM, announced that, rather than dilute, it would withdraw from India.[64] So, after its own dilution, ICL stood alone as India's foreign manufacturer of large computer systems. Because of the high barriers to the Indian market erected by FERA, these regulations became a source of protection from foreign competition for ICL and other multinationals.

Multinationals that remained in India did not, however, have to sell existing foreign equity to local investors. They could choose instead to issue fresh equity to those investors, in conjunction with a proportionately smaller increase in foreign shares. In fact, multinationals issued new equity to dilute their stock holdings as frequently as they sold off existing shares, according to a central bank survey reported in Figure 2-14. Through such issuances, for example, Gabriel India added a second foreign collaborator while reducing its total foreign equity from 50 percent to 39 percent.[65] This dilution scheme not only

---

64. For ICL's negotiations with the Indian government, see Joseph M. Grieco, *Between Dependency and Autonomy: India's Experience with the International Computer Industry* (Berkeley: University of California Press, 1984), esp. pp. 87–88, 95–96.

65. Data from interviews held during 1982 with senior managers of Gabriel India, reported in Dennis J. Encarnation and Sushil Vachani, "Foreign Ownership: When Hosts Change the Rules," *Harvard Business Review*, September–October, 1985, p. 154.

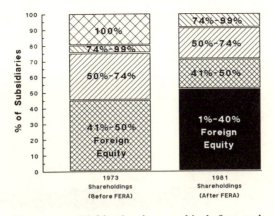

Figure 2-13. Multinational ownership before and after FERA, 1973, 1981

SOURCE: Reserve Bank of India, *Foreign Collaboration in Indian Industry: Fourth Survey Report, 1985* (Bombay, 1985), pp. 60–61.

facilitated local financing; it also resulted in an increase in the number (but not the proportion) of foreign shares. Thus, equity dilution funded the growth of minority foreign-owned affiliates in India.

Even when equity dilution did not result in the infusion of new foreign capital, growth still remained possible, through local equity offerings alone (see Figure 2-14). Ciba-Geigy, for example, increased the total equity base of its Indian subsidiary by 27 percent while it reduced its shareholdings to 40 percent.[66] The funds from the new equity, which sold at 40 percent over book value—a common response in India's inexperienced stock market—contributed nearly one-third of the total capital necessary to undertake expansion in 1983 and 1984. By issuing fresh equity exclusively to local investors, with no change in the absolute number of foreign shares, Ciba-Geigy and other multinationals also continued to grow as a result of equity dilution.

Finally, a few multinationals sold new equity to local investors, simultaneously selling existing foreign shares (see Figure 2-14). By employing this scheme, British-American Tobacco (renamed ITC) reduced its foreign ownership from 94 percent in 1968 to 75 percent in 1969, 60 percent in 1974 (following FERA), and 40 percent in 1976. The company embarked on this strategy of "phased Indianization" after it had realized, in the late 1960s, that the government was un-

---

66. Data from interviews held during 1983 with senior managers of Ciba-Geigy, reported in ibid., pp. 153–54.

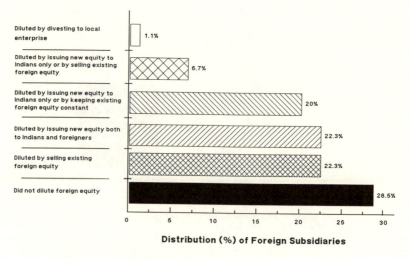

Figure 2-14. Multinational responses to FERA, 1973–1981
SOURCE: Same as for Figure 2-13.

likely to grant majority foreign ownership to a subsidiary in an industry (tobacco) that remained closely tied to agriculture, required little new technology or large capital investments, and had minuscule prospects for exports.[67] So, even before the passage of FERA, ITC chose to divest voluntarily and to look for new business opportunities as a legally defined "Indian" company. In the process of diversifying, minority foreign-owned ITC became, by the mid-1970s, one of India's twenty largest business houses.[68]

Not all multinationals that were forced by government to dilute their foreign shareholdings assumed a minority equity position after dilution, however. Those multinationals that qualified for government exemptions (for instance, by investing in the technology-intensive chemical industry) could still retain more than 40 percent foreign equity. Unilever, for example, still retained majority ownership in Hindustan Lever after issuing fresh equity to Indian investors. Moreover, in conjunction with this new infusion of Indian equity, Unilever also increased the number (but lowered the proportion) of shares it owned in its Indian affiliate. That increase in foreign shares did not, however, result from a new infusion of capital from abroad. Rather, in compliance with FERA, Unilever sold to local investors

67. Data from interviews held during 1982, 1983, and 1984 with senior managers of ITC, reported in ibid., pp. 153–54.
68. Khurana, *Growth of Large Business*, Table 8.9.

70

equity in a second Indian affiliate (minority foreign-owned Lipton) and then reinvested the proceeds of that sale back into Hindustan Lever.[69] By retaining more than this substantial ownership in a now larger Indian subsidiary, Unilever joined Imperial Chemical (also a majority shareholder after dilution) and the nearly one-fifth of all multinationals that simultaneously diluted their foreign shareholdings under FERA (see Figure 2-14) and expanded their equity base. In the process, Imperial Chemical and Unilever retained majority shareholdings in two of India's twenty largest business houses.

When they sold equity to Indian investors, multinationals made certain to disperse those shares widely, among many individual shareholders, each with a small holding. In 1980, for example, more than 89,000 Indians held 47 percent of Hindustan Lever's stock, while Unilever held the remaining block of shares.[70] Unilever therefore exercised unchallenged managerial control over its Indian operations, because majority foreign ownership was not essential so long as local shares were widely distributed. For example, more than 11,000 Indian nationals owned 57 percent of Chesebrough-Ponds (India) after the foreign parent reduced its share to 40 percent.[71] With foreign equity tightly held and local equity widely distributed, multinationals continued to control the operations of their Indian subsidiaries after equity dilution.

A wide dispersal of local shareholdings also served to minimize the number of large share blocks purchased by Indian private enterprises. In fact, between 1973 and 1981 takeovers of foreign subsidiaries by local enterprises remained negligible (see Figure 2-14). Even when a foreign company operated in partnership with a single local enterprise, that multinational diluted its equity through a wide public offering. For example, in their equal-partnership joint venture, Burroughs and Tata each sold 12.5 percent of their holdings to the Indian public in order to reduce Burroughs's (and Tata's) holdings below 40 percent—an issuance the public oversubscribed one hundred times.[72] Thus, multinationals operating minority foreign-owned joint ventures ensured that dilution did not result in a hostile takeover, nor in any reduction of managerial control.

In subsidiaries with more than 40 percent foreign equity, multina-

69. Data from interviews held during 1983 with senior managers of Hindustan Lever, reported in Encarnation and Vachani, "Foreign Ownership," pp. 155, 157–58.

70. Data from the annual reports of Hindustan Lever, reported in ibid., p. 157.

71. Data from the annual reports of Chesebrough-Ponds (India), reported in ibid., p. 157.

72. Data from interviews held during 1982 and 1983 with senior managers of both Burroughs and Tata & Sons.

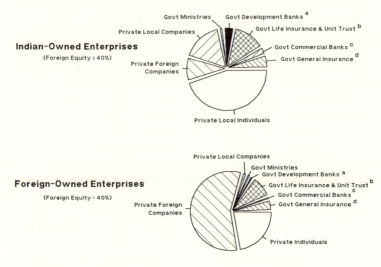

Figure 2-15. Foreign and local equity in private enterprise, 1978
SOURCE: Same as for Figure 2-6.
[a]Includes the Industrial Development Bank of India, the Industrial Credit and Investment Corporation of India, and the Industrial Finance Corporation of India, and the several State finance and industrial development corporations.
[b]Includes the Life Insurance Corporation of India and the Unit Trust of India.
[c]Includes the State Bank of India, plus the fourteen largest privately owned commercial banks nationalized in 1969.
[d]Includes the General Insurance Corporation of India.

tionals further reduced the prospects of mergers and acquisitions. As late as 1978, according to Figure 2-15, local enterprises owned negligible shares in these subsidiaries. By contrast, in Indian companies with less foreign equity, intercorporate holdings remained much more common; such holdings became a distinguishing characteristic of enterprises affiliated with Indian business houses. By limiting these holdings, multinationals diminished the possible loss of managerial control to Indian business houses and other local enterprises.

Typically, during public offerings, state financial institutions emerged as the only big institutional investors. Indeed, they often became the largest single Indian shareholders after dilution (see Figure 2-15). Still, compared to local enterprises, state financiers invested much less frequently in multinationals. Their reluctance to invest in foreign subsidiaries can be explained, at least in part, by history: Between 1956 and 1966, when foreign investment in India peaked (see Figure 2-9) along with the foreign proportion of private equities (see Figure 2-4) and industrial assets (see Figure 2-1), state financiers showed little inclination to own or underwrite the shares of Imperial Chemicals and other foreign-owned branches and subsidiaries (see Figure 2-5). (State financiers did, however, evidence a greater propensity to lend to multinationals, but that propensity still fell well below the lending rates enjoyed by local enterprises.) Over the next decade government shareholdings in foreign enterprises hardly changed, despite bank nationalization and the government's insistence that multinationals dilute their equity holdings. By 1978, as we can see from Figure 2-15, the state significantly reduced government shareholdings in enterprises with 40 percent or more foreign equity.

Even though equity dilution seldom diminished foreign managerial control, a few multinationals declined to expose their Indian operations to the risks associated with minority foreign ownership. Both IBM and Coca-Cola, for example, refused to dilute their shareholdings to the extent demanded by government; instead, they simply left India. Countless potential entrants, on the other hand, shied away. Indeed, after IBM and Coca-Cola exited during 1977, the number of new equity investments fell to an all-time low. In that year multinationals tied equity to less than 10 percent of all contracts supplying foreign technology (see Figure 2-9). Nevertheless, most multinationals already operating in India stayed on after FERA simply because their affiliates remained highly profitable.

Securing high profits and retaining control over the distribution of these local earnings—both of these objectives explained the original establishment by multinationals of majority foreign-owned subsidiaries in India. Between 1960 and 1981, as we can see from Figure 2-16, those subsidiaries typically enjoyed rates of profitability that remained higher than the rates attained by minority foreign-owned joint ventures. And compared with Indian private enterprise, majority subsidiaries repeatedly generated profits that proved at times to be 50 percent larger than those earned by Indian private enterprise.

Even in the same industry, majority foreign-owned subsidiaries have generally been much more profitable than local enterprises.[73] In fact, during 1981 electrical goods represented the only industry in which local enterprises performed as well as majority subsidiaries. Elsewhere, in machinery and machine tools, these foreign subsidiaries proved to be twice as profitable as local enterprises. With foreign ownership came technological, marketing, and managerial skills oth-

73. Reserve Bank, *Collaboration: Fourth Survey*, p. 16; data are for majority foreign-owned subsidiaries, minority affiliates, and wholly Indian enterprises with foreign technology licenses.

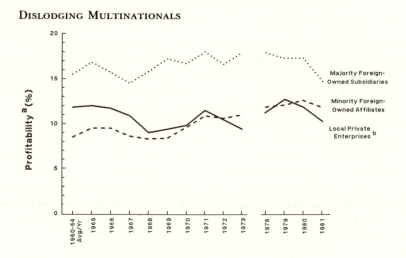

Figure 2-16. Profitability of multinationals and Indian enterprises, 1960–1981

SOURCES: Same as for Figure 2-12.

[a]Gross profit (profit after depreciation but before tax and interest payments) as a percentage of total capital employed (total assets less accumulated losses).

[b]Includes only firms with foreign technology but no foreign equity.

erwise unavailable to local enterprises—skills that generated high returns on foreign investment.

Similarly, majority subsidiaries have generally been more profitable than have minority foreign-owned affiliates operating in the same industry. In fact, again during 1981, pharmaceuticals became the only industry in which joint ventures performed as well as majority subsidiaries; in pharmaceuticals, moreover, subsidiaries and joint ventures alike remained nearly three times more profitable than local enterprises. Otherwise, in metal products and most other industries, majority subsidiaries consistently outperformed minority ventures. Majority ownership assured that multinational parents controlled the distribution of those profits which accrued from their supply of foreign capital and skills.

Often, majority subsidiaries retained these profits locally and then used them to fund expansion and diversification within India. In 1965 the retained earnings of majority subsidiaries were sixteen times larger than new infusions of foreign equity; in 1970 they were thirty-four times larger.[74] Before multinationals turned to the Indian equity market to dilute their shareholdings, these internally generated re-

74. Reserve Bank, *Collaboration: Second Survey*, pp. 9, 34–37.

sources represented the most important local source of capital. They allowed multinationals to retain their financial independence from Indian shareholders and lenders.

Even after the passage of FERA in 1973, retained earnings continued to be an important source of local financing. However, by the late 1970s retained earnings in majority foreign-owned subsidiaries had fallen off precipitously, as multinational parents repatriated their Indian earnings. Still, in 1981 retained earnings in majority subsidiaries were three times larger than foreign equity.[75] Moreover, retained earnings continued to constitute more than two-fifths of the net income among these subsidiaries, following a pattern evidenced earlier, beginning in 1965.[76] As new infusions of foreign capital dwindled, multinationals relied on these internally generated sources of capital to complement local equity offerings.

Higher profitability often followed such offerings. For example, between 1979 and 1984, after ICL had sold off 60 percent of the equity in its wholly owned subsidiary (and after its competition with IBM in India had ceased), net income grew 15 percent (compounded) annually on annual sales growth of 25 percent.[77] Chesebrough-Ponds undertook the same dilution scheme adopted by ICL, and during the four years following dilution, after-tax profits grew 57 percent.[78] Equity dilution assured these multinationals of continued access to the profitable Indian market, and the profits generated by their investments assured multinationals of the funds necessary to finance their continued growth.

Such high profitability kept multinationals interested in India, and only a slight liberalization in government policy, beginning in the early 1980s, was required to revive foreign investments once again. In fact, the response from multinationals followed immediately: between 1981 and 1982 the number of new direct investments nearly tripled, while in rupee value, equity inflows grew sixfold (see Figure 2-9). Japanese multinationals now joined a new wave of American and German enterprises; at last, British enterprises no longer accounted for more than one-half of the foreign equity invested in either majority or minority foreign-owned affiliates.[79]

75. Reserve Bank, *Collaboration: Fourth Survey*, pp. 12–13, 72–74.

76. Reserve Bank, *Collaboration: Second Survey*, pp. 34–37; Reserve Bank, *Collaboration: Fourth Survey*, pp. 12–13, 72–74.

77. Data from interviews held during 1983 with senior managers of ICL (India), reported in Encarnation and Vachani, "Foreign Ownership," pp. 157–58.

78. Data from interviews held during 1983 with senior managers of Chesebrough-Ponds (India), reported in ibid., p. 157.

79. Reserve Bank, *Collaboration: Fourth Survey*, p. 15.

By 1984 annual equity inflows from these multinationals had reached the highest level ever recorded in the history of independent India (see Figure 2-12). Still, the average new foreign investment remained quite small, seldom involving more than 40 percent foreign-owned equity, and investment continued to concentrate in only those sectors targeted by the government. In one such sector, electronics, Xerox established with a single Indian partner one of the largest of these new minority foreign-owned joint ventures, but only after Xerox had failed in attempts to retain 50 percent ownership.[80] In 1984 Xerox's equity investment of $3.3 million—combined with the record flurry of other foreign equity inflows—still represented less than 1 percent of total equity investments made by the Indian private sector during that year.[81] In other words, even in the midst of policy liberalization, multinationals found themselves nearly excluded from bargaining over access to finance.

Dislodging Multinationals: Stage One

By restricting multinationals through FERA (1973), the government satisfied a widely shared and long-standing belief in India that domestic ownership of assets and control over their use brought the nation both material and symbolic benefits. To many Indians, these gains seemed well worth subsidizing, even at the expense of higher prices, reduced quality, and supply scarcity. Already we have seen that among the strongest early supporters of this economic nationalism were the managers of Indian business houses, who had obvious incentives to advocate and support policies that promoted local ownership and control. Thus, on the eve of political independence, G. D. Birla, J. R. D. Tata, and other Indian industrialists, in the so-called Bombay Plan (1944), called for sharp reductions in India's reliance on foreign financing.

In fact, majority foreign-owned subsidiaries became the principal targets of these industrialists, since multinationals channeled through

80. Data from interviews held during 1985 with senior managers of Rank-Xerox Ltd. (U.K.), reported in Sanjeev K. Mehra, "Entry Strategies of Foreign Computer and Electronics Companies in India: 1977–86" (unpublished paper, Harvard Business School, March 14, 1986).
81. For the total investments made by the Indian private sector during 1984, see Indian Investment Center, *Indian Economy at a Glance* (New Delhi, January 1985), p. 14. For total foreign direct investment made during that same period, see Indian Investment Center, *Foreign Investment in India* (New Delhi, May 1985), p. 4.

their subsidiaries capital (bundled with technological, marketing, and managerial skills) adequate to challenge the preeminence of Indian business houses. Indeed, even after FERA and into the 1980s, the subsidiaries of two multinationals ranked among India's twenty largest business houses. Moreover, foreign control no longer necessitated majority ownership: a minority foreign-owned (but foreign-controlled) affiliate and a transformed British managing agency could also be counted among India's largest business houses during the 1980s.

Still, as business managers, Tata and Birla gained tremendous advantages by supporting nationalistic economic policies. They managed India's greatest business houses, which represented local institutional innovations shaped partly in response to India's weak capital markets. To mobilize financing, these home-grown conglomerates pooled resources and thereby reduced the cost of capital below prices prevailing in India's inefficient financial sector. Then, to distribute these resources, internal hierarchies channeled to favored associates such funds as could not be readily procured locally. Thus, in the mobilization and distribution of capital, business houses developed economies of scale. The change granted houses increased financial independence and ultimately allowed them to substitute for foreign enterprises operating in India. Their success emerged most clearly when Indian business houses acquired majority equity ownership in, and later exerted managerial control over, former colonial British enterprises (known locally as managing agencies). Historically, this Indianization of foreign capital had largely run its course by 1957, but it reappeared (although with less disastrous effects on foreign management) during the forced equity dilutions of the 1970s and 1980s.

Of course, over the country's first four decades of independence, business groups and other local enterprises were neither uniformly nor always hostile to foreign enterprise. In fact, among Indian business houses, Tata led the way in collaborating financially with multinationals. Several of its affiliated companies established joint ventures that exploited each partner's different endowments and capabilities: Tata's market access, for example, and the access of multinationals to scarce foreign exchange and (as we shall see in the next chapter) technology. Such diverse capabilities, rationally linked, yielded several mutually advantageous agreements between business houses and multinationals. In turn, their collaboration reinforced a second political demand: freedom from government interference in agreements privately negotiated. Managers with the most to gain from this cornerstone of capitalism acknowledged obvious incentives to join together in pursuit of their shared interests. Shortly after independence, as a case in point, Indian industrialists (joined by landed agriculturalists and small traders) successfully pressed the new government to include the ownership of private property in the Indian constitution as a "fundamental right." But (as we shall see in Chapter 4) such collective action in pursuit of an interest shared across large, diverse groups proved to be difficult to initiate and sustain; instead, the trading of different endowments and capabilities proved far more common.

Just as business houses were not always or unanimously hostile to multinationals, so government agencies also varied their policies in response to changes in their environment. Indeed, fifteen years earlier, those same government regulators that implemented FERA had actually encouraged foreign shareholdings by endorsing policies shaped by a very different rational calculus, in the wake of the 1957 foreign exchange crisis. During the following decade, through the mid-1960s, when local enterprises wanted to receive scarce government approvals to expand, public policy stipulated that they must secure foreign financing—and, preferably, foreign equity—to support all necessary imports of machinery and raw materials. Thus, throughout India's longest period of sustained industrial growth, government policies insisted that local enterprises and multinationals become more financially interdependent.

The success of government regulators in promoting interdependence always remained limited, however. Until the passage of FERA, the few multinationals that entered India received government permission to retain ownership of their Indian operations. As a result, as late as 1973 multinationals channeled over two-thirds of all foreign equity into majority foreign-owned subsidiaries, leaving little dependence on capital from state financial institutions or local industrial enterprises. In negotiations with potential local partners and the inevitable government regulators, multinationals expected to secure undisputed managerial control—the best single indicator of their bargaining power. By granting multinationals both equity ownership and managerial control over their Indian operations, private capitalism opened up greater opportunities for them in India.

Subsequently, however, the options available to multinationals diminished, until by the mid-1970s most foreign equity in India became concentrated in a limited number of minority foreign-owned joint ventures. Many such ventures involved local enterprises unaffiliated with business houses. However, by the 1980s even these independents had joined business houses by significantly reducing their (already limited) dependence on foreign financing. Yet that reduction did not result from an increase in the number of alternative foreign suppliers of financial resources. To the contrary, for India, foreign direct investment fell off precipitously after the government restricted majority foreign holdings, beginning in the late 1960s. And foreign commercial lending was not then viewed as an economically or politically viable substitute for foreign equity. (Concessional aid was typically disbursed to specific projects, principally in agriculture.) In any case, India's foreign exchange requirements actually remained limited, since multinationals increasingly relied on reinvested earnings, and not on fresh inflows of foreign debt or equity, to finance their growth. With the emergence of local financing, multinational parents could no longer exercise unambiguous control over the financing of their own subsidiaries in India.

Such foreign control diminished further as a result of two institutional innovations initiated by the state. First, the emergence of state financial institutions increased the interdependence of public and private finance in Indian business houses and other local enterprises. As those enterprises increasingly relied on state financial institutions for nearly all domestic and foreign-currency loans—and for growing shares of corporate equity—they also reduced their financial dependence on multinationals. Second, the state emerged as the principal financier of its own entrepreneurship. Central economic planning assured that state-owned industrial enterprises increasingly cornered the largest share of local investment. Thus, the emergence of these state industrial enterprises and financial institutions greatly increased local control over the mobilization and distribution of finance for industrial development. With that increased local control came a diminution in the power of multinationals to shape the process and outcome of bargaining.

In fact, the scale economies enjoyed by state-owned industrial enterprises provided them with an even greater amount of financial independence than that enjoyed by Indian business houses, an independence that bolstered state enterprises in their bargaining with both multinationals and local enterprises. Indeed, Indian SOEs consistently reinforced their independence by refusing to enter private capital markets or, on those rare occasions when they did collaborate financially, by insisting on majority state shareholdings. In practice, state entrepreneurs had little choice but to eschew financial interdependence with private enterprise, since directives issued by central ministries tightly restricted their bargaining range. As a result, the Indian government directly owned and controlled a greater share of the industrial economy than did private enterprise.

So long as these SOEs did not substitute for private enterprise, state capitalism received wide support among business managers. On the eve of political independence, for example, the country's leading industrialists endorsed (again, in the Bombay Plan of 1944) a mixed capitalist economy in which a strong public sector complemented a growing private sector. They envisioned a state that would enter markets unexploited by private enterprise, one that would mobilize capital otherwise unavailable. Indeed, for many Indians, some industries that the state entered early and with little opposition from private enterprise—such as steel and airlines—symbolized the economic value of their newfound nationhood. But state capitalism, like private capitalism or economic nationalism, did not receive consistent support from private enterprise. The bank nationalization of 1969, to cite only one example, prompted vociferous debate and widespread controversy.[82] Thus, when state capitalism substituted for private ownership of assets or private control over markets, serious conflict erupted (as we shall see in later chapters).

Yet, even within a sector (finance) that evidenced such conflict, the actual operation of state capitalism at least reduced (where it did not eliminate) hostilities between Indian business houses and government institutions. In this case, central ministries and parliamentary committees charged state financial institutions to invest in priority industries and to optimize returns on their portfolio of holdings. To achieve these objectives, financial institutions had little choice except to invest in large enterprises, typically owned by business houses. The rational calculus of state financiers thereby increased the interdependence between the state and business houses, while it reduced much of the political conflict inherent in the nationalization of India's financial markets. Similarly, the rational calculus of Indian business houses also promoted interdependence and worked to lessen conflict. Managers found no alternative to state financial institutions for securing most long-term debt, nearly all foreign currency, and new equity. In particular, the absence of any private alternative, foreign or domestic, drastically limited their options. Then, with business and government each able to constrain the choices of the other, state financial institutions and private industrial conglomerates crafted mutually advantageous agreements, largely without interference from the same political forces that had nationalized India's financial markets.

Multinationals, by contrast, gained little from state capitalism in India's financial markets. Unlike business houses, they seldom negotiated with sources of local capital; instead, they had to confront gov-

82. Veit, *India's Second Revolution*, pp. 109–24.

ernment regulators charged with limiting foreign ownership in the economy. In these negotiations, the influence exerted by multinationals over the bargaining process became severely limited during the 1970s because multinationals had been all but excluded as sources of new finance, or even as catalysts for mobilizing other foreign sources. With this restricted bargaining range—especially notable with regard to finance—most majority foreign-owned subsidiaries operating in India after 1973 finally had to accede to government demands for equity dilution if they hoped to maintain an existing stream of earnings.

Few other options allowed multinationals to satisfy government regulators, given their absolute dependence on state licenses to continue operations in India. One alternative—exit—seemed especially unattractive in view of India's tight restrictions on imports (as we shall see in a later chapter), at a time when growing competition among multinationals in the same industry virtually assured that some other foreign competitor would enter the Indian market. Later, in the 1980s, when India began to open up new markets to multinationals, these alternative sources of foreign capital (and foreign technology) multiplied, thus diminishing even further the prospects for multinationals to secure majority equity ownership.

Meanwhile, although FERA did create innumerable opportunities for conflict between multinationals (who often sought majority ownership) and government regulators (who sought to limit that ownership), the implementation of this legislation generated new opportunities for managers in business and government to forge mutually advantageous agreements within the law. For example, in exchange for an existing multinational's agreement to continue operations in India, government regulators themselves acceded to the demands of foreign enterprises that equity dilution be accomplished through a wider distribution of shares, rather than through mergers with local enterprises. As a result, foreign managerial control was not diluted along with foreign equity, even when foreign holdings stood at less than 40 percent.

In other words, Indian government regulators finally proved unable to dictate conditions to multinationals, even after these supranational enterprises had lost much of their power in bargaining. Here, as we shall see in the next chapter, one important constraint on the bargaining range of government regulators derived not from finance but from technology, where multinationals often exercised nearly complete control over access to those product and process innovations deemed essential for India's industrial development.

CHAPTER THREE

Technology

Even as it celebrated political independence, India remained technologically backward.[1] In fact, the new nation lacked everything except the rudiments of a machinery industry. Necessary imports came from a wide variety of sources, filling every Indian industry with an incredible mixture of machine types. For each type, local manufacturers had to stock numerous spare parts, which could be obtained only through a long foreign-dominated supply line. In its basic design, moreover, imported machinery often included costly labor-saving features that proved inappropriate for a nation of abundant manpower but scarce capital. Adaptations became essential, yet they also remained difficult to make, and technological inefficiencies resulted. India also experienced severe shortages of skilled workers, engineering technicians, and professional managers—a shortfall in human technology which reminded Indians of their colonial inheritance. For earlier, British managing agencies had attempted to overcome these same problems by drafting human resources and procuring machinery from outside of the country. In effect, these managing agencies created and maintained a virtual monopoly over the limited technology that entered India.

During the final decades of the British Raj, however, this colonial monopoly began to be threatened by a new and different breed of foreign corporation: the multinational. Unlike the managing agency, the multinational often generated and adapted technologies internally; then it moved to exploit them, by expanding operations at home and abroad. In addition to their more readily available machin-

1. Michael Kidron, *Foreign Investments in India* (London: Oxford University Press, 1965), pp. 11, 23–24, 36–40.

82

ery and management skills, the technologies of multinationals also included patented processes and products, and even know-how shared among employees—all intangible assets not easily replicated by competitors. In truth, the more unusual these technologies and related marketing skills, the more reluctant were multinationals to sell them on open markets, either to British managing agencies or to other potential competitors. Instead, multinationals typically insisted that their more advanced technological (and marketing) assets be dispersed only to captive affiliates, which bundled technology with foreign ownership and related managerial control. So, multinationals invested directly in Indian branches and subsidiaries. Also, they licensed their less unusual products and processes, and supplied foreign technicians to impart operational skills not easily procured on more open markets. But again, multinationals sought to limit the future activities of potential competitors largely by means of contractual provisions. Overall, using both technology licensing and direct investments, multinationals slowly eclipsed British managing agencies. And they emerged, in turn, as the principal purveyors of foreign technology into India.

Yet long before that eclipse was complete, a new force—the Indian business house—also began to pose a palpable threat. Like British agencies, Indian houses imported machinery and licensed other foreign technology. But like multinationals, they employed that technology to dislodge colonial managing agencies—and eventually to dislodge multinationals themselves. The eventual success of Indian business houses, however, was not apparent early in the process. Indeed, for Indians poised on the eve of political independence, the financing both of technology transfers and of internal innovations and adaptations proved especially difficult, as did the recruitment of technicians and managers. To overcome these constraints, only Tata, Birla, and a few other large Indian industrialists nurtured organizations capable of mobilizing and distributing sufficient financial and human resources. Not until much later did the state supplement their internal financial resources and establish separate training centers for managers and engineers. And later yet, enterprises and agencies of the state independently and actively engaged in the importation, adaptation, and generation of technology. But that replacement process, as we shall see, required both time and opportunity.

INDIAN BUSINESS HOUSES

The acquisition of former colonial agencies by private industrial conglomerates brought with it mature technologies in textiles and other industries where Indian enterprises had long enjoyed peculiar advantages. Indian business houses then used these native technologies, plus new tie-ups with emergent multinationals, to expand rapidly. Bangur, for example, emerged from relative obscurity at the end of World War II by gobbling up several small British managing agencies, and—at the same time—moving to establish five joint ventures with multinationals, which brought to that business house new foreign technology. As a result of its insatiable appetite for both colonial enterprises and new foreign tie-ups, Bangur soon ranked (1960s) among the ten largest business houses in India. Of course, Bangur was not unique, since foreign technology figured prominently in the growth of several business houses over the first forty years of Indian independence.

In fact, the combination of foreign with local technologies proved to be a practical key to growth. Tata, as we saw in Chapter 2, began a close association with several British agencies around the time of independence. And by 1958, one-half of its 120 affiliated companies had also entered into joint ventures with multinationals that supplied capital goods and technology licenses.[2] One of these joint ventures, a partnership with Daimler-Benz, expired in 1962, after Tata had modified foreign technology to satisfy Indian conditions. To adapt that technology and to develop local innovations, Tata invested in several R&D centers, and it employed the largest number of technical personnel in the private sector.[3] Professionally trained managers later joined them, but not in all business houses, many of which (like Birla) remained more family owned and less professionally managed. By combining these local skills and innovations with technology licensing and capital-goods imports, Tata managed to retain its ranking as India's largest business house, through independence and into the 1970s.

For Tata, Bangur, and other Indian houses, the old managing agency system remained useful as a means of mobilizing and distributing technology, since interlocking directorates and management pools conserved scarce human resources. Only in this way could a limited number of professional managers (Tata) or a few family members (Birla) coordinate the large number of diversified companies

2. R. K. Hazari, *The Structure of the Corporate Private Sector: A Study of Concentration, Ownership and Control* (Bombay: Asia Publishing House for the Planning Commission of the Government of India, 1966), Table 8.3, pp. 336–37.
3. For Tata's tie-up with Daimler-Benz and the R&D activities of Tata's second-largest affiliate (TELCO), see Baldev Raj Nayar, *India's Quest for Technological Independence*, vol. 2: *The Results of Policy* (New Delhi: Lancers, 1983), pp. 146–57.

affiliated with a business house. Among these affiliated companies, integrated production facilitated the transmission of product and process innovations from suppliers to buyers, and across potential competitors. To transfer product innovations, Birla channeled information horizontally among the country's second-largest grouping of textile mills; then, to transfer process innovations, another Birla enterprise supplied affiliated mills with automatic looms and other equipment used to weave textiles. Tata organized similarly to distribute product innovations in steel from the country's largest mill at independence, a Tata affiliate, to a second Tata affiliate, which manufactured commercial vehicles. By continuing to control the distribution of local and foreign technology in India, business houses retained their dominant position in the Indian economy long after the emergence of state enterprises.

Of course, the early dominance of Indian business houses as conduits for foreign and local technologies had important implications for their bargaining with multinationals and other foreign suppliers. For several years after independence, multinationals—if they hoped to enter the Indian market—had little choice but to supply technology to enterprises controlled by private industrial conglomerates. These multinationals were seldom left powerless, however, in their dealings with business houses. To the contrary: As soon as other local buyers of technology emerged, collaboration between multinationals and business houses fell off. Similarly, business houses were not bereft of power in their dealings with multinationals. Indian houses increasingly relied on government financiers and regulators, along with competition among foreign suppliers, to acquire technology unbundled from foreign capital. They then mixed foreign and local innovations to expand at home and abroad. Such expansion, whether it employed local or foreign technologies, always required government permission. And securing that permission became a unique and valued skill of Indian business houses.

Securing Government Licenses

When it considered a firm's application to enter or expand in an industry, the new state of India paid close attention to technology choices. Still, for nearly a decade, government regulators equivocated on questions about imported technology: they welcomed technology licensing and machinery imports but remained reticent about foreign financing. In this uncertain political environment, itself complicated by the upheavals that independence and its aftermath wrought, foreign collaboration with Indian enterprises naturally remained limited. Between independence and the foreign exchange crisis of 1957, India averaged only thirty-five new foreign collaborations annually (see Figure 2-9). Indeed, as late as 1959, fewer than one out of every eight industrial licenses issued by the government entailed any foreign tie-up, according to Figure 3-1.

But by 1964 everything had changed.[4] In that year, one out of every two new industrial licenses entailed foreign collaboration (see Figure 3-1). This rapid influx of foreign technology reflected a reversal in government policy, as the 1957 foreign exchange crisis immediately constrained prospects for the rapid industrialization envisioned in the Second Plan (1956–61). Following that crisis, government regulators, in their evaluation of the technology necessary to industrialize, began both to encourage local enterprises to procure imports of machinery and other technology tie-ups, and to finance these imports through new infusions of foreign equity. Through the mid-1960s, Indian enterprises that included foreign technology in their investment proposals thus increased their prospects for securing government approvals to enter or expand in an industry.[5]

In need of government permits and requisite technology, Indian business houses rushed to license foreign product and process innovations (see Figure 3-1). In 1956, on the eve of the Second Plan and India's first decade of sustained industrial growth, Indian business houses cornered two-fifths of all foreign technology licenses granted by the government. Three years later, in 1959, fresh inflows of foreign collaboration in India doubled. Tata, Bangur, and other Indian business houses again cornered most of the increase, holding one out of every two foreign technology licenses approved by government that year. Subsequently, their share of foreign technology just entering the country fell off, even as new foreign collaboration in Indian industry doubled again. Still, through the mid-1960s, Indian business houses each year secured anywhere from one-quarter to one-third of

4. For an early analysis of the rapid influx of foreign technology into Indian industry, see National Council of Applied Economic Research, *Foreign Technology and Investment: A Study of Their Role in India's Industrialization* (New Delhi, 1971); for a reanalysis of NCAER (and RBI) data see V. N. Balasubramanyam, *International Transfer of Technology to India* (New York: Praeger, 1973).

5. All-India Association of Industries, *Report of the Working of Foreign Collaboration Undertakings in India* (Bombay, February 1968), pp. 1–15; India (Republic), Ministry of Industrial Development, Internal Trade and Company Affairs, *Report of the Industrial Licensing Policy Inquiry Committee*, P. Dutt, Chairman (New Delhi: Manager of Publications, 1969): *Main Report*, pp. 137–38. Hereinafter cited: Licensing Policy Inquiry, *Main Report*; or Licensing Policy Inquiry, *Appendices* and volume number.

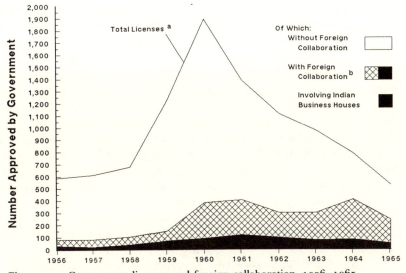

Figure 3-1. Government licenses and foreign collaboration, 1956–1965
SOURCES: Same as for Figure 2-9; plus, Subhendu Dasgupta, "Trend and Pattern of Foreign Collaboration in Indian Business Houses: A Quantitative Analysis" (unpublished manuscript, Department of Economics, University of Calcutta, March 1978), Table 5, pp. 13–15 (based on unpublished data gathered by the Industrial Licensing Policy Inquiry Committee, cited in Figure 2-5).
[a]Includes all annual government-approved licenses for establishing new undertakings, substantial expansion, new articles of association, carrying on existing business, and shifting production sites.
[b]Includes all annual government-approved foreign tie-ups (technology only, finance only, finance and technology combined).

all such government-approved technology licenses. Thus, a few powerful business houses remained the principal channels for foreign technology entering India.

That technology was never evenly distributed across business houses, however. As we can see from Figure 3-2, all seventy-three Indian business houses secured between 1956 and 1966 over two-fifths of all fresh government approvals permitting foreign collaboration. The largest twenty houses received one-quarter of these technology licenses, and the largest two—Tata and Birla—together secured over one-tenth of all new government approvals to collaborate with multinationals. Tata, Birla, and other business houses later employed this foreign technology to establish or expand industrial capacity. Between 1956 and 1966 India's largest houses tied foreign technology to nearly two-fifths of their government-approved applications. By contrast, private enterprise as a whole tied foreign collaboration to less than one-third of all fresh licenses issued by the government. Compared with other local enterprises, then, Indian business houses led the way in actively utilizing foreign technology to enter or expand productive capacity.

Indian business houses also extended their success in securing government permits for technology licenses to include government quotas on imports of machinery and other capital goods (see Figure 3-2). Indeed, they became even more successful: Between 1956 and 1966 all seventy-three business houses requested and received government permission to import over three-fifths of all capital goods (compared with two-fifths of all technology licenses), which then entered India's private sector. Birla alone secured roughly one-sixth of all such machinery imports, having inundated government regulators with applications for quotas. Tata, by contrast, submitted fewer applications for imports and secured a higher percentage of approvals—testimony to Tata's skills in lobbying with regulatory agencies. Together, Birla and Tata received government permission to import one-fifth of all the capital goods entering India during the country's first decade (1956–66) of sustained industrial growth. Again, compared with other local enterprises, Indian business houses more actively utilized imports of capital goods, along with technology licenses, to establish or expand productive capacity.

By receiving the lion's share both of government quotas to import capital goods and of government permits to license foreign technology, Indian business houses actually prevented other local enterprises from securing innovations from abroad—since, in any industry, government regulators allocated to private enterprise a limited number of permits and quotas, in accordance with plan priorities. That allocation procedure, along with central planning itself, thus behaved like a zero-sum game. In this game the benefits of securing scarce permits and quotas greatly exceeded the actual cost of the machinery imported and technology licensed. Indeed, during the early 1960s, one government commission estimated that import quotas were worth (annually) 100 to 500 percent more than the actual face value of imported goods—given the increased profits that accrued to holders of these quotas, but not to other enterprises excluded from gaining access to foreign machinery and other imports.[6] According to conser-

6. India (Republic), Ministry of Home Affairs, *Report of the Committee on the Prevention of Corruption*, C. Santhanam, Chairman (New Delhi: Manager of Publications, 1964), p. 18.

7. Anne O. Krueger, "The Political Economy of the Rent-Seeking Society," *American Economic Review* 64 (June 1974):294, Table 1.

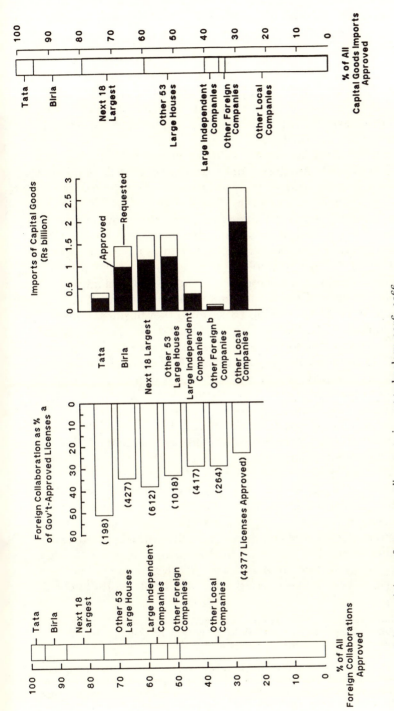

Figure 3-2. Private recipients of government licenses to import technology, 1956–1966

SOURCE: Same as for Figure 2-5, at *Main Report*, pp. 48–50, and *Appendices: Volume III*, pp. 1–3.

[a]Includes all annual government-approved foreign tie-ups (technology only, finance only, finance and technology combined) as a proportion of that year's total licenses for establishing new undertakings, substantial expansion, new articles of association, carrying on existing business, and shifting production sites.

[b]Excludes foreign companies also included either under business houses (e.g., ICI) or under large independent companies (e.g., Hindustan Lever).

vative estimates for 1964, those added benefits amounted to Rs 10 billion—or roughly 7 percent of India's national income.[7] Such value increased the competition among Indian enterprises to secure government quotas and permits. And it increased prospects of illicit behavior among business managers (seeking to influence the probability of receiving a permit) and government administrators (seeking to allocate quotas for personal gain).

For Indian business houses the value of government quotas and permits was especially apparent, since continued growth depended on machinery imports and technology licenses.[8] Here, Birla represented the most extreme example, closely followed by Tata. Both actively employed foreign technology to retain their ranking as India's two largest business houses. Similarly, between 1959 and 1969 Mafatlal moved from tenth to third in rank, thanks in large part to its active pursuit of foreign technology and, as noted in the previous chapter, to its receipt of sizable government loans (see Figure 2-5). Comparable infusions of foreign technology also aided Shri Ram's rise from ninth to sixth. Below the top 10, several other business houses— including Sarabhai, Kirloskar, Mahindra, and Bajaj—also relied heavily on foreign technology to grow. (Sarabhai, for example, moved from seventeenth to thirteenth place among Indian conglomerates by ranking among the private sector's four largest importers of capital goods and four greatest licensees of foreign technology.) By contrast, most remaining industrial conglomerates refrained from actively licensing foreign technology. In 1966 at least thirty-five of the country's fifty-three Indian-owned business houses maintained five or fewer such agreements. And, in the absence of this foreign technology, only a few of these houses experienced rapid growth.[9]

While fresh infusions of foreign technology remained integral to the growth of Indian business houses, their relative importance nevertheless declined between 1959 and 1966 (see Figure 3-1). Yet, for the private sector as a whole, such foreign infusions increased steadily, beginning in the late 1950s, until they peaked in 1964. In that year, as we saw above, one out of every two fresh government licenses issued to private enterprise involved foreign technology. Indian busi-

8. Unless otherwise noted, data in this paragraph from Licensing Policy Inquiry, *Appendices: Volume III*, pp. 1–3, Table III-A (3); Rakesh Khurana, *Growth of Large Business: Impact of Monopolies Legislation* (New Delhi: Wiley Eastern, 1981), Tables 8.7 and 8.10.

9. For example, Modi—ranked fifty-fifth in 1963—entered into only five technological collaboration agreements with multinationals during 1956–66; yet, by the mid-1970s, Modi ranked among India's twenty largest houses. At the opposite extreme, Thapar declined from fifth to ninth place between 1959 and 1969 despite active foreign collaboration. For sources, see n. 8.

ness houses, however, did not share in this deluge of technology licensing. In 1964 business houses contracted only one out of every five new technology licenses approved by government regulators. In other words, just as Indian industry increased its relative dependence on new foreign technology, Indian business houses increased their relative independence from multinationals. With that greater independence, business houses began to insist that foreign technology be unbundled from foreign capital and, by inference, freed of foreign managerial control.

Bundling and Unbundling Capital

For a decade after the 1957 foreign exchange crisis, government policy actually discouraged the unbundling of foreign technology and foreign capital. Instead, as we have already seen, with little foreign exchange at its disposal, the Indian government encouraged local enterprises to secure foreign loans and especially equity to finance the technology necessary for rapid industrial growth. Local enterprises that secured foreign financing thus improved their prospects for receiving government approvals to import new technology. So, in the years immediately following India's first foreign exchange crisis, the dependence of Indian business on technology bundled with capital increased—and actually peaked in the early 1960s, according to Figure 3-3.

Then, between 1961 and 1966, such bundling figured in more than one-tenth of all permits freshly issued by the government to establish or expand industrial capacity. In 1962 alone, new licenses for technology bundled with foreign capital nearly equalled technology licenses independent of any foreign financing. And in 1964, at the peak of foreign collaboration in Indian industry, foreign technology tied to foreign capital figured in nearly one out of every six capacity licenses issued that year by the government. Again, government regulators promoted the further interdependence of multinationals and local enterprises—this time by insisting that imports of foreign technology be financed with foreign debt and (especially) foreign equity.

By the end of the decade, however, India had drastically reduced its dependence on fresh inflows of foreign technology generally, and of bundled technology specifically (see Figure 3-3). Between 1964 and 1971 India cut by two-thirds its reliance on all new technological infusions to establish or expand productive capacity. And by 1971 most such infusions entailed no foreign financing. In fact, foreign financing figured in fewer than one-fifth of all technology licenses approved by government during 1971, compared with one-third in

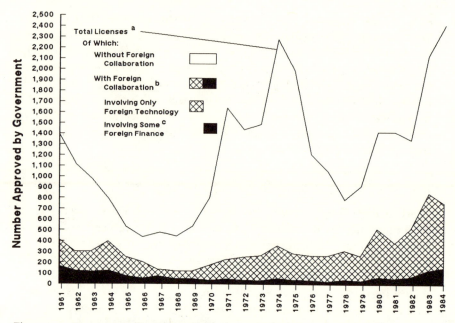

Figure 3-3. Government licensing and foreign collaboration, 1961–1984

SOURCES: Same as for Figure 2-5 (at *Main Report*, p. 45) and Figure 2-9; plus *Statistical Outline of India: 1978* (Bombay: Tata Services, 1977), p. 116; *Statistical Outline of India: 1982* (Bombay: Tata Services, 1982), p. 123; and *Statistical Outline of India: 1984* (Bombay: Tata Services, 1984), pp. 125, 127.

[a]Includes all annual government-approved licenses for establishing new undertakings, substantial expansion, new articles of association, carrying on existing business, and shifting production sites.

[b]Includes all annual government-approved foreign tie-ups (technology only, finance only, finance and technology combined).

[c]Includes agreements for finance only, and for finance and technology combined.

1964 (and nearly one-half in 1961). Foreign financing of technology imports did not again emerge as central to the entry and expansion decisions of Indian industry until the 1980s, and even then bundled licenses approved annually by government regulators did not, as a proportion of all licenses, approach the levels of the early 1960s.

In fact, changes in government policy forced this decline of technology bundled with capital. Beginning in the late 1960s, in the throes of another foreign exchange crisis, government regulators reversed course and began to limit overseas financing of technology imports in an effort to reduce foreign remittances. (It was widely assumed then in India and elsewhere that technology bundled with capital included more hidden charges than did technology licensing alone.) By 1973 new foreign financial collaborations in Indian industry reached their lowest point in more than a decade (see Figure 3-3). In that year the Foreign Exchange Regulation Act (FERA) codified the government's preference for foreign technology supplied independently from foreign capital, or at least with less foreign equity attached. Not all enterprises, however, could immediately exert their independence, since— as noted in the previous chapter (Figure 2-10)—unaffiliated enterprises in 1973 depended more heavily than did business houses on foreign financing of technology imports.

Among the many Indian business houses, individual reliance on foreign financing of technology imports varied widely. Again, it is instructive to compare the divergent strategies adopted by Tata and Birla, India's two largest conglomerates and most active collaborators with multinationals: Tata (joined by Mafatlal and Thapar among the ten largest houses) relied heavily on foreign technology bundled with foreign finance (see Figure 2-10). By contrast, Birla (and most other Indian conglomerates) demonstrated a clear preference for foreign technology *untied* from foreign capital. Indeed, among the top ten houses, Shri Ram became conspicuous for its independence from foreign financing of any type, despite its active pursuit of foreign technology.[10] To pay for new infusions of such technology, Shri Ram and other Indian business houses secured the lion's share of government-disbursed foreign currency loans, as noted in the previous chapter (see Figure 2-5). Here, government financing became an important substitute for debt and equity otherwise supplied by multinationals. Also, it facilitated the unbundling of foreign technology from foreign capital in dealings with those multinationals seeking access to the Indian market.

Diversifying Suppliers

In addition to Indian government financing, international competition among foreign technology suppliers also operated to unbundle foreign technology from foreign financing. In industries with abundant infusions of new foreign tie-ups, the dependence of Indian enterprise on foreign financing declined very rapidly. Electronics, for example, experienced the greatest infusion of new foreign collaborations (23 percent annually) between 1973 and 1980—and electronics over this period also evidenced the largest proportionate reduction in foreign licenses that bundled capital with technology, according to

10. Licensing Policy Inquiry, *Appendices: Volume II*, pp. 3–93.

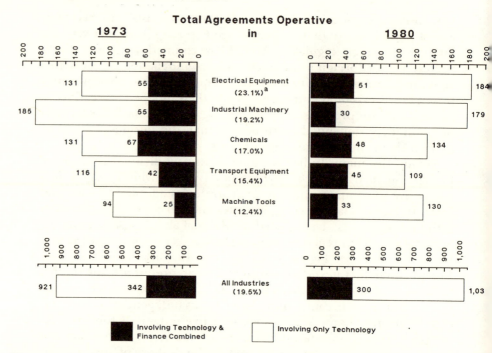

Figure 3-4. Foreign technology and finance in Indian industries, 1973, 1980

SOURCES: India (Republic), Directorate General of Technical Development, *Handbook of Foreign Collaboration: 1973* (New Delhi: Manager of Publications, 1974), and *Handbook of Foreign Collaboration: 1980* (New Delhi: Manager of Publications, 1980).

Note: Includes all government-approved foreign tie-ups (technology only, finance only, finance and technology combined) still operative in either 1973 or 1980, and under the purview of the Directorate General for Technical Development.

[a]Numbers in parentheses represent compound annual growth rates of agreements between 1973 and 1980, using stocks of foreign collaboration in 1973 as the base.

Figure 3-4. At the opposite extreme during the 1970s, transport equipment experienced smaller inflows of new technology (roughly 15 percent annually), and such equipment recorded the greatest proportionate increase in technology licenses bundled with foreign capital. Machine tools further exemplified that same extreme: Here, even more limited infusions of new foreign technology easily offset the retirement of existing licenses and maintained that industry's ratio of bundled to unbundled agreements. Thus, in transport equipment and machine tools, the small number of new suppliers of foreign technology granted local enterprises little choice but to accept more technology bundled with foreign capital.

Yet in electronics, as well as in industrial machinery and chemicals, local enterprises could choose among a full range of new foreign suppliers (see Figure 3-4). So, they increasingly unbundled foreign technology from foreign capital. Consider chemicals, for example, a broadly defined industry that, along with industrial machinery, accounted for the largest percentage of total foreign collaborations then operative in India. In the chemical industry between 1973 and 1980 the number of newly signed foreign collaboration agreements almost equalled the number retired. Yet, the proportion of agreements that bundled technology with capital nearly halved. Independent companies and large business houses, as shown in the previous chapter, also experienced that decline (see Figure 2-11). In fact, the two houses that relied heavily on bundled contracts in 1973, Tata and Kilachand, had retired them all by 1980. In so doing, they exemplified a larger process: Indian enterprises acted to reduce their dependence both on foreign financing of technological imports and on new infusions of that technology—for which they now substituted local adaptations and innovations.

Mixing Foreign and Indigenous Sources

India's modest research and development (R&D) expenditures contributed greatly to that country's reduced dependence on foreign technology, especially on technology bundled with foreign capital. Not only did these expenditures generate new product and process innovations, but they also adapted foreign technology to local conditions. Consider another example from the chemical industry: Sarabhai initially acquired pharmaceutical and related technologies through a minority foreign-owned joint venture with Merck Pharmaceuticals. Over the life of this joint venture, Sarabhai repeatedly modified Merck's technology to satisfy local conditions and invested in product innovations appropriate to India. When that joint venture's technical and financial agreements expired in 1969, Sarabhai assumed full control. Thus, during the late 1960s Sarabhai reduced its foreign technology remittances, just as it increased its local R&D expenditures. It thus followed a pattern consistent with other joint ventures, as shown in Table 3-1.

At the same time, as data in this table indicate, these joint ventures began to spend more of their sales on local R&D than did wholly locally owned enterprises with unbundled technology licenses—enterprises that during the late 1960s spent roughly equal (albeit

Table 3-1. Foreign technology in Indian enterprises and multinationals, 1960–1981

Period	State-owned enterprises[a]	Local private enterprises[a]	Minority foreign-owned joint ventures	Majority foreign-owned subsidiaries
	Average number of technology licenses per firm			
1960–64	2.9	1.8	1.6	1.6
1964–70	4.2	1.8	1.7	1.9
1970–73	NA[b]	1.6	1.6	1.8
1977–81	4.2	1.5	1.6	1.6
	Average number of foreign technicians on site			
1960–64	229.8	2.8	6.4	12.2
1964–70	149.7	2.6	6.4	18.8
1970–73	NA	0.7	2.1	4.3
1977–81	25.0	0.3	0.8	6.3
	Foreign remittances for royalties and fees[c]			
1960–64	NA	0.42%	0.63%	0.46
1964–70	0.61%	0.30	0.43	0.49
1970–73	NA	0.24	0.29	0.23
1977–81	0.28	0.25	0.23	0.05
	Expenditures for local R&D[c]			
1964–70	0.79%	0.30%	0.40%	0.67%
1977–81	0.66	0.67	0.66	0.75
	Restrictive clauses[d] in foreign technology agreements[e]			
1960–64	NA	46.1%	56.4%	43.8%
1964–70	54.0%	60.2	65.4	40.7
1970–73	NA	65.2	63.5	52.6
1977–81	62.4	72.3	58.7	67.4

SOURCES: Reserve Bank of India, *Foreign Collaboration in Indian Industry: Survey Report, 1968* (Bombay, 1968), pp. 11, 21, 27, 34, 40, 50, 55, 58, 69, 73, 77, 80, 92, 96; Reserve Bank of India, *Foreign Collaboration in Indian Industry: Second Survey Report, 1974* (Bombay, 1974), pp. 30, 42, 46, 50–51, 66, 69–70, 77, 80, 84–85, 88, 91, 92, 93, 102, 130, 138; Reserve Bank of India, *Foreign Collaboration in Indian Industry: Fourth Survey Report, 1985* (Bombay, 1985), pp. 44, 67, 81, 97, 99, 108, 123, 127, 129, 135, 149, 152, 155, 160, 166, 169, 171, 178–79, 194, 214, 220.
[a]Includes only enterprises with technology tie-ups and with no foreign equity.
[b]Not available.
[c]As percentage of total sales.
[d]Includes prohibitions on exports and minimum payment provisions.
[e]Technology licenses with restrictive clauses as a percentage of all technology licenses.

small) proportions of their sales on local and foreign technology. However small, these proportions actually exceeded the local R&D expenditures of another group of wholly Indian-owned enterprises— namely, enterprises that did *not* license foreign technology—according to a separate study of the country's top three hundred companies conducted in 1971.[11] That is, among wholly Indian-owned enterprises, those that licensed foreign technology spent more of their total sales on local R&D than did those that licensed *no* foreign technology. And both types of wholly locally owned enterprises spent even smaller proportions of their sales on local R&D than did joint ventures that bundled foreign technology with foreign equity. At a bare minimum, Indian enterprises licensing bundled and unbundled foreign technology had to adapt that technology to local conditions, which required that they invest accordingly. Again, for Sarabhai and others producing a broad range of products—including chemicals, industrial machinery, and transport equipment—these local adaptations and innovations eventually allowed them, during the late 1970s, to retire existing foreign licenses (see Figure 3-4).

As a result, between 1977 and 1981 foreign technology remittances declined further as a percentage of sales, while local R&D expenditures increased. In fact, for both joint ventures and local licensees these local expenditures actually began to exceed foreign remittances for royalties and technical fees (see Table 3-1). As enterprises reduced their dependence on foreign technology generally, and bundled technology specifically, they seem to have broadened their search for local alternatives. These alternatives, in turn, granted joint ventures and local licensees a newfound independence from the foreign technology of multinationals. Put another way: In Indian enterprises free of foreign capital and in joint ventures with multinationals, local expenditures on R&D operated to reduce the degree of dependence on new infusions of foreign technology.

For local enterprises the critical turning point occurred in 1973, when FERA and new tax incentives combined to encourage expenditures on local R&D. Over the next four years the number of in-house R&D facilities operating in the private sector also doubled, reaching more than three hundred by 1977.[12] (In that year, the entire Indian private sector spent nearly eight-tenths of 1 percent of its sales on R&D—double comparable expenditures by state-owned industrial enterprises.[13]) Indeed, a few of the R&D facilities operated by Indian business houses built reputations that extended well beyond India's borders, including Tata's center for research on commercial vehicles

11. V. Shriram and Associates, *Top 300 Companies: Imports, Exports, Foreign Collaboration Agreements, and R&D* (New Delhi: Economic and Scientific Research Foundation, 1979), pp. 127–28, 131–33.
12. Nayar, *India's Quest*, 2:328, Table 6.2.
13. Shriram, *Top 300 Companies*, p. 136, Table 6.14, and p. 143, Table 6.19.

and Bajaj's facility for the development of two-wheel scooters.[14] Having retired earlier collaboration agreements with Mercedes and Vespa, respectively, Tata and Bajaj now contributed to a larger trend: the reverse flow of technology out of India—yet another sign of their growing technological independence from multinationals.

Reversing the Flows

Indian business houses spearheaded the outflow of foreign technology from India by investing in joint ventures abroad. In 1977, at the height of this investment, ten of India's twenty largest business houses owned nearly one-half of all Indian joint ventures that manufactured in other developing countries.[15] Another one-fifth were owned by smaller business houses. (A wide assortment of Indian companies unaffiliated with business houses owned the remainder.[16]) Nearly all of these Indian enterprises held minority equity in their joint ventures abroad, obtained through the capitalization of technology and machinery.

Textiles accounted for the largest number of overseas joint ventures, and that industry typified the reverse flow of technology. In fact, India's largest producer of textiles, Birla, established in 1956 the first successful Indian joint venture outside the country, a textile mill in Ethiopia.[17] Birla, like most other Indian textile manufacturers, actively exploited its own technological achievements at home to expand production abroad. In fact, foreign technology licensing was relatively uncommon in India's textile industry: In 1971, for example, barely one-quarter of the country's eighty largest textile manufacturers licensed foreign technology, while over one-half of the coun-

14. Nayar, *India's Quest*, 2:146–62, for a discussion of foreign licensing and local R&D in Tata and Bajaj.

15. Dennis J. Encarnation, "The Political Economy of Indian Joint Industrial Ventures Abroad," *International Organization* 36 (Winter 1982):37, Table 1.

16. These independent Indian enterprises established a majority of the projects still under implementation. However, given the high rate of failure and abandonment at that stage—roughly 45 percent in 1976—and the greater accumulated experience of large business houses in overseas operations, independent companies were unlikely to increase their relative share of joint ventures vis-à-vis business houses. For example, all five projects in Malaysia that reported delay or no progress as of 1977 were initiated by independent Indian companies. See ibid., pp. 37–38; for rates of failure and abandonment, see Indian Institute of Foreign Trade, *India's Joint Ventures Abroad* (New Delhi, 1978), pp. 80–81.

17. In 1960 the mill began production and subsequently supplied half of Ethiopia's textile market; for further details, see Indian Investment Centre (IIC), *Joint Ventures Abroad* (New Delhi, 1977), p. 16.

try's three hundred largest private corporations licensed their technology.[18] By 1977 Birla and other technologically self-sufficient textile manufacturers established one-fourth of the sixty Indian joint ventures manufacturing in other developing countries.[19]

Another two-fifths of these joint ventures manufactured abroad a range of light engineering goods, employing the same technology they used in India. In both the textile and light engineering industries, product and process technologies used in India and other developing countries changed infrequently, employed much more labor than capital, and granted few economies of scale in manufacturing.[20] Besides these investments, another one-fifth of all Indian joint ventures then manufacturing in developing countries concentrated in cement, paper, and other such raw material–intensive industries. Here, Indian enterprises also enjoyed peculiar technological advantages that could be easily exploited in other developing countries with endowments similar to those in India.

Much of the technology used by Indians abroad could be traced to earlier adaptations of foreign R&D to Indian conditions. Again, consider Sarabhai: after acquiring foreign technology through a joint venture, modifying that technology to Indian conditions, acquiring all foreign shareholdings, and retiring related licensing agreements, Sarabhai Chemicals expanded its operations abroad. By 1980 Sarabhai's pharmaceutical facilities were in production or under construction in Kenya, Indonesia, Malaysia, and Thailand. Several other business houses—Birla, JK, Kirloskar, Tata—followed a similar path of first licensing, then adapting, and finally exporting technology to joint ventures abroad. Along with Sarabhai, they accounted for nearly one-tenth of all foreign technology licenses operative in Indian industry during 1973, and they owned during 1977 two-fifths of all Indian joint ventures manufacturing in other developing countries.[21]

Among these houses, Kirloskar, Sarabhai, and Tata not only collaborated at home more and invested overseas more, but they also produced abroad many of the same products for which they originally had sought foreign collaboration in India. Only Birla established several joint ventures overseas in traditional Indian industries (principally cotton and jute textiles) for which, as noted above, indigenous

---

18. Shriram, *Top 300 Companies*, p. 42, Table 2.5.

19. IIC, *Joint Ventures Abroad*, Annexure VII, pp. 71–101.

20. K. Balakrishnan, "Indian Joint Ventures Abroad: Geographic and Industry Patterns," *Economic and Political Weekly* (Bombay): *Review of Management*, May 29, 1976, pp. M35–M48.

21. Encarnation, "Indian Joint Ventures Abroad," p. 49, Table 4.

Indian technology was readily available.[22] With these notable exceptions, then, Indian business houses that heavily licensed foreign (typically unbundled) technology in India also established the greatest
number of joint ventures abroad.

The Price of Unbundling

Business houses could not move abroad with impunity; instead, the
same licenses that granted Indian enterprises access to foreign technology also worked to restrict the subsequent use overseas of that
licensed technology. In their licensing agreements, for example, foreign suppliers commonly inserted contractual provisions which prohibited exports from the Indian houses that employed their technology. Other provisions insisted on minimum payments for the use of
that technology exclusively in India, even when sales lagged. When,
on the other hand, domestic sales soared, foreign suppliers charged
additional royalties, above the minimum threshold, in proportion to
these sales. Over time, the incidence of these and other restrictive
clauses in foreign licensing agreements increased, especially when the
state toyed with minimum export guarantees and other performance
requirements as ways of earning scarce foreign exchange. Restrictive
clauses also multiplied when Indian business houses and other local
enterprises reduced the bundling of foreign technology and capital.

Over the twenty years between 1961 and 1981, as noted above,
foreign financing of technology imports generally declined (see Figure 3-3), as foreign suppliers increasingly insisted that local enterprises with no foreign shareholdings sign contracts restricting their
use of foreign technology (see Table 3-1). Finally, Indian business
houses and other Indian-owned private enterprises were especially
affected. By contrast, state-owned enterprises (SOEs) continued to
confront a lesser insistence on restrictive clauses in their licensing
contracts with multinationals and with other foreign suppliers of
technology.

STATE-OWNED ENTERPRISES

In 1947 the limited services provided by the central government
benefited little from new infusions of foreign technology. Instead, the

22. Ibid. J. K. also licensed less foreign technology in India than did other large
houses investing abroad but had more extensive overseas operations than did other
houses.

Indian state relied almost exclusively on capital goods (e.g., the rail-roads and power plants) and managerial skills (e.g., in public admin-istration and postal services) left behind by the British. Two decades after independence—into the 1960s—the state's entrepreneurial ac-tivities remained limited (see Figure 2-1), as did the state's licensing of foreign technology. Between 1956 and 1966, at the height of foreign collaboration in Indian industry, Tata and Birla each licensed more foreign technology (102 and 146 agreements, respectively) than did all state-owned industrial enterprises combined (71 agreements).[23] Thus, for more than twenty years foreign technology in SOEs re-mained notable for its absence.

With central economic planning all of this changed, however. Dur-ing the late 1960s and through the 1970s state investments grew dramatically, until they eventually outpaced investment in the private sector (see Figure 2-2). As we saw in the previous chapter, the state concentrated most of this new investment in a few (so-called non-departmental) enterprises—notably twenty-three of the twenty-five largest corporations in India, including the top ten. By 1973 these enterprises were operating in selected industries—especially steel, en-gineering, chemicals, and mining—that required new infusions of foreign technology (see Figure 2-3). During that year these few SOEs operated under license to roughly the same number of foreign sup-pliers of technology as did the hundreds of firms controlled by India's ten largest business houses (107 versus 109 agreements still opera-tive).[24] The pattern became familiar: like Indian business houses, state-owned enterprises increasingly relied on foreign technology to grow.

Yet, in contrast to those private industrial conglomerates, Indian SOEs seldom bundled foreign technology with foreign capital. Dur-ing 1973, for example, state enterprises financed fewer than one out of every one hundred technology licenses through foreign suppliers, compared with one out of every three for the country's fifty-three Indian-owned business houses (see Figures 3-5 and 2-10). (Among the 10 largest business houses, only Shri Ram and Scindia relied less frequently on bundled technology than did the state.) As noted ear-

23. Licensing Policy Inquiry, *Main Report*, Table II, p. 48, and Table III, p. 49.
24. Data on foreign collaboration in Indian SOEs from Figure 3-5. Data on foreign collaboration in the ten largest business houses through 1973 from Subhendu Dasgup-ta, "Trend and Pattern of Foreign Collaboration in Indian Business Houses: A Quan-titative Analysis," manuscript (Department of Economics, University of Calcutta, March 1978), Table 11, pp. 24–26 (based on the same data gathered by the Directorate General for Technical Development and reported in Figure 2-10).

lier, central economic planning and the nationalization of the country's financial sector assured a few SOEs of financial independence and managerial autonomy.

The financial and managerial independence of state enterprises, and their growing importance as conduits for foreign technology, held important implications for their bargaining with multinationals and other foreign suppliers. Namely, Indian SOEs routinely secured technology unbundled from foreign capital; and in those selected industries dominated by SOEs, multinationals found themselves forced to supply unbundled technology to enterprises controlled by the state—if they wished to gain access to the Indian market. Alternative buyers hardly existed. Again, like Indian business houses, these SOEs also relied on competition among foreign suppliers, and on a mixture of foreign and local innovations, to secure the technology they demanded. Yet multinationals were not entirely powerless in their dealings with SOEs, as they proved again by imposing a variety of contractual provisions to limit the uses of their technology.

Unbundling Technology and Diversifying Suppliers

To secure foreign technology independent of foreign equity, state enterprises moved beyond more traditional sources of such technology to include several communist governments that did not invest in overseas equity. During 1973, for example, Indian SOEs called upon the Soviet Union and other Eastern Bloc countries to supply unbundled technology in one out of every six licenses these SOEs signed. State investments in steel, petroleum, fertilizers, and pharmaceuticals during the 1950s and 1960s depended heavily on technology from these countries.[25] By contrast, private Indian enterprises relied little on technology supplied by centrally planned economies, and they remained less successful in unbundling foreign technology as we can see from Figure 3-5. Over the remainder of the 1970s, foreign technology in the Indian private sector increased only marginally.

Already we have noted how regulatory policies and local R&D expenditures combined to reduce the dependence of business houses and other private Indian enterprises on product and process innova-

25. For examples, see Padma Desai, *The Bokoro Steel Plant: A Study of Soviet Economic Assistance* (Amsterdam: North Holland, 1972); P. J. Eldridge, *The Politics of Foreign Aid in India* (New York: Shocken Books for the London School of Economics and Political Science, 1969).

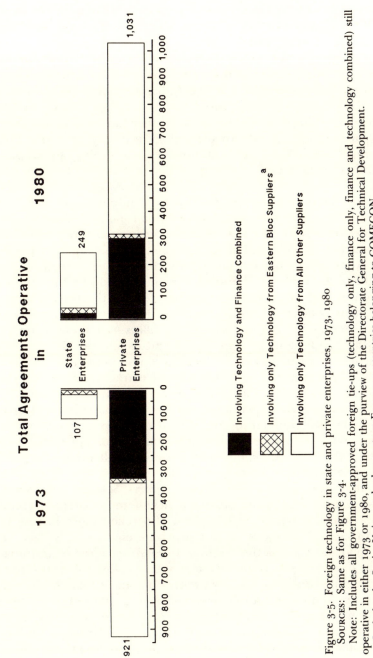

Figure 3-5. Foreign technology in state and private enterprises, 1973, 1980

SOURCES: Same as for Figure 3-4.

Note: Includes all government-approved foreign tie-ups (technology only, finance only, finance and technology combined) still operative in either 1973 or 1980, and under the purview of the Directorate General for Technical Development.

[a]Includes the Soviet Union and other eastern European countries belonging to COMECON.

tions from abroad. Indian state enterprises, on the other hand, experienced no similar reduction. To the contrary: Between 1973 and 1980, as total foreign collaboration in the Indian private sector increased marginally, technology licensing by Indian SOEs doubled (see Figure 3-5). During 1973 SOEs accounted for one-ninth of all such technology licenses operative in the Indian economy; by 1980 their share of all licenses had increased to one-fifth. Of course, foreign suppliers based in the Soviet Union and other Eastern Bloc countries participated in this growth of technology licensing by SOEs; even more important in the long term, however, was technology supplied by multinationals based in North America, western Europe, and Japan.

This increased dependence on technology supplied by multinationals eventually led to increased foreign financing of technology imports. Between 1973 and 1980 bundled agreements grew eightfold, from less than 1 percent of all technology licenses operative in SOEs (1973) to nearly 10 percent (1980). By contrast, between these two dates the total number of bundled agreements held by Indian business houses and other local enterprises fell. In the private sector, government policies, local investments in R&D, and increased competition among foreign technology suppliers—all these again reduced the bundling of foreign capital and technology. Indian state enterprises, on the other hand, experienced no comparable reduction in bundled agreements. Still, they signed markedly fewer bundled agreements overall than did private enterprises. Indeed, during the 1970s central economic planning and the nationalization of India's capital markets continued to save SOEs from relying extensively on multinationals to finance massive infusions of foreign technology.

Much of that new technology entered only a small number of SOEs, which signed multiple licenses, typically involving several multinationals along with a few Eastern Bloc suppliers. Seldom did a private firm, whether Indian or multinational, license more foreign technology than did the typical SOE—which also relied more heavily on foreign technical personnel than did private enterprise. In fact, between 1960 and 1964, at the height of foreign collaboration in Indian industry (see Figure 3-3), the average SOE employed over two hundred foreign technicians—nearly twenty times more than the average majority foreign-owned subsidiary, and over a hundred times more than business houses and other private Indian enterprises (see Table 3-1). Compared to these private enterprises, then, Indian SOEs during the late 1960s typically paid twice as much in royalties and fees.

By the late 1970s and early 1980s, however, state enterprises had cut their foreign remittances for technology in half, thus bringing them more in line with remittances in the private sector (see Table 3-1). In fact, across the Indian economy, such remittances declined between the 1960s and the 1980s. Here, a significant drop in the employment of foreign technical personnel throughout Indian industry—but especially in state enterprises—helps to explain the overall decline. (Yet, during 1977–81, SOEs still employed four times more foreign technical personnel than did the next-largest employer, majority foreign-owned subsidiaries.) In addition to declining foreign employment, Indian industry generally— and SOEs specifically— also reduced the cost of individual technology licenses. Therefore, as the number of technology agreements signed by all state enterprises increased during the 1970s, foreign remittances for royalties and technical fees actually declined as a percentage of sales. So, too, did relative expenditures on local R&D.

Developing Indigenous Sources

Prior to the 1970s the growth of local R&D expenditures by Indian SOEs actually outpaced the otherwise rapid growth of their foreign technology remittances (see Table 3-1). Consequently, by the late 1960s these SOEs had begun to spend more of their sales, both on foreign technology *and* on local R&D, than did private enterprise. Much of this difference between state and private enterprises actually eroded over the decade of the 1970s, following a marked decline in the proportion of SOE sales spent on foreign technology. While state expenditures on local R&D also declined as a percentage of sales over that decade, they did so less precipitously. As a result, within SOEs the existing gap between local R&D expenditures and foreign technology remittances widened. By the early 1980s local expenditures were 2.5 times larger than foreign remittances—and they had settled to a level that was roughly comparable to the private sector's own R&D expenditures. Indeed, within the private sector, majority foreign-owned subsidiaries spent more of their sales on local R&D than did Indian SOEs.

These state enterprises channeled most of their local expenditures into forty-five in-house R&D facilities in operation as of 1977.[26] Like their private-sector counterparts, many of these government centers not only invested in local product and process innovations; they also adapted to local conditions the foreign technology licensed or other-

26. Nayar, *India's Quest*, 2:328, Table 6.2.

wise purchased by SOEs. A few of these R&D facilities, however, relied very little on foreign technology to supplement their own in-house work. For instance, the state's sole computer manufacturer, the Electronics Corporation of India (or ECIL), sought no foreign licenses or purchases until 1984.[27] Instead, ECIL supplemented its own R&D expenditures on commercial products with additional government expenditures earmarked for "noncommercial" uses—in defense, atomic energy, and space research. These noncommercial R&D activities actually accounted for nearly four-fifths of all government R&D expenditures, with the remainder going largely to the forty-five in-house R&D centers mentioned above.[28]

Added together, the government's commercial and noncommercial expenditures on local R&D grew nearly three times faster between 1959 and 1979 than did India's national product.[29] Despite these R&D activities, the records of official inquiries documented many cases in which SOEs rejected local technological alternatives, favoring instead new foreign tie-ups.[30] Like government regulators of private enterprise, central ministries—in pursuit of rapid industrialization—often preferred foreign product and process innovations to untested local technologies. Although FERA (1973) eventually altered the preferences of government regulators, it had minimal effect on central ministries. Instead, these ministries continued to promote, during the 1970s and 1980s, the value of interdependence between state-owned industrial enterprises and multinationals.

MULTINATIONALS

While the Indianization of colonial managing agencies served to eliminate most foreign enterprises from textiles and other industries with low technological barriers to entry,[31] this process did little to

27. In 1984 ECIL entered into a technology licensing contract with Control Data; for further details, see India (Republic), Department of Electronics, *Annual Report: 1984* (New Delhi: Manager of Publications, 1985), p. 60.

28. Nayar, *India's Quest*, 2:329, Table 6.3.

29. Shriram, *Top 300 Companies*, p. 122, Table 6.2.

30. For several case studies, see India (Republic), Parliament, House of the People, Committee on Public Undertakings, 1975–76, *Eighty-Ninth Report: Foreign Collaboration in Public Undertakings*, Fifth Lok Sabha (New Delhi: Lok Sabha Secretariat, 1976), pp. 174–277. Numerous scholars have also examined this issue. Instructive is V. V. Bhatt, "Decision Making in the Public Sector: Case Study of Swaraj Tractor," *Economic and Political Weekly* (Bombay): *Review of Management*, May 3, 1978, pp. M30–M45.

31. Kidron, *Foreign Investments in India*, p. 40.

displace those multinationals in possession of unique managerial and technological assets that had already catapulted them abroad. Like Imperial Chemicals (ICI), most multinationals moving to India invested in majority foreign-owned subsidiaries, indeed, during the early 1960s (at the peak of foreign investment), multinationals concentrated nearly three-quarters of their foreign equity in majority subsidiaries. Such concentration typically gave foreign parents 80 percent of all shareholdings, with the remainder distributed widely. In fact, Indian financial institutions evidenced little proclivity to own these shares (see Figure 2-5). Though the concentration of foreign equity in majority subsidiaries subsequently fell off, as late as 1973 multinational parents continued to invest more than three-fifths of all their foreign equity in subsidiaries (see Figure 2-12), where they owned 75 percent of the shareholdings. Like transformed British agencies before them, ICI and other multinationals entered India directly, without the assistance of joint-venture partners.

Naturally, the ability of multinationals (and transformed colonial agencies) to finance from abroad their technology imports held important implications for subsequent bargaining over access to technology. In practice, government regulators had little choice but to allow these multinationals to continue bundling foreign capital and technology. Later, however, as technology unbundled with capital became more readily available, these same regulators would deny additional licensing of bundled technology. Even so, multinationals with investments already operating in India turned to local product and process innovations for growth. And new foreign entrants continued to view technology licensing as less risky than equity investments, and therefore as a preferred first step toward entering the huge Indian market. To enter, however, government licenses were required.

Securing Government Licenses

We have already noted that government regulators, after the foreign exchange crisis of 1957, rewarded multinationals that supplied technology coupled with capital. Again, consider ICI. Between 1956 and 1966 that single multinational received 1 percent of all new government licenses approving foreign collaboration.[32] Only eight other industrial conglomerates—all owned by Indians—could boast that they had received more. In addition, ICI received approval for nearly

---

32. Licensing Policy Inquiry, *Appendices: Volume III*, pp. 1–3, Table III-A (3). In fact, ICI and all other multinationals received more than one-tenth of all government approvals for establishing or expanding industrial capacity in India.

three-quarters of the machinery and capital goods it requested. ICI then employed these foreign technologies in nearly two-thirds of all government-issued permits it received to establish or expand manufacturing capacity. None of the other top ten industrial conglomerates—all Indian-owned except for ICI—evidenced such a dependence on technology licensing.[33] With this technology, by 1969 ICI had moved into fourth place among India's industrial conglomerates, up from nineteenth in 1963.[34] In this, ICI exemplified a larger trend: The increasing prominence of foreign technology in the rapid growth of multinationals.

For former colonial British agencies, continued growth also depended on government permission to import capital goods and license technology. Bird-Heilgers, for example, diversified into chemicals and away from jute and mining through new infusions of foreign technology and capital (see Figure 2-11). Between 1956 and 1966 Bird-Heilgers tied foreign collaboration to one-quarter of its government-approved applications to establish or expand industrial capacity.[35] As a result, Bird-Heilgers continued to rank among India's twenty largest business houses into the 1970s, when Indian shareholders finally assumed managerial control. Similarly, Parry joined the ranks of the top twenty during the 1970s by expanding its production of chemicals and fertilizers through several technology licenses.[36] Between 1956 and 1966 foreign capital and technology figured into one-fifth of Parry's government-approved expansion plans.[37] By contrast, five other former colonial agencies— all of which survived the initial wave of Indianization, but licensed no foreign technology between 1956 and 1966—-did not survive into the 1970s.[38] In retrospect, their reluctance to tie up with foreign technology suppliers seems symptomatic of a failure to adapt to the new exigencies of an industrializing economy.

With government regulators readily approving applications to im-

---

33. Ibid. Of India's seventy-three Indian and foreign-owned business houses in 1966, only Kirloskar (with assets ranked twenty-third among these houses) boasted more foreign collaboration among its industrial licenses (forty-nine of fifty-one) than did ICI.

34. Khurana, *Growth of Large Business*, Tables 8.7 and 8.10.

35. Licensing Policy Inquiry, *Appendices: Volume III*, p. 3, Table III-A (3).

36. With this new technology, between 1963 and 1971 Parry moved from fifty-second to twenty-third in rank among India's business houses. By contrast, Bird-Heilgers actually fell in rank (from ninth to eighteenth) over this same period but still remained in the top twenty houses. For this change in rank, see Khurana, *Growth of Large Business*, Tables 8.7 and 8.10.

37. Licensing Policy Inquiry, *Appendices: Volume III*, p. 5, Table III-A (3).

38. Ibid., pp. 3–6, Table III-A (3).

port technology, licensing agreements signed by multinationals reached their peak numbers during the late 1960s. Between 1964 and 1970 majority foreign-owned subsidiaries, on average, paid royalties for two technology licenses and employed nearly twenty foreign technicians (see Table 3-1). No other type of private enterprise operating in India depended so heavily on foreign products, processes, and skills to grow; only state enterprises became more dependent. With this government-approved technology, multinationals (along with transformed colonial agencies) grew faster than did Indian business houses, or Indian private enterprise generally. Accordingly, the share of foreign ownership in the Indian private sector reached its highest point (20 percent) in the late 1960s (see Figure 2-4).

During the early 1970s, however, a reversal in government policy—capped by tightened foreign exchange restrictions (FERA, 1973)—sharply reduced inflows of foreign technology and skills. In majority foreign-owned subsidiaries—the principal targets of FERA—the employment of foreign technicians fell off dramatically, and the incidence of technology licensing began to decline (see Table 3-1). After 1973 and FERA, a few majority subsidiaries also reduced their reliance on foreign technology bundled with foreign capital. ICI, for example, retired by 1980 two of the eight bundled agreements it had operated earlier (through 1973) in the chemical industry (see Figure 2-11). By the late 1970s most other multinationals also looked abroad less frequently for new technology to use in India. As a result, during the early 1980s majority foreign-owned subsidiaries paid negligible royalties on fewer technical licenses, in marked contrast to remittances before the enactment of FERA (see Table 3-1). And, for their part, minority foreign-owned affiliates reduced their payments on a stagnant number of technical agreements, keeping in step with the rest of Indian industry.

The uncertainties introduced by FERA regarding foreign ownership and control also led multinational parents to tighten contractual provisions that guided the use of their technology in majority foreign-owned subsidiaries. Prior to FERA, by contrast, the foreign parents of these subsidiaries had insisted on fewer restrictive clauses—fewer, in fact, than those contracted by minority affiliates and by all local enterprises, state and private (see Table 3-1). Here, greater managerial control over the use of foreign technology in majority subsidiaries had precluded any need for contractual restrictions. But with FERA in force, new infusions of foreign technology became rarer, and its uses far more restricted. So, majority subsidiaries operating in India began to look for local technological alternatives.

Mixing Foreign and Indigenous Sources

Their search actually began before FERA, as the government during the late 1960s began to tighten its restrictions on foreign ownership (see Table 3-1). In fact, between 1964 and 1970 majority foreign-owned subsidiaries typically spent a greater proportion of their sales on local R&D than did either minority foreign-owned affiliates or (by even greater margins) private Indian enterprise with foreign technology tie-ups.[39] During this period only state enterprises outspent majority subsidiaries, but by the 1980s even this difference was eradicated. As SOEs secured multiple technical licenses—involving several multinationals—and relied more heavily than enterprises in the private sector on foreign technical personnel, their expenditures on local R&D fell off. By contrast, into the 1980s majority subsidiaries increased their local expenditures as the number of foreign technicians and technology licenses continued to decline. So did minority affiliates and wholly Indian-owned enterprises with technology licenses. But their increased expenditures on local R&D still did not match the expenditures by majority subsidiaries.[40] For these subsidiaries, then, local R&D emerged during the 1980s as an important supplement to new infusions of technology from abroad in industry after industry, according to surveys conducted by India's central bank and reported in Table 3-2.

Again, let us consider the chemical industry. Between 1978 and 1981 that broadly defined sector accounted for two-fifths of all expenditures on local R&D undertaken by those private and state enterprises engaged in some form of foreign collaboration.[41] Here, majority foreign-owned subsidiaries spent 2.5 times more of their sales on local R&D than did local enterprises, whether private or state-owned (see Table 3-2). Minority foreign-owned affiliates also spent more than did local (state or private) enterprises with no foreign shareholdings, but less than majority subsidiaries. Faced with a net reduction in foreign collaboration in the chemical industry during the 1970s (see

---

39. A separate survey of R&D expenditures by India's largest private corporations also shares this conclusion, see Shriram, *Top 300 Companies*, pp. 139, 144–45 (Table 6.20).

40. Sanjaya Lall arrives at the same conclusion in a separate econometric study of R&D expenditures in India during 1978; see his "Multinationals and Technology Development in Host Countries," in Lall, ed., *Multinationals, Technology and Exports: Selected Papers* (New York: St. Martin's, 1985), pp. 122–23, and Appendix table, pp. 129–30.

41. Reserve Bank of India, *Foreign Collaboration in Indian Industry: Fourth Survey Report, 1985* (Bombay, 1985), p. 178.

Table 3-2. Local R&D by multinationals and Indian enterprises across industries, 1978–1981

	State-owned enterprises[a]	Local private enterprises[a]	Minority foreign-owned joint ventures	Majority foreign-owned subsidiaries
Chemicals	0.40%	0.40%	0.73%	1.02%
of which:				
Industrial	0.30	0.30	0.67	1.03
Pharmaceuticals	3.15	0.34	0.96	1.44
Transport equipment	0.61	0.40	0.91	0.67
Electrical machinery	4.22	0.91	1.06	0.49
Other machinery and machine tools	0.48	0.97	0.51	0.54
All other[b]	0.08	0.47	0.24	0.34

SOURCE: Reserve Bank of India, *Foreign Collaboration in Indian Industry: Fourth Survey Report, 1985* (Bombay, 1985), pp. 81, 109, 136, 160, 178.
Note: For all firms capital expenditures are underestimated given inadequate data for 1977–78; current expenditures exist for all years.
[a]Includes only firms with technology tie-ups and no foreign equity.
[b]In manufacturing, petroleum, plantations, mining, and services.

Figure 2-11), multinationals seemed to respond with new infusions of local technology.[42]

One of these multinationals was Unilever, whose active mixing of foreign and indigenous technology exemplified a corporate strategy pursued, at least in part, by many others.[43] During the 1970s Unilever's subsidiary, Hindustan Lever, added basic chemicals to the detergents, soaps, and other consumer goods that made up its product lines. This addition reflected the high priority given to chemical manufacture by the government, and it also fit Hindustan Lever's plan for backward integration. Between 1973 and 1980 Hindustan Lever continued to rely on technology bundled with its parent's equity to produce chemicals (see Figure 2-11). At the same time, in India, Hindustan Lever expanded its research facility—one of the largest in the country's private sector—and there achieved several important technological advances. (Most notably, the company found ways to sub-

42. Lall argues that, in addition to chemicals, the same conclusion applies to engineering goods; see Lall, "Multinationals and Technology," pp. 122–23, 129–30.
43. Data from interviews held during 1978, 1982, and 1983 with senior managers of Hindustan Lever, reported in Dennis J. Encarnation and Sushil Vachani, "Foreign Ownership: When Hosts Change the Rules," *Harvard Business Review*, September–October 1985, pp. 155, 157–58.

stitute locally abundant, typically inedible oils for imported, edible tallow in the manufacture of high-quality soap—a substitution that saved the country scarce foreign exchange.) So highly valued were these investments in local R&D that government regulators granted Unilever an exemption from the equity dilution requirements of FERA, thus permitting Unilever to retain majority equity ownership in Hindustan Lever. As we shall see in the next chapter, other multinationals also received in FERA specific exemptions for employing "sophisticated technology" in their Indian subsidiaries. And, by the late 1970s, they had established nearly one-half of India's in-house R&D centers.[44] For multinationals, then, investing in local research and development facilitated continued access to the Indian market, even when new foreign suppliers of technology competed to enter.

Competing with Suppliers

During the 1980s competition among suppliers of foreign technology reached unprecedented heights, as multinationals flooded India with product and process innovations. In fact, during the five years between 1979 and 1984 the number of these innovations exceeded all comparable inflows into India during the country's first twenty-five years of independence (see Figure 2-9). Two-fifths of that new foreign technology and capital during the 1980s entered two broad, related industries: electrical equipment and electronics.[45] To attract new products and processes into these industries, the Indian government began to liberalize restrictions on foreign trade and investment. And it spearheaded a buying spree that promised to increase by 43 percent annually the size of the Indian market for electrical equipment.[46] Even though the electrical equipment industry was singled out by government as a model for future policy changes in other industries, it nevertheless exemplified a larger process: During the 1980s changes in government policy dramatically increased the Indian demand for product and process innovations from abroad.

While both a liberalization of government policy and, correspondingly, a mushrooming of Indian demand were required to accelerate new infusions of foreign technology, even together the two were not sufficient to attract attention from foreign suppliers. In addition, cer-

44. Lall, "Multinationals and Technology," p. 119.

45. Indian Investment Centre, *Foreign Investment in India* (New Delhi, 1986), pp. 12–13.

46. Department of Electronics, *Annual Report: 1984*, esp. p. 59; "Gandhi Opens Up Electronics Industry," *Financial Times* (U.K.), January 15, 1985, pp. 1, 5.

tain changes in the international market had to take place. Again, consider electrical equipment. Before the 1980s multinationals had little incentive to invest directly or to license technology, given the small size of that tightly restricted Indian market. Instead, they concentrated their operations outside India, in faster growing segments of the world market that afforded easier access. But during the 1980s growth in that larger world market slowed considerably, just as Indian demand for electrical equipment began to take off. In fact, by 1984 India represented one of few national markets projected to grow rapidly. Thus, by rushing to India, multinationals actually were also responding to conditions in the global market.

Even in the attractive Indian market of the 1980s, however, the vast majority of multinationals sought to license technology rather than to invest directly. By 1984, for example, foreign direct investment inflows had reached the highest level ever recorded in the history of India; yet, four-fifths of all new foreign collaborations that year involved no foreign financing (see Figure 2-9). Those few multinationals that entered India by bundling foreign capital with technology still found that the government remained insistent: Foreign equity must not exceed 40 percent of total shareholdings. In the rapidly growing electrical equipment industry, for example, only three multinationals had invested directly to serve the Indian market by 1986; by then, each owned no more than 40 percent of the equity in their joint ventures.[47] Instead, the vast majority of multinationals operating in the Indian electrical equipment industry—ten multinationals by 1986—entered the Indian market by licensing technology.

These multinationals preferred such licensing to direct investment for various reasons. In the electrical equipment industry, for example, most agreements were one-product, one-time transfers of technology, which occurred immediately after the government had liberalized rules regarding technology sales and tightened import restraints on finished goods.[48] To sidestep these restrictions, foreign

47. Of these three, ICL originally owned 60 percent of the equity in the Indian subsidiary it had established in 1963, whereas both Burroughs and Xerox initially owned 50 percent in the affiliates they established in 1977 and 1981, respectively. In addition, three other multinationals established wholly foreign-owned subsidiaries that did not service the Indian market but were instead 100 percent export-oriented. Data from interviews held during 1985 with senior managers in Burroughs and Xerox.

48. Data from interviews held during 1985 with senior managers in multinationals currently operating in the Indian electrical equipment industry, or considering such operations. The companies included Burroughs, Control Data, Data General, Digital Equipment, Hewlett-Packard, ITT, NCR, Prime Computer, Rank-Xerox, Texas Instruments, and Xerox.

suppliers linked sales of imported components to technology licenses, until those components could finally be produced in India. Until such local production commenced (which often took five years), technology licensing was a means for multinationals to sell components in a growing market otherwise closed to them. Moreover, by acquiring some information about the Indian market through technology licensing, multinationals positioned themselves to invest directly in that market later, should the government further liberalize its policies.

Even then, multinationals might still prefer technology licensing to direct investment, especially if they operated in an industry in which product and process innovations experienced rapid obsolescence in world markets.[49] That is, multinationals often licensed technology in India (and in other developing countries) that had already begun to exhaust sales opportunities in the more lucrative markets of industrialized nations. The time between initial product introduction and later technology licensing could be long; nonetheless, during the 1970s that lag was reduced significantly. In the computer industry, for example, Joseph Grieco reports that the lag between the first introduction of computer systems into India and their earlier introduction in the United States declined from eight and a half years (1967–72) to two and a half (1978–80).[50] "This marked an improvement," according to Grieco, "in the degree to which Indian users obtained the most recently developed systems available internationally."[51]

His conclusion, however, fails to acknowledge that the average life cycle of computer products worldwide had also declined rapidly over this period. Data General, for instance, first introduced a new product line into the U.S. market in 1980; over the next five years the company significantly upgraded or replaced products in that line seven times.[52] Only after sales had ceased in the United States did Data General (in 1986) license in India the technology for that product line. Similarly, Data General's competitors—Prime Computer, NCR, and Hewlett-Packard—introduced into India those products already in their final year of sales in the United States.[53] Only Tandy

---

49. For a further discussion and empirical verification of this rationale for licensing technology, see David J. Teece, "Technology Transfer by Multinational Firms: The Resource Cost of Transferring Technological Knowhow," *Economic Journal* 87 (June 1977):242–61.

50. Joseph M. Grieco, *Between Dependency and Autonomy: India's Experience with the International Computer Industry* (Berkeley: University of California Press, 1984), Table 9, p. 45.

51. Ibid., p. 44.

52. Data from interviews held during 1985 with senior managers of Data General.

53. In the case of Prime, this meant two years after the product had been introduced

introduced a product (already five years old) into India as much as two years before ending sales of it in the United States. Thus, in computers at least, the innovations Indian industry licensed were typically in the final phase of their short life cycles in more advanced markets.

Still, Indian enterprises needed this technology—and probable upgrades later—just to stay competitive.[54] Such intense competition among local enterprises further discouraged more direct investment by multinationals, as did the dramatic swings over the previous two decades in government policy regarding the electrical equipment industry.[55] It was equally risky, of course, to ignore the Indian market when international competitors took advantage of environmental changes. For multinationals faced with such contradictory pressures, technology licensing represented the first step toward gaining greater access to the Indian market, but one that could be easily reversed if the Indian environment again became hostile.

DISLODGING MULTINATIONALS: STAGE TWO

In recent years multinationals have rushed to supply India with technology. During 1984 alone they licensed twice as much foreign technology as they had during the entire first decade of Indian independence. Indeed, from 1947 to 1958 multinationals responded only very cautiously, both to India's lackluster economic performance (during its First Plan, 1951–56) and to the general ambivalence with which the new nation treated all foreign business. That ambivalence, in turn, reflected emergent India's pursuit of two often competing drives: to industrialize as rapidly as possible, but also to become technologically self-reliant on products and processes especially appropriate to India's endowments. Like the other variants of economic nationalism we have already examined, the development of indigenous technologies appeared to convey a combination of economic and political benefits that exceeded in value all obvious costs, such as higher

---

in the United States; in the case of NCR and Hewlett-Packard, three years. Data from interviews held during 1985 with senior managers of Hewlett-Packard, NCR, Prime Computer, and Tandy Corporation.

54. For example, eight of the eleven top Indian minicomputer manufacturers licensed technology from new foreign entrants; data from interviews during 1985 with senior managers from two of these manufacturers—ICIM and IDM.

55. For example, in the computer industry government policy experienced three identifiable swings during the 1960s and 1970s; see Grieco, *Between Dependency and Autonomy*, esp. pp. 103–49. During the 1980s the industry entered its fourth policy regime; see "Byte is Right!" *Economic Scene* (Bombay), January 1985, pp. 20–31.

prices, reduced quality, and scarce supply. Accordingly, Indian nationalists began early to demand sharp reductions in their country's dependence on foreign technology. For them, such technology remained synonymous with British domination, a connection that could be alleged as late as the 1960s, since British enterprises continued for many years to supply India with the bulk of its foreign technology. From the beginning, Indian industrialists more generally feared that *all* well-ensconced foreigners, by exploiting unique product and process innovations, would prove difficult to dislodge from the domestic market. They also feared that foreign technology—left alone—would displace Indian skills, even from textiles and other industries in which Indian enterprises had long enjoyed special advantages.

To thwart these technological challenges, J. R. D. Tata and G. D. Birla directed India's two largest industrial conglomerates to invest in local R&D and to adapt necessary foreign technology to native conditions. Indeed, as institutions, Indian business houses themselves represented specialized domestic responses to native conditions; in particular, to strong local demand for product and process technologies (along with managerial skills) that could not be readily procured. To overcome such technological constraints, business houses pooled the financial and human resources necessary to generate innovations and adaptations; they then distributed these products and processes through internal hierarchies to affiliated companies. By exploiting such scale economies, business houses finally achieved a level of technological independence which often allowed them in India to substitute for foreign enterprises. That substitution began in jute and cotton textiles, and eventually spread to tea, light engineering, and insurance—all technologically mature industries only minimally dependent on new infusions of foreign technology.

But outside of these mature industries, India's technological resources remained meager, and local hostility to foreign technology began to matter less. Indeed, both business and government recognized that indigenous technologies alone would inevitably fail to satisfy India's strategy for an increasingly ambitious industrialization, beginning with the Second (1956–61) and Third (1961–66) Five-Year plans. During the decade ending in 1966, then, government regulators—charged with approving virtually every aspect of a firm's technology choice—more readily approved those applications that included foreign technology. Still, to pay for such technology, India had little foreign exchange after the crisis of 1957, so government regulators encouraged local enterprises to secure foreign equity—and, less frequently, foreign loans—to help finance technology imports. Thus, during India's longest period of sustained industrial growth, the state actively stimulated the financial and technological interdependence of local and foreign enterprises.

To these government incentives, both business houses and multinationals responded immediately. Foreigners began to flood India with technology to satisfy the seemingly insatiable demand of Indian houses. Indeed, through the mid-1960s foreign collaboration figured prominently in the investment decisions of Indian business houses, just as technology licensing became the principal avenue for multinationals to gain limited access to the Indian market. At times, foreign equity accompanied that technology, providing both a way to finance such imports and a method of assuring foreigners some managerial control. Yet the modest number of multinationals investing directly in India paled alongside the far larger number that restricted their Indian operations merely to licensing technology. For those unbundled licenses, multinationals received large (in contrast to later periods) royalty payments, monopolized future Indian imports, and restricted subsequent uses of their technology, while business houses and other local licensees received the rights to make use of foreign products and processes within India. Thus, by trading their different endowments and capabilities, multinationals and local enterprises rationally constructed mutually advantageous economic agreements. By sharing an interest in the sanctity of these agreements (as we shall see in the next chapter), at least a few of these local enterprises acted politically to defend private capitalism.

Indian business houses secured the lion's share of government-approved technology licenses early on, but by the mid-1960s such technological collaboration typically involved Indian enterprises unaffiliated with the largest houses. In fact, smaller business houses often employed massive amounts of foreign technology to leapfrog over larger competitors more reluctant to license technology from abroad. And outside of these industrial conglomerates, new foreign tie-ups increased rapidly, as independent entrepreneurs sought to catapult out of the ranks of small-scale industry. Indeed, these unaffiliated independents became the most likely partners for multinationals seeking to license their technology in India—especially during the 1970s, when business houses further reduced their relative dependence on foreign technology. Such growing technological self-reliance, in turn, granted business houses greater financial independence from multinational suppliers of technology imports. By the 1980s that independence had spread across the Indian private sector, as unaffiliated companies joined business houses to reduce still further their reliance on foreign financing of technology imports. This increasing ability of Indian business houses—and, later, unaffiliated local enterprises—to unbundle technology from finance indicated their growing bargaining power in dealings with multinationals.

To enhance that bargaining power, local enterprises sought addition leverage from the Indian government. In response, state financiers, we have already noted, supplied selected business houses with foreign exchange, thus reducing each house's financial dependence on multinationals. Using that financial independence, these houses increasingly demanded that foreign technology be unbundled from foreign capital. Simultaneously, government regulators also insisted that bundled technology—when permitted at all—be accompanied with less foreign equity. As a result, with the passage of FERA in 1973, foreign financing of technology imports reached its lowest point since the beginning of rapid Indian industrialization; during the rest of the decade, foreign financing remained very low. For local enterprises seeking foreign technology free of foreign equity, then, FERA actually improved their bargaining position with those multinationals seeking access to the Indian market.

As they became available, alternative sources of foreign technology also served to enhance the bargaining position of Indian enterprises. Even after FERA became law, fresh inflows of foreign technology did continue, as competition among multinationals for access to the Indian market escalated. During the 1970s and 1980s many new logos appeared, when multinationals based in the United States, West Germany, and (most recently) Japan finally managed to supplant British enterprises as the preeminent suppliers to India of foreign technology. In fact, this heightened interest by multinationals reflected not only an increase in local demand for foreign technology but also critical changes in international markets (for example, a general slowdown of sales), which limited their options elsewhere. In India the effects proved exciting: For once international competitors had offered to supply technology unbundled from foreign capital, and at a lower price, the bargaining position of IBM (or any other multinational seeking majority foreign-owned subsidiaries in negotiations with government regulators and local enterprises) seriously eroded. Power had shifted elsewhere.

In India, while royalties and technology bundling declined, expenditures by private enterprise on local R&D grew (as a percentage of sales). FERA and other government constraints on new technology inflows stimulated these local expenditures, as did tax incentives inaugurated at the same time. Providing testimony to their successful development of new products and processes, and to their rapid adaptation of foreign technology to local conditions, Indian business houses expanded abroad in ever-increasing numbers during the 1970s and 1980s, where they set up manufacturing plants, especially in other economically less-developed countries. Now, through this reverse flow of technological innovations and adaptations, Indian business houses and multinationals had made themselves more complexly interdependent, in India and abroad.

Yet these changes in the domestic and international supply of technology had no corresponding effect on relations between multinationals and SOEs. Increased expenditures by state enterprises on local R&D, their diversification of foreign sources of technology, the constraints of FERA—even the financial independence of SOEs from multinationals—*none* of these factors did much to stem the dependence of SOEs on foreign technology. They remained dependent. Of course, given limited government investments early in India's history, that dependence had developed more slowly than did the private sector's reliance on foreign technology. But once state enterprises began to expand across the Indian economy, foreign collaboration jumped sharply, just when it had begun to fall off in the private sector. Indeed, compared with private enterprise, the average state enterprise (even in the same industry) continued into the 1980s both to secure a greater number of technology tie-ups and to rely more heavily on foreign technical personnel. Together, these conditions meant that a greater proportion of SOE sales were spent on royalties and other remittances. Even after 1973 and FERA, moreover, the interdependence of state enterprises and multinationals remained high; the trend may have actually been increasing.

That interdependence, based on the rational trading of different endowments and capabilities, served to generate mutually advantageous agreements between multinationals supplying technology and SOEs controlling access to markets. (By contrast, comparable technological linkages between SOEs and Indian business houses remained virtually nonexistent.) For a few multinationals, in fact, SOEs represented the only possible partners, given the state's dominant position in certain sectors of the economy and the reduced need of private enterprise for foreign technology. Though the activities of the state as entrepreneur did generate a certain level of support among multinationals for some version of state capitalism, the preeminence of the state as technology regulator served far more influentially to encourage conflict. Implementation of FERA, for example, invoked vociferous debate concerning a multinational's choice of technology;

yet, at the same time, the implementation of this restrictive legislation also produced new opportunities for managers in business and government to forge mutually advantageous agreements within the law. In exchange for increased expenditures on local R&D, for example, government regulators granted Unilever and other multinationals shareholdings in their subsidiaries greater than those held by foreigners who proved less inclined to undertake such expenditures. A few multinationals operating in India thus managed to reverse the obsolescence of earlier bargains and also to supplement their operations with new infusions of technology from abroad.

Even new foreign entrants into India tried to guard against future obsolescence by tightening those contractual provisions that guided the use of their technology in all types of firms—majority subsidiaries, joint ventures, and Indian licensees. The technology they sold in India typically was experiencing rapid obsolescence abroad. Multinationals held in abeyance their newer technologies, to be used as a future bargaining chip should access to the Indian market be threatened by business competitors or government regulators. In fact, government regulators simply could not dictate conditions to multinationals, even when these foreigners had lost much of their earlier bargaining power. The most important constraint on government regulators remained India's ongoing (and, during the 1980s, increasing) demand for product and process innovations, developed both at home and abroad. In 1985 Indian enterprises seeking to expand their industrial capacity secured more foreign technology from multinationals than ever before in the history of independent India. So long as multinationals controlled access to such technological innovations, through new infusions from abroad or through local investment, they simply could not be dislodged. Instead, they continued to gain (albeit restricted) access to the Indian market.

CHAPTER FOUR

Markets

> We shall be able to use our own iron ore and with our own hands produce steel; and then use the steel to produce more machinery to produce more steel and tools; and also to produce machinery to make more consumer goods. We will then not have to worry about foreign exchange every time we wish to start a new factory as we do now. Our dependence on foreign supplies will be greatly reduced. The main obstacle to rapid industrialization being thus removed, we shall be able to increase production and employment quickly and raise the level of living.[1]

With this vision of national self-reliance, India's economic planners embarked on four uninterrupted decades of inward-looking industrialization. Their task was formidable. At independence, the country imported most of its machinery and related technology. As for steel, one Indian business house (Tata) and a single British managing agency (Martin Burn) operated India's only mills, but their production failed to meet domestic demand. Indeed, most industrial conglomerates in India proved unable or unwilling to provide the large, risky investment necessary to substitute for imports of steel (or machinery). Consequently, India exported its iron ore to foreign suppliers, who increased their own overseas production and employment to satisfy the Indian market. None of these foreign suppliers—and few multinationals generally—saw sufficient reason to shift their production to India so long as they could ship goods to that market from existing facilities abroad. These (cheap) imports further discouraged domestic

---

1. Attributed to Professor P. C. Mahalanobis, first director of the Indian Statistical Institute, by Ved Mehta in *The New India* (New York: Penguin Books, 1971), p. 192.

investment by local industrial conglomerates, as did their inability (or unwillingness) to export anything except India's bountiful raw materials. Consequently, in 1947 India suffered from insufficient investment to supply markets at home and abroad, and both domestic production and employment lagged.

The foreign exchange crisis of 1957 changed all this, especially the government's response to that crisis and to languishing investment after a decade of political independence. With the imposition of import quotas, Tata and other business houses positioned themselves to fill the void being created by a reduction in foreign supplies. Then, even foreign suppliers began to consider Indian investments. But only a few multinationals arrived, and most Indian business houses, with the notable exception of Tata, preferred to invest in consumer goods and in other markets requiring less of their scarce capital and employing available technological skills. To fill the remaining void, the state intervened. Carrying forward a series of British wartime controls (and the nationalist movement's plans for development),[2] the new government required all enterprises operating in India to secure government permission either to enter virtually any market or to expand an existing position in any market. These controls further inhibited exports and reserved several domestic markets for the state's own enterprises. Through the government's use of both regulatory policies and direct investments, independent India moved a long way toward achieving the level of national self-reliance envisioned at independence.

THE STATE

As we have noted, in 1947 state-owned enterprises (SOEs) were remarkable mostly for their absence from the market. Of course, the central government provided limited services—public administration, transportation, communications, defense—while a few State governments also generated electricity, mined coal, and operated a few other vital infrastructures. By the early 1970s, however, the situation had largely altered, as SOEs held over one-third of all corporate

2. For British wartime controls, see B. R. Tomlinson, *The Political Economy of the Raj, 1914–1947: The Economics of Decolonization in India* (London: Cambridge University Press, 1979), passim. For the development plans of the Indian National Congress before independence, see Francine R. Frankel, *India's Political Economy, 1947–1977* (Princeton: Princeton University Press, 1978), pp. 28–70; A. H. Hanson, *The Process of Planning: A Study of India's Five-Year Plans, 1950–1964* (London: Oxford University Press, 1966), esp. pp. 28–44; Michael Kidron, *Foreign Investments in India* (London: Oxford University Press, 1965), esp. pp. 25–26, 66–69.

assets in India (see Figure 2-1). Most of these investments, the state concentrated in a small number of firms—notably, twenty-three of the twenty-five largest enterprises in India, including all of the top ten. As we saw in Chapter 2, central economic planning and the nationalization of the country's financial sector assured these few SOEs of financial independence and managerial autonomy. Once established, moreover, state enterprises readily licensed foreign technology from both multinationals and Eastern Bloc countries. Each SOE typically held multiple licenses, involving several foreign suppliers, in marked contrast to private enterprise. As a result, SOEs generally paid a higher proportion of their sales on royalties and technical fees, but these foreign remittances seldom exceeded SOE investments in local R&D. As we saw in Chapter 3, by employing India's scarce foreign exchange to license other technology, SOEs often managed to reject foreign financing of technology imports, and by investing in their own adaptations and innovations, they also managed to extend managerial control over the use of foreign and local technology in India.

Finally, the financial and managerial independence of state enterprises combined with their active procurement of technology at home and abroad to create important advantages in subsequent bargaining over access to markets. Namely, these financial and technological resources allowed state enterprises to corner markets as yet untapped by private enterprise, as well as to invade markets previously dominated by Indian business houses and multinationals. Expansion in these markets followed a pattern of vertical and horizontal integration, which granted to SOEs control across several industries basic to industrialization. In the beginning, however, before the inception of most SOEs, the state restricted—and all but eliminated—foreign and domestic competition in the markets it then proceeded to enter.

Protecting Markets

To segregate the Indian market from the rest of the world, India first imposed quantitative restrictions on imports. Continued imports (and not, say, a simultaneous reduction in export receipts) caused the country's first foreign exchange crisis, in 1957, according to official government inquiries: "As a result of liberal import policy and private capital's indulgence in an import spree, India squandered most of its foreign exchange reserves on consumer goods."[3] In response, the

3. India (Republic), Parliament, House of the People, Estimates Committee, 1967–68, *Thirteenth Report*, Third Lok Sabha (New Delhi: Lok Sabha Secretariat, 1968), p. 310.

Indian government rejected tariffs and other market mechanisms; instead, it directly administered quotas to license foreign exchange for practically every use in the economy. Briefly, these quotas and India's scarcity of foreign exchange combined to restrict foreign access to the Indian market.

Accordingly, imports plummeted. Before the foreign exchange crisis of 1957, India imported more than 50 percent of most capital goods and processed inputs.[4] Just a few years after that crisis, however, India needed only one-half as much in imports, according to the data reported in Figure 4-1. As nationalists had hoped, machinery imports experienced very sharp declines, with domestic production being fed increasingly by Indian-made iron and steel. Local production also substituted for imports of other metals, as well as for imported chemicals. By 1980, overall, imports of chemicals, metals, and most machinery had been sliced in half.

In contrast to these capital goods and processed inputs, imports of consumer goods accounted for only a small proportion of domestic supply prior to the 1957 crisis.[5] And following that crisis, domestic production of consumer goods quickly substituted for these already limited imports (see Figure 4-1). Such import substitution proved less successful, however, in industries dependent on special climatic conditions (e.g., food), or on natural resources (e.g., nonmetal minerals). With these notable exceptions, after 1957 quotas and scarce foreign exchange increasingly eliminated foreign exporters as competitors in the Indian market.

Once competition from imports had been eliminated, the government set out to restrain competition among those producers left to operate in the now-protected domestic market. Again, it imposed quantitative restrictions—this time, numerical ceilings on the industrial capacity of each public and private enterprise. Regulators distributed licenses until planned ceilings in targeted (not actual) production had been achieved. Since available licenses over any plan period had to be limited, the licensing system, like the government-run financial system, behaved like a zero-sum game; that is, a gain for one firm diminished the market prospects for all others.[6]

SOEs became especially successful in securing licenses from government regulators. Between 1956 and 1966, for example, state en-

4. India (Republic), Ministry of Finance, *Economic Survey: 1975–76* (New Delhi: Manager of Publications, 1976), p. 109.

5. Ibid.

6. Bhagwati and Desai provide the best description of this zero-sum game: "Capital issues controls, licensing and the permission to import machinery are the principal points at which *entry* into an industry is controlled by the government. The net effect of

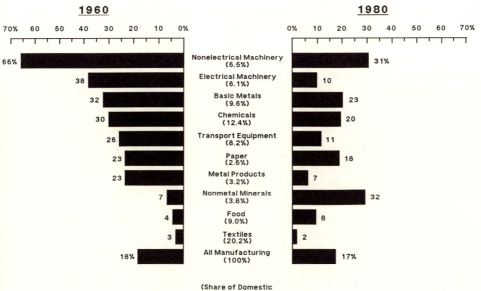

Figure 4-1. Market shares of imports in Indian industries, 1960, 1980
SOURCE: Isher Judge Ahluwalia, *Industrial Growth in India: Stagnation since the Mid-Sixties* (Delhi: Oxford University Press, 1985), p. 119, Table 6.3.

terprises gained government approval for more than four-fifths of the applications they submitted, compared with a two-thirds rate of approval for the private sector as a whole.[7] Yet, even with this high

this system is to make the entry of new competitors impossible—as the government will not allow the creation of any more capacity than current, estimated demand. It thus rules out the elimination of inefficient current producers by efficient, *new entrants*. It *also* rules out the possibility of the more efficient, *current* units expanding and eliminating the inefficient, current units: expansion by current units is as much subject to control within targets as expansion through new firms. (This elimination of competition is applicable even to the *utilization* of existing capacity. Materials and exchange are frequently allocated on a *pro rata* basis rather than to efficient producers.) If, then, competition from efficient rivals at home is ruled out by economic planners, what about foreign competition? Here again, competition has no chance! The use of import quotas rules out the possibility of competition from abroad. We are thus in an economic situation where the possibility of competition from potential entry by domestic and foreign rivals in minimized." Jagdish N. Bhagwati and Padma Desai, *India: Planning for Industrialization* (London: Oxford University Press for the OECD, 1970), pp. 271–72, emphasis in original. Also see Jagdish N. Bhagwati and T. N. Srinivasan, *Foreign Trade Regimes and Economic Development: India* (New York: Columbia University Press for the National Bureau of Economic Research, 1975).

7. India (Republic), Ministry of Industrial Development, Internal Trade and Company Affairs, *Report of the Industrial Licensing Policy Inquiry Committee*, P. Dutt, Chairman (New Delhi: Manager of Publications, 1969), *Main Report*, p. 48. Hereinafter cited:

rate of success, SOEs secured less than 4 percent of the total number of government licenses during the decade ending in 1966; the remainder went to private enterprise. In both sectors these government licenses were highly valued, since they guaranteed their holders access to the Indian market and protection from local competitors, much as trade quotas assured them of protection from imports. Unimpeded by local and foreign competition, licensed SOEs proceeded to integrate their domestic production both horizontally and vertically. Such integration granted SOEs greater control over the various Indian markets they entered.

Integrating Domestic Production

The systematic integration of state production began soon after independence, with the government's first Industrial Policy Resolution (1948), which placed the ownership and management of all railway transport under the exclusive jurisdiction of the central government. Legislated monopolies also existed in other basic infrastructures—posts, telegraph, telephone, radio—and the 1948 resolution ruled out future competition in all these markets, leaving the government to control the supply of most industrial infrastructures.

Outside of these monopolies, the state began either to compete with private suppliers or to acquire their assets. As a step toward vertical integration, new SOEs started to manufacture locomotives for the national railways, in competition with Tata. The state also expanded horizontally in the transport sector by acquiring (through mutual agreement) the country's only existing airline, also owned by Tata. Friendly takeovers, usually involving private firms experiencing financial problems, expanded across the service sector, especially after the government's second Industrial Policy Resolution (1956) included shipping among a dozen (so-called Schedule A) industries, whose future development became the exclusive responsibility of the public sector. More often, however, the state provided industrial infrastructures by investing in new start-ups, as we see in Figure 4-2.

By contrast, according to this figure, hostile acquisitions of otherwise healthy companies occurred far more frequently in the financial sector. The 1956 resolution called upon the state "to foster institutions to provide financial aid to the private sector."[8] At the time of this

---

Licensing Policy Inquiry, *Main Report,* or Licensing Policy Inquiry, *Appendices* and volume number.

8. India (Republic), "Industrial Policy Resolution" (April 30, 1956), para. 10, as

resolution, the government also acquired the largest (and foreign) commercial bank, as well as all private life insurance companies. With these acquisitions, as we saw in Chapter 2, the state dramatically increased its control over the allocation of financial resources (through debt and equity), as well as the actual mobilization of those domestic savings (in the form of insurance premiums and bank deposits) being channeled to private enterprise (see Figure 2-4). The state also eliminated its principal foreign competitor, the British-owned Imperial Bank of India. A decade later, in 1969, the state removed Indian business houses from another crucial segment of the financial market by nationalizing the country's fourteen largest commercial banks. Through additional nationalizations and new investments, the government systematically cut out nearly all private suppliers of financial services, leaving it with a near monopoly of the market.

Once the government had its own industrial and financial infrastructure in place, its attention shifted to processed inputs and other manufacturing (see Figure 4-2). In the 1956 resolution steel joined the list of Schedule A industries reserved for the state. At that time, private producers and imports accounted for all steel supplied in the country. Soon, steel mills rivaled the railroads as the largest repository of government investment; and with that investment the state's control over the market grew. By 1974 the Steel Authority of India (SAIL)—the largest corporation in India, which controlled all government investments in this industry—produced nearly two-thirds of the country's steel ingots, as we see in Figure 4-3. The remainder, we noted above (see Figure 4-1), was divided almost equally among imports and local private producers.

After constructing new steel mills, the state emerged as a fully integrated producer. Steel production intensified demand upstream for coal and iron ore—two Schedule A industries that also became the preserve of SOEs. And downstream, the expansion of the national railroads accelerated the demand for coal and steel. So, government investments in these industries grew, as did the public sector's share of total national production. Most of that production originated in a small number of firms; in fact, SAIL exercised control over the steel mills, plus the coking coal and iron ore mines, while a single company controlled the entire national railroad. By the 1970s the state had integrated these few, large enterprises vertically—from industrial infrastructures, to mining, to processed inputs. Such integration of a

---

reprinted in India (Republic), Planning Commission, *Programmes of Industrial Development: 1956–61* (Delhi: Manager of Publications, 1956), p. 436.

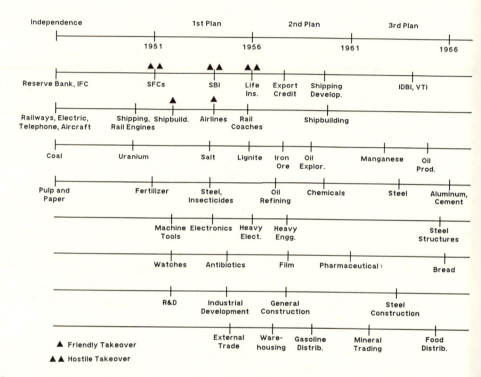

Figure 4-2. State-owned enterprises: horizontal diversification and vertical integration, 1947–198
SOURCE: Willis Emmons, "From Independence through the Fifth Five Year Plan: The Indian
State as Entrepreneur" (unpublished paper, Harvard Business School, May 23, 1985), Exhibit 1, p
68.

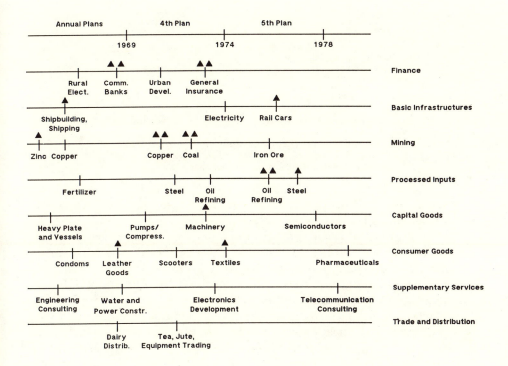

Annual Plans   4th Plan   5th Plan

1969   1974   1978

Finance

Rural Elect.   Comm. Banks   Urban Devel.   General Insurance

Basic Infrastructures

Shipbuilding, Shipping   Electricity   Rail Cars

Mining

Zinc   Copper   Copper   Coal   Iron Ore

Processed Inputs

Fertilizer   Steel   Oil Refining   Oil Refining   Steel

Capital Goods

Heavy Plate and Vessels   Pumps/ Compress.   Machinery   Semiconductors

Consumer Goods

Condoms   Leather Goods   Scooters   Textiles   Pharmaceuticals

Supplementary Services

Engineering Consulting   Water and Power Constr.   Electronics Development   Telecommunication Consulting

Trade and Distribution

Dairy Distrib.   Tea, Jute, Equipment Trading

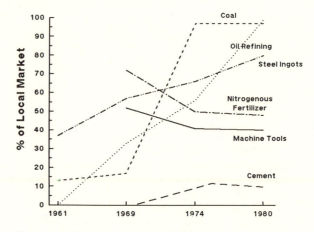

Figure 4-3. Market shares of SOEs in Indian industries, 1961–1980
SOURCE: India (Republic) Ministry of Finance, Bureau of Public Enterprises, *Public Sector Survey*, vol. I (New Delhi: Controller of Publications, selected years).

few buyers and suppliers across industries assured state domination of key industrial markets.

Only after this vertical integration of the iron and steel industry was well underway did the government move further downstream, principally into capital goods (see Figure 4-2). Indeed, government-run railroads, mines, and steel mills intensified the demand for heavy plant and equipment (another Schedule A industry), as well as for machine tools. The 1956 resolution included machine tools in a second list of industries (so-called Schedule B industries) in which both state and private enterprises were to coexist, with the government to take a lead role in future development. Before 1956 a few private firms supplied some of these capital goods locally, but we noted above that most continued to be imported. Subsequently, new state-owned suppliers dominated the markets they entered. By 1969 a single government enterprise supplied over one-half of all domestically produced machine tools (see Figure 4-3). These investments further integrated the public sector and made the state a formidable competitor in industries in which it coexisted with private enterprise.

The 1956 resolution greatly increased the number of Schedule B industries in which public and private enterprises potentially competed, principally in the processing of raw materials. Fertilizers proved to be among the first of these industries to attract government investment, and by 1969 two SOEs produced nearly three-quarters of

India's nitrogenous fertilizer (see Figure 4-3). Smaller investments entered the cement and aluminum industries, to establish correspondingly lower levels of state production relative to private output. Again, these investments contributed to the decline in India's imports; in aluminum, for example, imports plummeted from two-thirds of total supply in 1956 to only 1 percent in 1974.[9]

Once the state had integrated buyers and suppliers in the steel industry, the petroleum industry captured the lion's share of new government investment. During the 1970s the state assumed all foreign equity in ventures previously owned by Amoco and Shell, following the expiration of their twenty-five-year contracts with the government. A second set of oil contracts expired in 1980, leaving the government additional monopolies in crude oil extraction and refining (see Figure 4-3). Subsequently, during the 1980s state investments in exploration and refining rivaled those in steel (see Figure 2-3). Through the vertical integration of the petroleum industry—from extraction to refining, to processing derivatives, to supplying those derivatives to government railways, electricity generators, and fertilizer plants—the state eventually replaced multinationals operating in the Indian market.

The state's preoccupation with the petroleum and steel industries, and the capital intensity of the investments they entailed, inhibited further integration downstream. In consumer goods until the 1970s, the only significant government investment supplied drugs and pharmaceuticals, another Schedule B industry. Subsequently, the government entered the ailing but employment-generating textile industry through several takeovers (see Figure 4-2). By comparison, the government invested more substantial sums in the service sector, initially as a means of providing technical consulting and construction services to a now-burgeoning public sector. In addition, government enterprises became involved as intermediaries in foreign trade, beginning in the mid-1950s, and in the domestic wholesale trade of food and other commodities, beginning in the mid-1960s. Still, private enterprises remained the principal suppliers of most services and consumer goods, and substituted for most imports.

Private enterprises actually expanded in several markets officially reserved for SOEs in the 1956 Industrial Policy Resolution.[10] One such reserved (or Schedule A) industry was coal; yet, for the next two decades, government regulators continued to grant licenses to private

9. Ministry of Finance, *Economic Survey: 1975–76*, p. 109.
10. Licensing Policy Inquiry, *Main Report*, pp. 105–6.

collieries, until planned ceilings in targeted capacity were achieved. Not until the mid-1970s did the government move to assert its market position (see Figure 4-3). And in the mining of other raw materials (iron ore, for example), as well as the manufacture of processed inputs (such as steel), private enterprise persisted into the 1980s. As for Schedule B industries in which the 1956 resolution called for the public and private sectors to coexist, and for the government to take a lead role—there, private enterprise enjoyed even greater access, as it continued to account for the bulk of national production. Thus, the segmentation of the Indian market into public, private, and mixed sectors restricted—but did not eliminate—market access by private enterprise.

Nevertheless, during the 1970s the state did threaten to upset this balance by reversing its earlier reluctance to engage in hostile takeovers of existing producers. As we saw in Figure 4-2, nationalizations expanded from the mining of new raw materials (copper, coal), to processed inputs (iron and steel), to industrial intermediates (steel products, machinery), to a variety of consumer goods (leather, textiles, bicycles). Upstream, for example, the nationalization of private collieries increased the public sector's share of coal production from 17 percent in 1969 to 97 percent in 1974 (see Figure 4-3); and the state's share of copper production grew from nothing to a complete monopoly in 1974.[11] Downstream, as well, the government finally consolidated its already dominant market position (in steel, for example), further integrated vertically its production (in machinery), and diversified horizontally into entirely new markets for state enterprises (in leather goods). Through such nationalizations, complemented by new investments, the state directly challenged the existing market shares of private enterprise. And the state further established itself as a viable alternative to both multinationals and those local industrial conglomerates seeking to operate in the protected and segmented Indian market.

INDIAN BUSINESS HOUSES

Before the expansion of SOEs, business houses held reign over the Indian market by first integrating and then managing an ever-expanding number of diversified enterprises. Among India's seventy-

11. Centre for Monitoring the Indian Economy, Economic Intelligence Service, *Public Sector in the Indian Economy* (Bombay, July 1978), p. 32, Table 3.5.

five or so business houses at independence, Birla diversified the most, operating more than a hundred companies in all sectors of the economy: from plantations (for coffee, jute, and tea) to processed foods, from mining to smelting, from machine tools to textile machinery, from textiles to garments, from electrical and engineering goods to automobile assembly, from chemicals to paper mills to newspapers. By contrast, Tata controlled fewer, less diversified companies, but that house also integrated its affiliated enterprises. Tata Engineering (TELCO), the second-largest corporation in the private sector, for example, bought most of its steel from another Tata affiliate (TISCO), at independence India's largest corporation. In a similar but more narrowly defined pattern of integration, ACC amalgamated eleven formerly independent cement companies and related machinery manufacturers. To control the Indian market, business houses coordinated buyers, suppliers, and potential competitors in a single conglomerate.

Even after SOEs began to flex their muscles in the Indian market, a few business houses, aided now by state financial institutions, managed to retain their market position. According to an official government commission, three private producers controlled, during 1963, more than 75 percent of the market in nearly all (1,133) of the (1,170) products surveyed.[12] In over one-third of these products, a single private producer controlled the entire market. Birla, for instance, controlled nearly two-fifths of the Indian market for automobiles, aluminum, refrigerators, and most paper lines in 1963.[13] A single Tata affiliate (TELCO) produced nearly two-fifths of all transport vehicles sold in India. And ACC's affiliated companies supplied one-third of the market for cement products and related machinery. By controlling giant shares of the Indian market, these business houses helped to reduce India's imports of processed inputs, machinery, and consumer goods (see Figure 4-1).

To operate in many different markets simultaneously, we saw in Chapter 3, business houses had to secure technology from several sources. As a beginning, the acquisition of former colonial agencies brought with it mature technologies in textiles and other industries in which Indian enterprises had long exercised peculiar advantages. Then, soon after independence, business houses supplemented these

12. India (Republic), Ministry of Finance, *Report of the Monopolies Inquiry Commission,* vol. 1 (New Delhi: Manager of Publications, 1965), Appendix C, Statement 1, pp. 225–372.

13. For the market shares of enterprises controlled by Birla, Tata, and ACC, see ibid., pp. 47–54.

modest resources with product and process innovations licensed from multinationals, based principally in Britain and then the United States. Once licensed, these innovations underwent extensive modifications, in response to local conditions; in fact, such modifications often supplanted the original technology, as did growing investments in local R&D. Of course, each of these sources of technology helped to enhance the market position of Indian business houses and to challenge the comparative standing of both existing multinationals and emergent state enterprises.

In addition, the continued dominance of Indian business houses—along with their several financial, technological, marketing, and managerial resources—exerted special influence in all subsequent bargaining over access to the Indian market. In particular, government regulators felt compelled to grant licenses to enterprises controlled by private industrial conglomerates as a means of satisfying many of their own objectives. Yet, in their dealings with business houses, these government regulators were never powerless. Quite the contrary: as the state tightened its antitrust legislation by enacting the Monopolies and Restrictive Trade Practices (or MRTP) Act of 1969, regulators encouraged business houses either to expand in those industries already accorded high priority by government or to move overseas and earn additional (scarce) foreign exchange, which the state also required. As a result, state regulators and Indian business houses grew highly interdependent, a symbiosis that benefited greatly from the political skills of India's industrialists.

Securing Licenses: The 1950s and 1960s

To secure government licenses and—equally important—to block competitors from obtaining such licenses *both* required some exercise of political skills, so the larger business houses maintained specialized "industrial embassies" in New Delhi, often run by former civil servants or military officers.[14] Smaller business houses and large independent companies used their sales or public relations offices in New Delhi to perform similar, albeit more limited, functions. By contrast, those enterprises with fewer financial and managerial resources, and located far from the capital, found it more difficult to conduct lengthy and repeated negotiations, requiring reams of data and correspondence, with the dozen or more regulatory agencies (in the

14. Stanley A. Kochanek, *Business and Politics in India* (Berkeley: University of California Press, 1974), esp. pp. 289–91, 295–96.

central government alone) which typically exercised some control over licensing.[15] Overall, in dealings with regulatory agencies, Indian business houses proved politically effective: Between 1956 and 1966, for example, the twenty largest business houses secured nearly one-fifth of all government-approved licenses, according to data gathered by official parliamentary inquiries and summarized in Figure 4-4. The two largest houses, Tata and Birla, together secured nearly one-tenth of all government approvals to initiate or expand productive capacity. No other business house secured so much as 1 percent of these government-approved licenses.

Here we can see that Tata and Birla employed fundamentally different strategies in pursuit of government licenses. On the one hand, Tata submitted far fewer applications for licenses and secured a much higher percentage of approvals—testimony to the skills of its "industrial embassy." By contrast, Birla inundated government regulators with applications for licenses, many of which government rejected. This low rate of approval reflected, in part, Birla's early submission of multiple applications for the same opportunity to expand in the domestic market. The decision rules adopted by government regulators often encouraged this practice, by granting licenses in sequence with the date of application (first-come, first served) until regulators achieved planned ceilings in targeted capacity in an industry.[16] By deftly responding to government regulators, Birla received more than twice as many licenses to enter the Indian market as did Tata, and nearly one-fifth of all licenses secured by India's seventy-three large business houses (see Figure 4-4).

Indeed, Birla's organizational capacity to respond to government at every level, from the lowest administrator to the prime minister, exceeded that of any other business house. In addition to its "industrial embassy" in New Delhi, Birla also dominated several industry associations (e.g., textiles) actively involved in government advisory bodies. Birla's control over these associations also gave it a powerful position in regional chambers of commerce (e.g., the Calcutta Chamber, representing much of eastern India) which, in turn, exercised much influence over the Federation of Indian Chambers of Commerce and Industry (FICCI). As India's preeminent (but not its only) national business chamber, FICCI enjoyed formal access to nearly all levels of

15. Dennis J. Encarnation, "The Indian Central Bureaucracy: Responsive to Whom?" *Asian Survey* 19 (November 1980): 1126–45.

16. For the operation of these decision rules, see Bhagwati and Desai, *India: Planning for Industrialization*, pp. 258–59, 269–72.

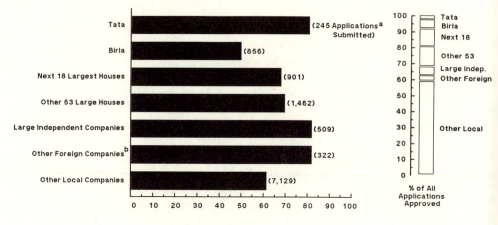

% of Applications Approved by Government

Figure 4-4. Private recipients of government licenses to expand in India, 1956–1966
SOURCE: Same as for Figure 3-2.
[a]Includes applications for establishing new undertakings, substantial expansion, new articles of association, carrying on existing business, and shifting production sites.
[b]Excludes foreign companies also included either under business houses (e.g., ICI) or under large independent companies (e.g., Hindustan Lever).

government policymaking. And its secretariat, the largest of any business association in India, actively engaged in examining and debating bureaucratic regulations and parliamentary legislation. Birla and the Calcutta Chamber were instrumental in the founding of FICCI, and they long influenced its secretariat. (Tata, by contrast, dominated the Bombay Chamber representing much of western India but never participated actively in FICCI.) Naturally, through FICCI plus a host of regional chambers, industry associations, and its own "industrial embassy," Birla enjoyed multiple points of access to government policymaking.[17]

Political contributions, channeled directly to prospective ministers or indirectly through party bosses, provided Birla and other business houses with additional access to policymaking. Long before independence G. D. Birla began to bankroll much of the independence movement, and he enjoyed a special relationship with Mahatma Gandhi and other nationalist leaders.[18] After independence, however, new

17. Kochanek, *Business and Politics*, esp. pp. 97–106, 131–41, 170–85, 274–78; also see S. R. Maheshwari, *Government Through Consultation: Advisory Committees in Indian Government* (New Delhi: Indian Institute of Public Administration, 1972).

18. G. D. Birla, *In the Shadow of the Mahatma* (Bombay: Orient Longman's, 1955), esp. p. 48.

restrictions limited (legal) company contributions to expenditures recorded in annual reports. Through 1969, these expenditures accounted for nearly 90 percent of all campaign financing reported to India's election commission.[19] During the critical elections of 1967–68 (when the Congress Party, for the first time in its history, lost a substantial number of seats in Parliament and several State assemblies), these contributions became critical to success. According to data gathered by Parliament, nearly four-fifths of all recorded company contributions during that election went to the ruling Congress Party.[20] And, again, Birla stood forth as the Congress Party's largest contributor.[21]

In sharp contrast to Birla, according to these data, Tata remained conspicuous for its large contributions to the Swatantra (Freedom) Party, India's first political organization devoted almost exclusively to the curtailment, if not elimination, of the "license, permit, quota Raj."[22] Tata and a few other Bombay business houses became instrumental in the establishment of the Swatantra Party during 1959 and even earlier, during 1956, in the founding of its predecessor, the quasi-educational Forum for Free Enterprise.[23] Subsequently, most major Swatantra supporters—like Tata—relied extensively on foreign financial and (especially) technological collaboration to grow.[24] Yet these resources proved insufficient to cast Swatantra as a serious challenger to the Congress Party in national politics. Nevertheless, Swatantra did periodically assume control over State governments,

19. Kochanek, *Business and Politics*, p. 232; A. H. Somjee and G. Somjee, "India," *Journal of Politics* 25 (March 1963): 251–66.

20. India (Republic), Parliament, House of the People, *Debates*, 4th Lok Sabha (April 22, 1969), pp. 52–54.

21. Ibid. During the 1967 elections, of the Rs 9.6 million contributed by India's seventy-three large business houses (and formally reported in their annual reports), Birla contributed Rs 1.7 million—nearly all of which (98.8 percent) went to the Congress Party.

22. In fact, the term "license-permit-quota Raj" was first termed by the Swatantra Party's founder, C. Ragagopalachari; see his *Licensing Power in India* (New Delhi: S. Chand, 1980), esp. pp. 3, 27.

23. Howard L. Erdman, *The Swatantra Party and Indian Conservatism* (Cambridge: Cambridge University Press, 1967), pp. 46–71.

24. During 1956–66 Tata sought foreign collaboration in 52 percent (93 of 198) of all government-approved licenses to establish and expand industrial capacity. As for other Swatantra supporters, the comparable ratio for Bajaj was 37 percent (20 of 54); for Khatau, 38 percent (8 of 21); for Scindia, 57 percent (4 of 7); for Walchand, 64 percent (34 of 53). In fact, during 1956–66, Tata, Walchand, and Bajaj were ranked second, fourth, and eighth, respectively, among active collaborators with multinationals. See Subhendu Dasgupta, "Trend and Pattern of Foreign Collaboration in Indian Business Houses: A Quantitative Analysis" (unpublished manuscript, Department of Economics, University of Calcutta, March 1978), Table 5, pp. 13–15 (based on unpublished data gathered by the Industrial Licensing Policy Inquiry Committee, cited in n. 7 above).

and following the 1967 elections it led the Congress opposition in Parliament.[25] By continuing its support of Swatantra, Tata recorded its long-standing opposition to government policies. But Tata never carried that opposition to an extreme;[26] the Congress Party still remained the largest recipient of Tata's campaign contributions.[27] By channeling most campaign contributions to the Congress Party, Tata and other business houses hoped to improve their chances of securing government licenses and other largess.

Occasionally, business houses joined together to finance the campaigns of politicians sympathetic to their position. ACC and Khatau, for example, owned the two largest amalgamations of cement producers, and they dominated the Cement Manufacturers Association. When the government sought to increase cement production during the late 1960s, ACC and Khatau, through their industry association, successfully advocated the decontrol of cement prices, as well as private control over the quasi-governmental body subsequently established to monitor sales and distribution. This new body received a small commission from the government for its management services, which it then used illegally to finance the campaigns of politicians who supported the continued decontrol of cement prices.[28] In the process, industry oligopolists behaved like political oligarchs, transforming business associations into political organizations.[29]

25. And in 1977 Swatantra was awarded the finance portfolio in India's first coalition government. See Dennis J. Encarnation, "A Rationalist Theory of Collective Action and the Policy Process: Capital-State Relations in India" (Ph.D. diss., Duke University, 1980), Table 6-2, p. 216; reprinted in Joseph M. Grieco, *Between Dependency and Autonomy* (Berkeley: University of California Press, 1984), Table 20, pp. 144–45.

26. Except for periodic flirtations, Tata and other Bombay houses actually preferred to stay aloof from Congress politics both before and after independence. See Stanley Wolpert, *A New History of India* (New York: Oxford University Press, 1977), pp. 276, 301; also see Claude Markovits, *Indian Business and Nationalist Politics, 1931–1939: The Indigenous Capitalist Class and the Rise of the Congress Party* (Cambridge: Cambridge University Press, 1985), esp. pp. 37, 76, 111, 178.

27. During the 1967 elections, of the Rs 0.8 million contributed by Tata (and formally reported in its companies' annual reports), two-thirds went to the Congress Party, while another one-third went to the Swatantra Party; see Parliament, House of the People, *Debates*, pp. 52–54.

28. The Cement Allocation and Coordinating Organization contributed Rs 3.4 million to the 1967–68 parliamentary elections, of which the largest proportion (43 percent) went to Swatantra Party politicians who advocated the total elimination of price controls. For further details, see S. N. Shrinivasan, *Party and Democracy in India* (New Delhi: Tata McGraw-Hill, 1977), p. 309; Kochanek, *Business and Politics*, p. 236, 253–55; and India (Republic), Parliament, House of the People, *Debates*, 4th Lok Sabha (November 23, 1967), pp. 237–38.

29. For another example, this time among business houses in Gujarat, see Howard L. Erdman, *Political Attitudes of Indian Industry: A Case Study of the Baroda Business Elite* (London: Athlone Press for the University of London Institute for Commonwealth Studies, 1971), esp. pp. 39–41.

Outside of national politics, business houses with a strong regional base also turned to the several State governments for political support. Most State banks and development corporations, for example, actively sought government licenses to establish joint ventures (otherwise known as joint-sector projects) with private entrepreneurs, especially in textiles, sugar, and other industries vitally important to local employment (see Figure 2-8). In their selection of partners, State financial institutions strongly preferred Indian business houses, with which the States shared equity ownership but not managerial control. Most State financial institutions preferred to leave day-to-day management to the project's private partner and then to use State-appointed directors for securing government licenses, government-supplied services (notably, electricity and rail transport), and additional government financing (especially foreign currency loans).[30]

The demonstrable success of business houses in gaining access to government and in securing government licenses prompted several parliamentary investigations into the functioning of the industrial licensing system.[31] All of these inquiries concluded that the system was permeated with a number of biases that favored large business houses such as Birla. During 1969, following these inquiries and a high tide of populist sentiment, the government abolished managing agencies, nationalized nine large commercial banks, outlawed company contributions to political campaigns, and enacted wide-ranging monopolies legislation (the MRTP Act). While all of these actions complicated subsequent efforts by business houses to secure government licenses, the monopolies legislation, in particular, seriously threatened all future expansion of business houses in the Indian market.

Securing Licenses: The 1970s and 1980s

In the views of most Indian industrialists, the MRTP Act of 1969 represented the most serious threat since independence to their continued market access. The act required that companies register with the newly created Monopolies Commission if: (1) their assets exceed-

---

30. Samuel Paul et al., "Joint Sector: Guidelines for Policy," *Economic and Political Weekly* (Bombay), December 9, 1972, pp. 2416–17.

31. The most important of these included the Mahalanobis Committee (1960–64), the Monopolies Inquiry Commission (1964–65), the Planning Commission study of industrial licensing done by R. K. Hazari (1966–67), the Parliament's study of industrial licensing done by its Estimates Committee (1966–67), the Administrative Reforms Commission study of economic administration (1967), and the Industrial Licensing Policy Inquiry Committee headed by P. Dutt (1967–69).

ed Rs 20 million; (2) they were financially interconnected with companies of that size; or (3) they sold more than 60 percent of any product or service produced in India. The act next required companies that satisfied these criteria, the so-called MRTP companies, to secure special government permission to expand production substantially, or to establish productive capacity in new product lines. The act also empowered the government to investigate the operations of registered companies when it suspected that these companies impeded domestic trade or had otherwise violated their industrial licenses. Finally, the act called upon the government to identify those industries "open" to MRTP companies, industries to be accorded high priority by government regulators evaluating proposals for expansion or new investment. In each of these ways, then, the MRTP Act sought to increase government's control over the access of industrial conglomerates to the Indian market.

While lobbying with the Monopolies Commission for special dispensations, Indian business houses frequently secured the support of other government agencies. A principal ally proved to be the government-appointed secretary for each industry's advisory council, a body dominated by industry oligopolists. That secretary was typically the senior administrator within the Directorate General for Technical Development (DGTD) charged with regulating technology imports and granting production clearances in that industry. Frequently, this DGTD administrator shared the perspective of an industry's largest producers: Between 1971 and 1977, for example, of the thirty-six applications referred to the Monopolies Commission, only two encountered objections from the senior administrator within the DGTD.[32] By contrast, the Directorate General for Small-Scale Industry, a separate agency, objected to all eighteen applications that

32. The advice of various government agencies—as well as of the applicant's competitors, suppliers, and buyers—appears in reports prepared by the Monopolies Commission, which carefully investigated only a few of the licensing applications submitted by MRTP companies. In fact, between 1971 and 1978, the government sought full reports from the commission in the thirty-six cases discussed here; the remaining cases, the government felt, did not merit such detailed evaluations. For titles and case descriptions, see the various annual reports of the Monopolies and Restrictive Trade Practices Commission; the best compendium is India (Republic), Ministry of Law, Justice and Company Affairs, *The Fifth Annual Report Pertaining to the Execution of the Provisions of the M.R.T.P. Act, 1969* (Faridabad: Manager of Publications, 1977), pp. 35–36. A member of the Monopolies Commission during this time, H. K. Paranjape, reviews the most important cases in his "Industrial Growth with Justice—India's Strategy," in Charan D. Wadhva, ed., *Some Problems of India's Economic Policy* (New Delhi: Tata McGraw-Hill, 1977), pp. 325–55. For further details, see Encarnation, "A Rationalist Theory: Capital-State Relations in India," pp. 110–13.

threatened the market position of its own constituency, firms with scant financial and managerial resources to influence government regulators.

By successfully lobbying government regulators, Indian business houses continued to secure access to the Indian market. Again, Birla's success stood out: Between 1971, when the Congress government issued its first MRTP order, and 1977, when that Congress government toppled, MRTP companies controlled by Birla secured licenses for nearly one-sixth of all new investment sought by all MRTP companies, according to the data summarized in Figure 4-5. To secure these licenses, Birla continued to rely on its familiar strategy: It inundated government regulators with multiple applications, recognizing that government would reject a large proportion of these applications (more than two-fifths).

By contrast, Tata continued to submit fewer applications than did Birla (see Figure 4-5), while securing government approval for nearly four-fifths of its smaller total. These new approval rates actually compared favorably with Tata's success during the 1950s and 1960s (see Figure 4-4). As a result, between 1971 and 1977 Tata secured the same number of government approvals as did Birla—testimony to the continued skills of Tata's "industrial embassy." That "embassy," for example, organized TELCO's suppliers, mostly small-scale enterprises, into a business association, which subsequently made separate representations before the Monopolies Commission and other regulatory agencies, endorsing TELCO's applications for expansion.[33] As a result, Tata neutralized one of its principal opponents within government, the Directorate General for Small-Scale Industries.

Even though Birla proved less successful than Tata in shepherding its applications through India's bureaucratic labyrinth, Birla nonetheless overcame this disadvantage by submitting multiple and early applications for large projects designed to corner a considerable amount of targeted capacity. In fact, each successful Birla application entailed sizable investments—up to four times the amount of those by Tata. Birla's assets therefore grew 12.5 percent compounded annually between 1969 and 1977, faster than the growth in Tata's assets (and faster than the growth in the corporate private sector as a whole).[34]

33. H. K. Paranjape discussed these activities in interviews held during 1977–78 and in a dissenting opinion before the Monopolies Commission. See India (Republic), Monopolies and Restrictive Trade Practices Commission, "Report on Tata Engineering and Locomotive Company Request for Substantial Expansion in Manufacture of Commercial Vehicles" (mimeographed, 1971).

34. Birla's assets in 1969 were Rs 4.2 billion, according to the government; see Rakesh

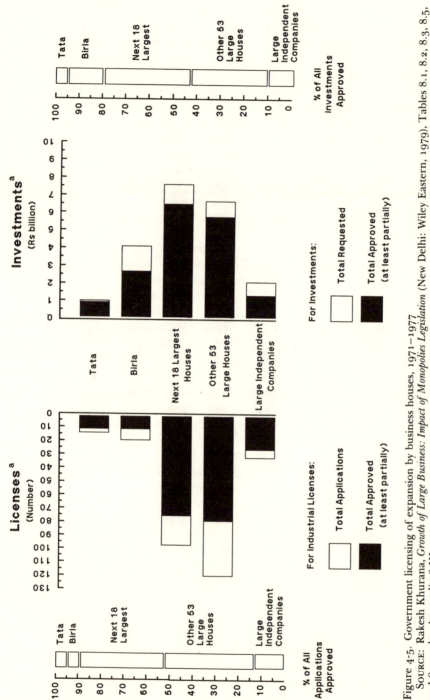

Figure 4-5. Government licensing of expansion by business houses, 1971–1977

SOURCE: Rakesh Khurana, *Growth of Large Business: Impact of Monopolies Legislation* (New Delhi: Wiley Eastern, 1979), Tables 8.1, 8.2, 8.3, 8.5, and 8.10, plus Appendix 8.III.

Note: Only for companies registered with the government under the terms of the Monopolies and Restrictive Trade Practices (MRTP) Act of 1969.

[a]Licenses and investment approved for plant and equipment associated with the substantial expansion of existing production or the establishment of new undertakings. More than 95 percent of all requested investment fell into these two categories, as distinct from mergers, acquisitions, takeovers, amalgamations, and divisions.

So, by 1977 Birla had steadily increased its assets beyond those of Tata, and finally it assumed the number-one rank among business houses.

In addition to Birla and Tata, ACC and Scindia (among the ten largest business houses) also remained successful in securing government licenses. Indeed, under the MRTP Act these two houses secured government approval for every application they submitted, applications with a total investment value greater than that sought by every other business house except Birla.[35] This enviable success of ACC and Scindia in securing government approvals reflected not only the political skills of their "industrial embassies" but also the high priority assigned by government to those industries—cement and ships, respectively—in which ACC and Scindia proposed to invest. Indeed, as we can see from Figure 4-6, government regulators approved nearly every application submitted by ACC, Scindia, and other MRTP companies seeking to expand in shipping and cement, as well as in machine tools, transport equipment, and industrial machinery.

Between 1971 and 1977 those industries expressly opened to MRTP companies together accounted for more than four-fifths of all investments approved by the Indian government (see Figure 4-6). Shipping alone accounted for two-fifths of all state-approved investments, while cement accounted for over one-tenth. Proposed investments to manufacture paper products contributed another one-tenth. But in marked contrast to shipping or cement, in the paper industry a few applicants competed for a very limited number of licenses, in a zero-sum game dictated by the government's production targets. A similar process was at work in both metallurgy and electrical equipment, where state enterprises (as noted above) continued to challenge Indian business houses for scarce government licenses. With several potential entrants seeking a few available licenses, approval rates in these industries remained low.

Approval rates stayed even lower in chemicals (see Figure 4-6).

Khurana, *Growth of Large Business: Impact of Monopolies Legislation* (New Delhi: Wiley Eastern, 1981), Table 8.10. In fact, new investments approved between 1971 and 1977 under the aegis of the MRTP Act (see Figure 4-6) equalled one-half of all Birla assets in 1969, when Parliament passed the act. By 1977 Birla's actual assets were Rs 10.7 billion, according to the government; see Rakesh Khurana, "Policy towards Large Business," in C. Rangarajan et al., *Strategy for Industrial Development in the '80s* (New Delhi: Oxford and IBH Publishing, 1981), p. 67. Between 1969 and 1974 private corporate assets grew 10 percent compounded annually, according to government estimates; see ibid., p. 68.

35. Khurana, *Growth of Large Business,* Tables 8.1, 8.2, 8.3, 8.5, and 8.10, plus Appendix 8.III.

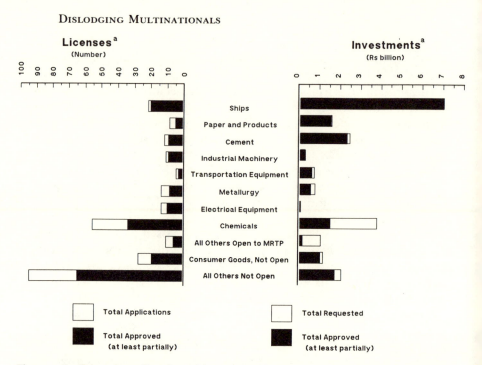

Figure 4-6. Government licensing of investments by business houses in Indian industries, 1971–1977

SOURCE: Same as for Figure 4-5.

Note: Only for companies registered with the government under the terms of the Monopolies and Restrictive Trade Practices (MRTP) Act opf 1969.

[a]Licenses and investment approved for plant and equipment associated with the substantial expansion of existing production or the establishment of new undertakings.

Between 1971 and 1977 MRTP companies seeking to enter or expand in the chemical industry submitted more applications than in any other industry (over one-sixth of their total applications, or one-third of all applications in "open" industries). In chemicals particularly, Indian business houses battled with large multinationals for access to scarce government licenses, and—as we shall see—generally fared better than did their foreign competitors. This time, the political skills of their "industrial embassies" combined with expanded government constraints on foreign expansion (e.g., FERA) to grant Indian business houses a distinct competitive advantage. Indeed, the stakes remained high: Although government regulators rejected nearly two-fifths of all chemical applications submitted by MRTP companies between 1971 and 1977, they nevertheless rewarded successful applicants in that single industry with nearly one-fifth of all the MRTP licenses they then approved throughout the entire economy (see Figure 4-6). The average size of approved investments remained relatively small, however, and chemicals continued to account for fewer than one-tenth of all investments approved by government. Again, applications for investments in chemicals and other targeted industries did not guarantee expansion to MRTP companies, since a large number of applicants continued to compete in a zero-sum game for a limited number of licenses.

Outside of these priority industries, new or expanded investments by MRTP companies remained ostensibly blocked. Nonetheless, MRTP companies continued to test the government's resolve to exclude them from attractive markets such as consumer products, but they did so through the submission of modest proposals requesting limited investment (see Figure 4-6). So fundamental were these (albeit limited) investments to the future expansion of MRTP companies that such applications eventually accounted for more than two-fifths of the total number they submitted, and this path led to impressive growth: Between 1971 and 1977 applications in these presumably "closed" industries fared better through the bureaucratic labyrinth than did applications for expansion in chemicals and a few other "open" industries. In fact, across industries, the government actually approved more than three-quarters of the total investment requested by MRTP companies, thus assuring business houses of continued access to the Indian market.[36]

In addition, existing producers often bolstered their market position without ever submitting applications for government permission to expand productive capacity. And once applicants had secured licenses, government regulators seldom made on-site inspections to guarantee compliance with the terms of the original permits. So, without requesting an expansion of capacity, existing producers exceeded their government-approved capacity in nearly one-tenth of the licenses they held, according to Figure 4-7. Indian business houses, otherwise restricted from expanding capacity under the MRTP Act, actively produced beyond the capacity the government formally permitted them to install.

No other local enterprise rivaled Birla in expanding market access through production in excess of licensed capacity. In fact, actual pro-

---

36. According to government estimates, between 1969 and 1974 growth in the total assets of the twenty largest business houses (9.7 percent compounded annually) kept pace with the growth of total corporate private assets (10.0 percent compounded annually); see Khurana, "Policy towards Large Business," p. 68.

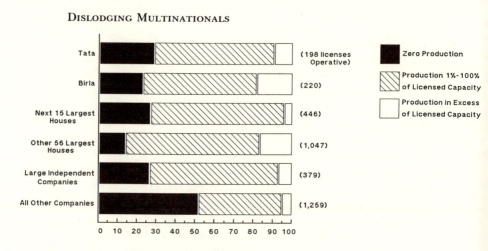

% of Licenses Operative

Figure 4-7. Capacity utilization in private enterprise, 1979
SOURCE: S. K. Goyal et al., *Functioning of Industrial Licensing System: A Report* (New Delhi: Corporate Studies Group, Indian Institute of Public Administration, 1983), pp. 24–25, Table II.2; p. 60, Table III.8; p. 66, Table III.10; p. 69, Table III.11; Appendices I, II, and IV, pp. 113–14, 123–26.

duction exceeded licensed capacity in nearly one-fifth of all the products Birla manufactured (see Figure 4-7). Yet another one-fifth of Birla's licenses went unimplemented (that is, zero production) as of 1979. Unlike many of its private competitors, however, Birla continued to encounter special difficulty in securing government approval for those applications it submitted (see Figures 4-4 and 4-5). So, for Birla in particular, production in excess of licensed capacity proved to be a viable alternative strategy for expanding access to the Indian market.

In contrast to Birla, Tata exceeded licensed capacity far less frequently and failed to implement its licenses more often (see Figure 4-7). Such underutilization of existing licenses fostered claims that Tata (and other houses) simply hoarded licenses to ensure monopolistic profits.[37] But that charge ignored the fact that zero production of licensed capacity proved endemic to Indian industry. In fact, fully one-fifth of Indian private enterprises did not implement their production licenses. Though the reasons for such underutilization re-

---

37. For one example of these charges, see S. K. Goyal et al., *Functioning of Industrial Licensing System: A Report* (New Delhi: Indian Institute of Public Administration, Corporate Studies Group, January 1983), p. 67.

main legion, among them we can distinguish a strategic consideration: Just as the expansion of existing production beyond approved
limits increased a firm's market access, the holding of government
licenses (whether utilized or not) served as an important barrier to
market entry for a firm's domestic and foreign competitors.

Although business houses proved able to maintain and in some
cases (e.g., Birla) even to expand their access to the Indian market in
spite of the MRTP Act, this legislation undoubtedly scared away innumerable investments. Seeking an alternative to the Indian market,
some of that investment went overseas. In one investigation, after
interviewing managers of Indian joint ventures operating in Africa
and elsewhere in Asia, government researchers concluded, "almost all
firms, especially those doing well, have unhesitatingly stated they
wanted to overcome MRTP" legislation by investing outside of India.[38] For these firms, then, the attraction of the domestic market
quickly gave way to the lure of overseas possibilities.

Invading Overseas Markets

Indian business houses controlled most of the firms that invested
abroad after passage of the MRTP Act.[39] Just as Parliament debated
that legislation, in 1969, the number of government licenses clearing
the establishment of joint ventures abroad jumped tenfold over the
previous year; of these, business houses secured four-fifths. During
the following year, 1970, fully 80 percent of all joint ventures in
production overseas (twelve of fifteen) were established by business
houses—up from 50 percent (three of six) in 1968. Over the 1970s,
however, the relative dominance of business houses in foreign operations eroded, as other Indian enterprises moved abroad. Nevertheless, Indian business houses still prevailed: By 1977 these houses had
established fully two-thirds of all Indian joint ventures in production
overseas, and nearly one-half of all government-approved projects
not yet completed.

Not all business houses showed the same proclivity to invest outside

38. Indian Institute of Foreign Trade, *India's Joint Ventures Abroad* (New Delhi, 1978),
pp. 74–75. In a separate study, managers of Indian firms operating in Mauritius and
the Philippines also cited constraints on the Indian market generally, and monopolies
legislation specifically, as the most compelling factors underlying the establishment of
overseas joint ventures; see Vinod Busjeet, "Foreign Investors from Less-Developed
Countries: A Strategic Profile" (DBA diss., Harvard Business School, 1980), pp. 57–58.

39. Dennis J. Encarnation, "The Political Economy of Indian Joint Industrial Ventures Abroad," *International Organization* 36 (Winter 1982):44–45.

of the Indian market, however. Birla, a principal target of the MRTP Act, became especially active overseas, and by 1977 it accounted for nearly one-fifth of all joint ventures in production. But Tata lagged far behind, as did most other MRTP companies. Indeed, direct investments abroad remained notably absent from the portfolios of three of India's ten largest industrial conglomerates, despite the presumed constraints imposed by the MRTP Act. And another three limited their overseas production in 1977 to a single joint venture for each. Therefore, with the important exception of Birla, most Indian business houses did not have the regulatory incentives or the requisite technology (and other assets) to invest aggressively overseas. Thus, by itself, the MRTP Act did not provide sufficient reason to invest outside of the protected home market.

To these regulatory policies must also be added the actual ebb and flow of the Indian market itself, especially the market for machinery. During 1967–68, and again during 1973–74, domestic recessions crippled Indian sales of capital goods. To fill idle capacity, Indian equipment manufacturers increasingly looked to export markets.[40] Unfortunately, the poor (or nonexistent) reputation of Indian-made machinery hindered foreign sales. In response, Indian business houses sought to establish captive markets for their equipment exports by investing directly in overseas buyers. Of course, such vertical integration had long been practiced in the Indian market. Birla, for example, was a manufacturer of automatic looms and other capital equipment used to weave textiles, and it remained one of India's three largest textile producers. When these textile companies established joint ventures abroad, they naturally bought their equipment from affiliated companies back in India. For Birla, the captive market for textile equipment eventually became quite large: By 1977 Birla had already set up five cotton mills and four jute mills overseas, and it planned to invest in several others. By integrating existing machinery suppliers at home with new equipment buyers overseas, business houses stimulated Indian exports of capital goods when sales fell off in the home market.[41]

40. Domestic recessions have been important determinants of Indian trade generally; see Martin Wolf, *India's Exports* (New York: Oxford University Press for the World Bank, 1982), esp. p. 124; Deepak Nayyar, *India's Exports and Export Policies in the 1960s* (Cambridge: Cambridge University Press, 1976), esp. p. 196.

41. Lecraw reported a direct linkage between foreign trade and foreign investment: 45 percent of the Indian joint ventures he surveyed in Thailand imported their machinery directly from India; see Donald J. LeCraw, "Direct Investment by Firms from Less Developed Countries," *Oxford Economic Papers* 29 (November 1977):454, Table VI.

Encarnation ("Indian Joint Ventures," pp. 39–43) shows that countries which hosted

Along with industrial recessions and regulatory policies back in India, trade restrictions in new overseas markets also spurred foreign investment by Indian business. Consider the case of engineering goods: During the 1960s and early 1970s such goods became India's fastest growing exports, especially to other developing countries, with Malaysia being the largest importer. During the mid-1970s, however, local competitors in Malaysia and other export markets, often stimulated by import tariffs, began to manufacture their own engineering goods and other products that, like Indian exports, remained undifferentiated in quality and sensitive to price fluctuations.[42] So, by 1977, twenty-four of sixty Indian joint ventures manufacturing in other developing countries were producing engineering goods, at a time when Indian exports of such products leveled off. Malaysia alone hosted one-half of these joint ventures. Thus, foreign trade and foreign investment continued to be inextricably intertwined as Indian business houses sought to enter new markets overseas.

Correlatively, the corporate strategies of Indian business houses and the foreign exchange policies of the Indian government also remained highly interdependent. Exports of Indian capital goods continued to be encouraged by Indian government policies, which insisted that Indian-made equipment—and not cash (except under extraordinary conditions)—be used to secure minority shareholdings in overseas ventures. These exports of equipment conserved scarce foreign exchange, an important objective of the government during the 1970s. At the same time, the Indian government readily approved applications from Indian manufacturers of engineering goods, whose export markets had been threatened by host government policies and local competitors. To offset falling export earnings, foreign investment ensured that at least a modicum of foreign exchange would continue to be repatriated to India through dividends and other remittances.[43] By the late 1970s business houses played a prominent

---

the largest number of Indian joint ventures also imported growing proportions of Indian capital goods, especially while that industry remained in recession in India. For example, between 1967 and 1973, as recessions crippled sales of capital goods in India, exports of Indian capital goods to Malaysia increased from 8.2 percent to 32.1 percent of all Indian exports to Malaysia. And by 1977 Malaysia was the principal host for Indian joint ventures abroad.

42. K. Balakrishnan, "Indian Joint Ventures Abroad: Geographic and Industry Patterns," *Economic and Political Weekly: Review of Management*, May 29, 1976, pp. M35–M48.

43. These remittances remained rather low, however. In 1978 dividends amounted to Rs 20 million, with fees for technical know-how adding another Rs 40 million; see "Indian Companies," *Business Asia*, p. 400.

role in achieving the government's objective—by securing scarce foreign exchange through trade and investment in overseas markets.

The growing interdependence of foreign exchange policies and foreign investment strategies held important implications for politics back in India. During 1977, for example, a proposal by the industries minister to expand the MRTP Act by banning the participation of the largest business houses in joint ventures abroad encountered stiff opposition from the commerce minister, who foresaw reductions in foreign exchange earnings. Indeed, according to a leading business daily, the commerce ministry feared "that any such ban would eliminate all chances of Indian companies going abroad," since "only . . . larger houses have the necessary technology" to compete in new markets.[44] In the end, arguments championed by the commerce ministry and endorsed by Indian business houses prevailed: Regulators continued to encourage Indian business houses to explore new investment opportunities in overseas markets.

Indian investment experiences abroad also exercised an important influence on the politics of foreign investment in India itself. By 1972 FICCI explicitly noted that linkage in a confidential memorandum submitted to a special parliamentary committee studying proposed amendments to India's Foreign Exchange Regulation Act (FERA): "As India is emerging as an exporter of enterprise and capital equipment which forms the basis for our joint ventures abroad," FICCI concluded, "it is important to be circumspect as regards the treatment we mete out to foreign enterprises and foreigners doing business in India."[45] In particular, FICCI questioned a disparity in the legislation that set the maximum Indian equity participation in joint ventures abroad at 49 percent but then set the maximum foreign equity participation in Indian affiliates lower, at 40 percent. FICCI anticipated that any such disparity in the law would have negative implications for the two-way flow of trade and investment: "Not only [may] such foreign capital and technology that we would like to attract in the interest of speedy economic growth not be forthcoming, but our own industries and business interests abroad may face similar disabilities."[46] Indeed, as Indian enterprises established joint ventures abroad in ever-increasing numbers, they sought the same political and econom-

44. *Economic Times* (Bombay), February 19, 1978, p. 1.
45. Federation of Indian Chambers of Commerce and Industry, *Correspondence and Relevant Documents Relating to Important Questions Dealt with by the Federation During the Year 1972* (New Delhi, 1973), pp. 55–64.
46. Ibid.

ic conditions in African and overseas Asian markets that foreign multinationals looked for in India.[47]

Multinationals

During the Indianization of colonial enterprises, discussed in Chapter 2, Indian business houses began to gain control over the country's largest industries, including jute, tea, light engineering, and insurance. By the mid-1950s, in fact, they typically dominated these domestic markets, as Indians easily overcame low financial and technological entry barriers to establish strong positions in the face of early foreign competition. At the same time, early nationalizations, especially in the financial sector, also eliminated foreign competitors from the Indian market. During the 1960s and 1970s those nationalizations spread into manufacturing and mining, further discouraging foreign competitors. Indeed, the nationalization of Martin Burn, in 1969, eliminated from the Indian scene the third-largest business house—and the most significant British agency to survive earlier efforts at Indianization. In effect, this hostile takeover of Martin Burn served to consolidate state control over the Indian steel industry, by nationalizing one of the country's two privately held mills. (Tata retained control over the other.) Later, in 1971, India nationalized its coal mines (thus assuming ownership of the chief assets of another surviving British-owned managing agency, Andrew Yule) and also acquired all foreign equity in two foreign oil companies (following the expiration of their contracts). In effect, then, by the early 1970s the state had dismissed all foreign competitors in markets it sought to control; at the same time, the state had also acquired the assets and technology necessary to dominate those markets, at least for the present.

Indianization did not, however, eliminate all foreign competitors. In fact, as noted in Chapter 3, a few former colonial agencies did combine newly acquired technological and marketing skills with preexisting financial and managerial assets to survive. Into the 1970s, for

47. By 1973 Indian business houses were fully aware of the impact that a "good investment climate" had on their operations abroad. Projects had to be abandoned or left unimplemented as a result either of political instability or of nationalization and indigenization policies in Ethiopia, Ghana, Nigeria, Tanzania, Uganda, and Zambia. For further discussion, see Encarnation, "Indian Joint Ventures," p. 56.

example, Bird-Heilgers still ranked among India's twenty largest houses, because it had moved from jute and mining into chemicals. Parry joined ranks by expanding its production of chemicals and fertilizers to supplement existing businesses in sugar and related food products. But by the 1980s only Parry survived the relentless Indianization of large (transformed) British managing agencies and still retained foreign directors on its board.

The descendants of these old colonial agencies were joined—and, at times, also displaced—by such multinationals as Imperial Chemical (ICI), which exploited at home and abroad a unique combination of technological and marketing advantages. ICI became so successful in using its assets that, in 1963, it produced 100 percent of all the industrial explosives made in India, as well as large proportions of chemicals and dyes.[48] With further improvements in its market position, ICI had catapulted by 1969 into fourth place among India's industrial conglomerates, up from nineteenth in 1963.[49] ICI, like most other multinationals operating in India, channeled more than two-thirds of its equity investments into subsidiaries (see Figure 2-12), retaining upwards of three-quarters of all shares. Like transformed British agencies before them, these multinationals usually entered the Indian market directly, without the assistance of a joint-venture partner.

Naturally, the continuing dominance of transformed British agencies and newer multinational enterprises—operating without the assistance of local partners but with technological and other resources— would exercise a special influence on subsequent bargaining over access to markets: As these foreign enterprises established an initial position in the Indian market independent of both Indian business houses and SOEs, this independent position granted them considerable managerial control over the subsequent horizontal diversification and vertical integration of their Indian operations. Not until the 1970s did the independence of these multinationals in the Indian market deteriorate, as a result of changes in government policy and an aggressive pursuit of technology by local enterprises. Until the 1970s, however, the few multinationals that entered India readily expanded their position in the market, aided by government regulators motivated to seek inflows of that technology necessary to increase domestic production.

48. Monopolies Inquiry Commission, *Report*, p. 60.
49. Khurana, *Growth of Large Business*, Table 8.10.

Entering the Indian Market

For a decade following independence the Indian government equivocated on the matter of foreign entry into the Indian market. On one hand, the government strictly prohibited foreign entry through takeover or portfolio investment. And it severely limited foreign entry through imports. On the other hand, the government sought foreign technology to develop particular markets. In this uncertain political climate few foreign enterprises actually entered India. Indeed, between 1948 and 1957 the country averaged fewer than forty new foreign collaborations annually, typically involving a joint-venture partner (see Figure 2-9). Thus, during the first decade of independence multinationals remained unimportant in the Indian market.

The foreign exchange crisis of 1957, we have already noted, changed all this. Following the crisis, for at least a decade government regulators actively encouraged foreign entry into markets requiring foreign technology, and foreign capital to pay for that technology. Indeed, between 1956 and 1966 ICI and other multinationals secured government approval for more than four-fifths of the applications they submitted to enter or expand in the Indian market (see Figure 4-4). In fact, the government's acceptance of applications submitted by multinationals matched the success enjoyed by SOEs, and that success was surpassed by only a handful of Indian business houses. Thus, during the second decade of political independence multinationals received the government's full blessings to enter and expand in the Indian market.

Like ICI, most of these multinationals entered the Indian market through majority foreign-owned subsidiaries. And like ICI, these multinationals often concentrated their investments in chemicals, as we can see from Figure 4-8. During 1961, at the height of foreign entry into the Indian market, only three industries—chemicals, petroleum, and food products, in that order—accounted for more than three-fifths of the existing foreign stock invested in majority subsidiaries. (By contrast, multinationals concentrated much smaller investments in minority foreign-owned affiliates—located in plantations, mining, and petroleum, followed far behind by chemicals and machinery.) And during the following decade, until 1971, foreign chemical manufacturers continued to enter the Indian market. Within this broad industry, foreign pharmaceutical companies typically invested in majority subsidiaries, where they exercised unchallenged

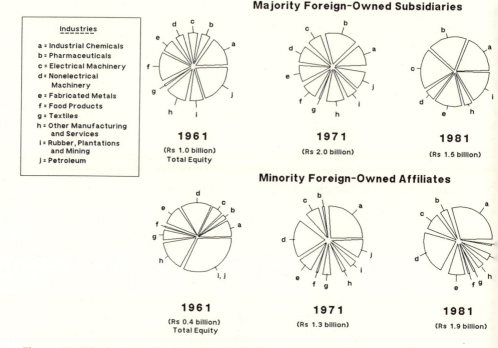

Majority Foreign-Owned Subsidiaries

Industries

a = Industrial Chemicals
b = Pharmaceuticals
c = Electrical Machinery
d = Nonelectrical
    Machinery
e = Fabricated Metals
f = Food Products
g = Textiles
h = Other Manufacturing
    and Services
i = Rubber, Plantations
    and Mining
j = Petroleum

1961
(Rs 1.0 billion)
Total Equity

1971
(Rs 2.0 billion)

1981
(Rs 1.5 billion)

Minority Foreign-Owned Affiliates

1961
(Rs 0.4 billion)
Total Equity

1971
(Rs 1.3 billion)

1981
(Rs 1.9 billion)

Figure 4-8. Distribution of foreign equity in Indian industries, 1961, 1971, 1981
SOURCES: Reserve Bank of India, *Foreign Collaboration in Indian Industry: Survey Report, 1968* (Bombay, 1968), pp. 15, 44 and, *Fourth Survey Report, 1985* (Bombay, 1985), pp. 14, 186.
Note: Includes year-end stocks of foreign equity.

managerial control. Indeed, in 1971 and subsequently, pharmaceutical subsidiaries accounted for nearly one-fifth of all foreign investment in majority foreign-owned subsidiaries (see Figure 4-8).

By contrast, multinationals manufacturing industrial chemicals typically entered the Indian market through minority foreign-owned affiliates. In fact, during 1971 affiliates producing industrial chemicals accounted for nearly one-quarter of all such minority ventures in India. In industrial chemicals, as we saw in Chapter 3, local enterprises began to acquire requisite technology in the international market (see Figure 3-5). So, entry and expansion in the Indian market by majority foreign-owned subsidiaries producing industrial chemicals became less likely there than in pharmaceuticals, where technological and marketing barriers to entry remained higher.

On the other hand, low technological barriers to entry forced majority subsidiaries to leave processed foods, textiles, and rubber (see

Figure 4-8). Some of these foreign enterprises entered into minority foreign-owned affiliates, but increasingly foreigners sold their assets (and market position) to Indian business houses and other local enterprises. In fact, by 1981 no majority subsidiaries, and only a few minority affiliates, produced food, textiles, and rubber. Outside of manufacturing, majority subsidiaries experienced a similar, precipitous decline in petroleum refining and assorted services, where—as noted above—state enterprises often displaced them.

For a few multinationals, partnerships with state enterprises represented one of the few means available to gain access to the Indian market. To these resulting joint ventures, foreign partners sold raw materials (as in the case of Madras Refineries) or, more frequently, capital goods and other technology (as in Madras Fertilizers).[50] In addition to providing immediate market access, partnerships with SOEs also facilitated later negotiations with government regulators and central ministries. Amoco, for example, settled for less than 26 percent of the shareholdings in Madras Refineries in order to edge out a Bechtel-led consortium for control over 49 percent of the equity in Madras Fertilizers.[51] And in both instances the government left top management in the hands of its foreign partner. Thus, in its insistence on being the majority shareholder the government prevailed, while the multinational secured both managerial control and a powerful political ally in securing government licenses.

More frequently, the few multinationals that established affiliates sought out private Indian partners. Initially, they collaborated with the largest business houses. By 1959, as we saw in Chapter 2, Indian business houses had secured nearly one-half of all government approvals for foreign tie-ups (see Figure 3-1). For Tata, this meant that one-half of its 120 affiliated companies became affiliates with foreign partners, who typically held minority shares.[52] Even after partnerships with the largest business houses began to fall off, Tata and seven other business houses still remained active in joint ventures, accounting in 1973 for one-sixth of all such affiliates in India (see Figure 2-10). For multinationals, close relations with Tata and other

50. Aurobindo Ghose, "Joint Sector and 'Control' of Indian Monopoly," *Economic and Political Weekly* (Bombay), June 8, 1974, p. 906.
51. These negotiations were the subject of an in-depth case study; see Ashok Kapoor, *International Business Negotiations: A Study of India* (New York: New York University Press, 1970).
52. R. K. Hazari, *The Structure of the Corporate Private Sector: A Study of Concentration, Ownership, and Control* (Bombay: Asia Publishing House for the Planning Commission of the Government of India, 1966), Table 8.3, pp. 336–37.

business houses not only tapped into existing distribution channels but also into political organizations with the necessary financial and managerial assets to guide licensing applications through regulatory agencies.

However, most multinationals entering the Indian market actually established their own organizational capacity to deal effectively with India's bureaucratic labyrinth. Few tried to borrow the existing organizations of business houses or state enterprises because, into the 1970s, multinationals typically invested in the Indian market through majority foreign-owned subsidiaries unaffiliated with any local enterprise. Even when they did invest initially through affiliates, by 1973 most of their local partners were also unaffiliated with business houses or with state enterprises. Having no local partner to provide requisite political skills, minority affiliates—like majority subsidiaries—often established "industrial embassies" (or their equivalents) to handle government relations.

Like these "embassies," most other business organizations established by foreign enterprise mirrored those established by Indian enterprise. Indeed, they sometimes predated Indian institutions.[53] Long before Birla and other Indian business houses had mounted their own organizational drive, a few British managing agencies (e.g., Andrew Yule) established "embassies" early on to deal with the British Raj; next, they helped to found—and then moved to dominate—industry associations (e.g., the Indian Tea Association), large regional chambers (e.g., the Bengal Chamber serving Calcutta and eastern India), and finally, the national Associated Chambers of Commerce and Industry (ASSOCHAM). Just as ASSOCHAM was FICCI's counterpart for foreign (and especially British enterprise), so too in each industry and region of the country, separate foreign and Indian business associations existed side by side, and both sets of organizations enjoyed formal access to government policymaking. Again, industry oligopolists behaved like political oligarchs, but now the oligarchs were foreign enterprises.

In their dealings with government regulators, multinationals and Indian business houses often employed similar tactics to secure government licenses. For example, Tata and foreign-owned Philips each organized their suppliers, usually small-scale enterprises, into business associations, which then made separate representations before government agencies to endorse the applications submitted by their large buyers.[54] Both foreign and local enterprises also employed in-

53. Kochanek, *Business and Politics*, pp. 119–30.
54. Interview held in 1978 with the Director of the Federation of Associations of

dustry associations to provide additional access to government decisionmaking. For example, the Indian-dominated Cement Manufacturers Association and the foreign-dominated Organization of Pharmaceutical Producers used their permanent offices in New Delhi—both staffed by former members of the government civil service—to relax price controls during the 1960s.[55] Only in the financing of political campaigns did foreign and local enterprises diverge markedly in their activities, since multinationals typically refrained from any significant involvement. Otherwise, through the 1960s foreign enterprises employed a variety of political and business organizations to help secure scarce government licenses.

Once in possession of these licenses, and free from foreign competition, multinationals operating in India used their considerable financial, technological, marketing, and managerial resources to control several Indian markets. Consider, for example, the distribution of market share among India's three hundred largest companies: In 1967, as we can see from Figure 4-9, multinationals collectively controlled more than 80 percent of the market for rubber and pharmaceuticals, more than 50 percent of the market for electrical equipment and food products, and more than 40 percent of the market for both industrial chemicals and nonelectrical machinery. Within each of these industries, one or two multinationals typically controlled the manufacturing and distribution of most products.[56] Outside of these industries, however, the several resources available to foreign oligopolists proved much less potent. Thus, only a very few multinationals producing metals and transport equipment—and an even smaller number producing cement and textiles—exploited their several (technological and marketing) advantages, to rule the Indian market.

By 1971 in most Indian markets the position of multinationals had stabilized (see Figure 1-1). But by 1982 their market share had seriously eroded (see Figure 4-9). In sharp contrast to a decade earlier, multinationals during 1982 controlled more than 50 percent of only

---

Small Industries of India. The interview concerned the federation's depositions made before the Monopolies Commission, first, on behalf of the 1971 request by Tata Engineering and Locomotive to expand substantially its manufacture of commercial vehicles, and second, on behalf of the 1974 request of Philips India to expand substantially its manufacture of light bulbs.

55. Kochanek, *Business and Politics*, esp. pp. 236, 313–14.

56. In pharmaceuticals, for example, a single producer, typically a multinational, supplied forty-nine of the ninety-seven products examined by the government's Monopolies Inquiry Commission (*Report*, pp. 247–49) in 1963. The top two producers accounted for all of the production of another twenty-one products; and the top three producers controlled the market for most remaining pharmaceutical products.

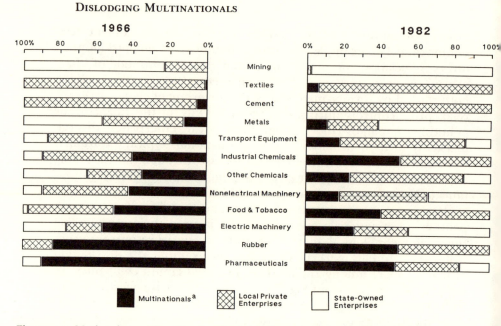

Figure 4-9. Market shares of multinationals and Indian enterprises, 1966, 1982
SOURCES: Same as for Figure 1-1.
^aClassified as multinational if foreign shareholding exceeded 20 percent, or if 20 percent of board of directors were foreigners, or if chairman/managing director were foreigners.

two markets—rubber and industrial chemicals—where both majority foreign subsidiaries and minority affiliates remained active (see Figure 4-8). Indeed, industrial chemicals represented one of the few industries in which multinationals improved their market position between 1966 and 1982. More often, their share of other Indian markets simply disappeared. Foreign pharmaceuticals and machinery companies experienced the most dramatic declines; their market shares were cut in half. Still, multinationals held 40 percent of the Indian market for pharmaceuticals (typically through majority foreign-owned subsidiaries), and an equal proportion of the Indian market for food products (exclusively through minority foreign-owned affiliates). In all other industries, however, multinationals lost much of their earlier standing, and in 1982 they held less than one-quarter of the Indian market.

Losing Market Share

Between 1966 and 1982 multinationals largely sacrificed the Indian market to business houses and other local-private enterprises (see

Figure 4-9). Just as the market share of multinationals in the rubber, electrical machinery, and pharmaceutical industries declined precipitously, so the share held by Indian business houses and other large private firms more than doubled. Indeed, as late as 1971 business houses controlled none of the largest pharmaceutical companies in India; yet in 1982 the Indian private sector held over one-third of the pharmaceutical market. In pharmaceuticals and most other industries, as we noted in Chapter 3, Indian business houses and other local private enterprises sought out foreign technology, unbundled it from foreign capital, and modified it to Indian conditions, often at the expense of multinational investors. (Sarabhai, for example, had retired in 1969 its earlier technical and financial agreements with Merck Pharmaceuticals and assumed full control over their joint venture.) Business houses also invested in local product and process innovations, as alternatives to foreign technology. Before 1966 Indian business houses and other local private enterprises employed that foreign and local technology to exclude multinationals from the Indian markets for textiles, cement, and (to a lesser extent) transport equipment. Then, during the 1970s they employed that foreign and local technology to attack the existing position of multinationals operating throughout the Indian market.

To combat multinationals, state-owned enterprises also utilized foreign and local technology (see Figure 4-9). Between 1966 and 1982 SOEs nearly tripled their market share in nonelectrical machinery, at the expense of multinationals. In addition, as we saw earlier, the state also nationalized the holdings of Martin Burn and improved its position in the market for metals and related products. In mining, other nationalizations hurt foreign enterprises. Even local private enterprises lost position in steel and mining (and, to a much lesser extent, textiles), mostly as a result of state investments. Indeed, large planned investments in steel and other metals, in machinery and other engineering goods, and in mining served to increase the state's share of production in these markets (see Figure 2-3). During the 1970s central economic planning thus served as a means for reducing the market shares of multinationals and, to a lesser extent, of Indian business houses. Here, the state was asserting its peculiar combination of powers.

Government regulatory policies also played a significant role in reducing the position of multinationals in the Indian market. In textiles beginning well before 1966, government regulators remained reluctant to grant multinationals access to the Indian market both because local technology seemed adequate and because it was being exported to Indian affiliates abroad. Similarly, in transport equipment, government regulators granted a limited number of licenses to business houses already in possession of foreign technology, often untied from foreign equity. Then, after 1966, monopolies legislation (the MRTP Act, 1969) and changes in foreign exchange regulations (FERA, 1973) importantly contributed to the demise of multinationals operating in the Indian market. The MRTP Act brought the operations of the largest multinationals under the close scrutiny of government regulators, while FERA brought all companies with more than 40 percent foreign equity under similar scrutiny. In combination, the two sets of regulations made it more difficult for multinationals (compared with Indian business houses and other local enterprises) to expand in the Indian market (see Figure 4-10).

Between 1971 and 1977, as we can see, foreign subsidiaries regulated by both FERA and the MRTP Act secured three-fifths of the investments they sought, while Indian companies subject only to the MRTP Act secured well over four-fifths. Among majority foreign-owned subsidiaries, ICI—ranked fifth among business houses the year (1969) Parliament enacted the MRTP Act—found it especially difficult to expand under the combined weight of that act and FERA. Between 1971 and 1977, ICI secured government approval for only 20 percent of its licensing applications, down from 80 percent during 1956–66.[57] Still, during the 1970s ICI secured one-tenth of the total government-approved investment sought by all MRTP companies with more than 40 percent foreign shareholdings. Most of that investment went into chemicals, one of the few industries expressly open to expanded investment by MRTP companies—an industry that, between 1971 and 1977, accounted for more than one-third of all license applications for "open" industries submitted by such companies. All of these applicants competed for a limited number of licenses in a zero-sum game defined by the government's production targets. As a result, applicants in the chemical industry experienced a lower rate of government approval than did their counterparts in other "open" industries (see Figure 4-6). And among all chemical producers, ICI fared worst, having three-quarters of its applications rejected by government regulators (compared with two-fifths for the industry as a whole).[58] Overall, such rejection had disastrous effects for the company: By 1977 ICI no longer ranked among India's top ten industrial conglomerates.[59] And by 1977 ICI was not alone; across

57. Khurana, *Growth of Large Business*, Tables 8.2; Licensing Policy Inquiry, *Appendices: Volume III*, p. 3, Table III-A (3).
58. Khurana, *Growth of Large Business*, Tables 8.2. and 8.5.
59. Ibid., Table 8.7.

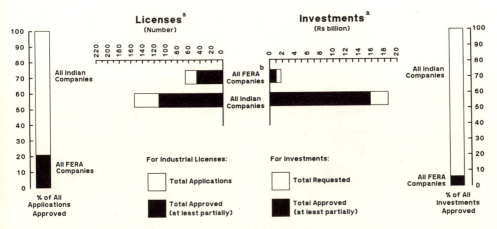

Figure 4-10. Government licensing of expansion by multinationals, 1971–1977

SOURCE: Same as for Figure 4-5.

Note: Only for companies registered with the government under the terms of the Monopolies and Restrictive Trade Practices (MRTP) Act of 1969.

[a]Licenses and investment approved for plant and equipment associated with the substantial expansion of existing production or the establishment of new undertakings.

[b]Companies with more than 40 percent foreign equity registered with the government under the terms of the Foreign Exchange Regulation Act (FERA) of 1973; all other companies are classified under FERA as Indian companies.

all industries, multinationals simply failed to secure government licenses more often than did local competitors also wishing to expand in the Indian market (see Figure 4-10).

Many of these multinationals, faced during the 1970s with diminished prospects for securing new government licenses, simply side-stepped the licensing system altogether and expanded production capacity on their own. As noted earlier, government regulators seldom made on-site inspections to see that existing producers were operating in accordance with their permits. So, without ever requesting an expansion of capacity, ICI and other existing foreign producers exceeded their government-approved capacity in nearly one-fifth of the licenses they held, double the comparable figures for Indian companies with less foreign equity, as we can see in Figure 4-11.

Even ICI's excesses seem minor, however, when compared with Unilever's persistent expansion of existing production beyond approved limits (see Figure 4-11). Here, Unilever probably represented

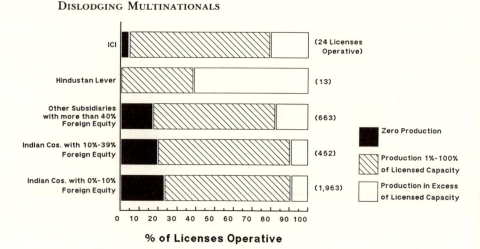

Figure 4-11. Capacity utilization by multinationals, 1979
SOURCE: Same as for Figure 4-7.

the most extreme example of multinational excess, for the company could not afford to let its licenses lay idle, in marked contrast both to most other multinationals and (especially) to local enterprises. Idle licenses meant high costs to Unilever, since it operated in an industry (consumer products) ostensibly closed to new or expanded investment by MRTP companies. More generally, whether through production in excess of approved limits or full utilization of existing licenses, Unilever, ICI, and other multinationals constantly fought to maintain—indeed, to improve—their market position, even after passage of the MRTP Act and FERA.

Diversifying Markets

In addition to illegally expanding production, Unilever also requested and secured government permission to diversify its existing operations.[60] During the 1970s Hindustan Lever (Unilever's Indian subsidiary) added basic chemicals to the detergents, soaps, and other consumer goods that made up its product lines. This increase reflected the high priority given such manufacture by the government

60. Data from interviews in 1978 and 1983 with senior managers of Hindustan Lever, reported in Dennis J. Encarnation and Sushil Vachani, "Foreign Ownership: When Hosts Change the Rules," *Harvard Business Review* 63 (September–October 1985):155, 157–58.

(chemicals became an open industry under the MRTP Act), while it conformed to the company's plans for backward integration. Later, in 1983, the subsidiary increased the proportion of its production in chemicals and other priority industries by selling its low-priority (by government standards) food business to a second Unilever affiliate (Lipton India), a separate Indian company with less than 40 percent foreign equity. In 1981 no majority foreign-owned subsidiaries processed foods; only minority foreign-owned affiliates did (see Figure 4-8). Instead, Unilever and other multinationals owning majority subsidiaries invested up to two-fifths of their equity in chemical plants. Just as Unilever diversified into chemicals, multinationals in 1982 finally achieved control over one-half of the Indian market for industrial chemicals (see Figure 4-9). Thus, Unilever's movement out of processed foods and into chemicals mirrored larger shifts in the overall pattern of foreign investment in India.

Again, Unilever's increased use of local technology and its diversification into overseas export markets also represented other patterns common to multinationals operating in India. As we saw in the last chapter, Hindustan Lever invested ever greater proportions of its sales in local R&D and achieved several technological breakthroughs in the manufacture of heretofore mature products (e.g., soap).[61] These achievements bolstered Unilever's claim that it both employed sophisticated technology and saved the country scarce foreign exchange (two other government priorities) by reducing imports and foreign technology licenses. Finally, Unilever further added to India's foreign exchange holdings by increasing the proportion of exports in its sales.[62] This represented a larger trend—at least according to data gathered by India's central bank—but the magnitude of that trend remains one hotly debated within India.[63]

61. Most notably, the company found ways to substitute locally abundant. typically inedible oils for imported, edible tallow in the manufacture of high-quality soap, a substitution that saved the country scarce foreign exchange. See ibid., p. 155.

62. Hindustan Lever's export sales tripled between 1977 and 1981, from Rs 170 million to Rs 430 million. The company exported not only its own products but also a variety of products manufactured by other, typically smaller Indian firms. In fact, Hindustan Lever was one of India's first licensed "export houses," promoted by the government as channels for products manufactured by smaller firms that were unable to export on their own. See ibid., p. 155.

63. Reserve Bank of India, *Foreign Collaboration in Indian Industry: Fourth Survey Report, 1985* (Bombay, 1985), pp. 138–39, 160–61; also see Sanjaya Lall and Sharif Mohammed, "Foreign Ownership and Manufacturing Export Performance in the Large Corporate Sector of India," *Journal of Development Studies* 20 (October 1983):63–64. For data and analysis challenging the conclusion that multinationals have added to India's exports and (especially) its foreign exchange holdings, see K. S. Chalapati Rao,

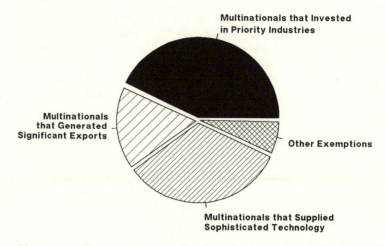

Figure 4-12. Government exemptions from foreign equity dilution below
40 percent, 1973–1981
SOURCE: Same as for Figure 2-13.

According to the Reserve Bank of India, Hindustan Lever and
other majority foreign-owned subsidiaries consistently exported more
than they imported following the passage of FERA. By contrast, before passage, they consistently had incurred trade deficits. Although
majority subsidiaries finally achieved small trade surpluses after
FERA, most minority affiliates, local private firms, and especially state
enterprises continued to run trade deficits. Moreover, this superior
trade performance by majority subsidiaries, according to the Reserve
Bank, remained visible in every industry during the late 1970s and
into the 1980s. Thus, to retain and improve their access to the Indian
market, as we can see in Figure 4-12, Hindustan Lever and other
majority foreign-owned subsidiaries pursued expansion into export
markets.

Under FERA, according to this figure, multinationals that: (1) exported a "significant proportion" of their production; (2) operated in
"high-priority industries"; or (3) employed "sophisticated technology"
could qualify to retain more than 40 percent of the shareholdings in
their Indian affiliates. Nearly a hundred multinationals finally met at

India's Export Policies and Performance: An Evaluation (New Delhi: Indian Institute of
Public Administration, Corporate Studies Group, 1988), esp. pp. 71–91; also see Indi-
an Institute of Foreign Trade, *Role of Transnational Corporations in India's Exports* (New
Delhi, 1981), pp. 11, 41–47.

least one of these conditions, but Unilever was among a mere handful to qualify on all three grounds. In 1982 approximately 60 percent of Hindustan Lever's sales generated foreign exchange, involved high technology, or operated in high-priority sectors—so the government allowed Unilever to retain its 51-percent share in one of India's twenty largest (by the late 1970s) industrial conglomerates.[64] The vast majority of multinationals, however, complied by diluting their equity holdings while retaining minority shares (see Figure 2-13). And a few multinationals—including IBM and Coca-Cola—chose to exit the Indian market rather than risk such dilution of managerial control.

Among the most successful multinationals to diversify operations through an equity dilution was ITC, originally a majority foreign-owned subsidiary of British-American Tobacco Company. Beginning with the MRTP Act of 1969, the government expressed special reservations about the operations of a large foreign subsidiary in an industry that remained so closely tied to agriculture, required little new technology or large capital investments, and held only limited prospects for export. So, by selling both fresh equity and existing stock, ITC reduced its foreign ownership from 94 percent in 1968 to 75 percent in 1969, 60 percent in 1974 (following FERA), and 40 percent in 1976. With each of these divestments, ITC further diversified its operations, from manufacturing to service industries, and from local marketing of a single product to exporting several products.[65]

Among multinationals operating in industries eventually accorded low priority by government, ITC did not stand alone. Colgate-Palmolive (India) also reduced foreign shareholdings to 40 percent and thereby retained its majority share of the fast-growing, highly protected toothpaste market. By comparison, Chesebrough-Ponds (India) not only maintained its existing market position but also managed to expand its manufacturing operations from one to four plants, to export nearly one-third of its sales, and to secure government approval to diversify its product line.[66] For these multinationals, as we saw in Chapter 2, continued operations in India—despite minority foreign ownership—proved quite profitable.

---

64. Data from interviews in 1983 with senior managers of Hindustan Lever, reported in Encarnation and Vachani, "Foreign Ownership," p. 155. During 1979 Hindustan Lever was ranked fourteenth by the government among India's largest business houses; see Goyal, *Industrial Licensing System*, p. 24.

65. Data from interviews in 1982 and 1983 with senior managers of ITC, reported in Encarnation and Vachani, "Foreign Ownership," pp. 155, 157, 160.

66. Data from interviews in 1983 with senior managers of Colgate-Palmolive (India) and Chesebrough-Ponds (India), reported in ibid. pp. 153, 157.

Even those multinationals operating in priority industries found that minority shareholdings improved access to the Indian market. For example, in pharmaceuticals Ciba-Geigy volunteered to dilute its equity to 40 percent (even though FERA required dilution only down to 51 percent), so that its subsidiary could benefit from being reclassified as an "Indian company." In return, that company was left free to produce pharmaceutical formulations valued at ten times the sale of its bulk drugs, or twice the manufacturing capacity permitted non-Indian producers.[67] Similarly, in computers, ICL diluted its foreign equity to 40 percent, to remain in the Indian market at the moment when IBM exited. ICL, Ciba-Geigy, and other such multinationals successfully retained managerial control over their expanded and diversified operations in India, even with minority foreign ownership. Their success encouraged other multinationals also operating in high-technology industries to enter India.

Entering India Anew: The 1980s

During the 1980s a growing number of multinationals invested in India, but now expressly for the purpose of using that nation as a base for exporting. Between 1981 and 1985, for example, American multinationals—the largest source of foreign investment in India during that period—secured government licenses for 127 direct investments in India, of which nearly one-fifth (23 of 127) exported *all* of their Indian production (see Table 4-1). The great majority of these firms (over three-quarters) produced electrical equipment and electronics, especially computer products and software, for which India supplied inexpensive but well-trained technicians. To attract investors, the Indian government streamlined its regulatory regime by establishing export processing zones and other means to simplify negotiations between multinationals and government regulators.[68] However, outside of electronics—in chemicals and most other industries—multinationals continued to invest in India to supply that market from within. In fact, they accounted for four-fifths of all U.S. multinationals entering India between 1981 and 1985.

Like these multinationals, most Indian enterprises that licensed foreign technology did so to service the domestic market. Indeed, in all

67. Data from interviews held in 1983 with senior managers of Ciba-Geigy (India), reported in ibid., pp. 153–54.
68. For a survey of these structures and procedures, see Dennis J. Encarnation and Louis T. Wells, Jr., "Sovereignty En Garde: Negotiating with Foreign Investors," *International Organization* 39 (Winter 1985):47–78.

Table 4-1.   U.S. multinationals entering India, 1981–1985

	Direct investments[a]		Techology licenses	
	Total number	Of which, number exporting total production	Total number	Of which, number exporting total production
Electrical equipment and electronics	51	18	93	2
Of which:				
Computers and related products	27	13	24	2
Industrial instruments and medical equipment	8	0	12	0
Computer software	6	3	3	0
Telecommuncations equipment	4	2	11	0
Other electrical equipment	6	0	43	0
Chemicals	9	0	62	0
Industrial machinery	7	0	53	0
Metals	12	2	29	0
All other	25	3	128	1
Total	104	23	365	3

SOURCES: Indian Investment Centre and Indo-U.S. Chamber of Commerce, reported in Sanjeev K. Mehra, "Entry Strategies of Foreign Computer and Electronics Companies in India: 1977-86" (unpublished paper, Harvard Business School, March 14, 1986).

[a]Includes all new government-approved foreign tie-ups involving finance only, or finance and technology combined.

industries, the number of Indian licensees who exported their production between 1981 and 1985 remained minuscule (see Table 4-1). When they did choose to export, these licensees often encountered obstacles erected by foreign suppliers who (as noted in Chapter 3) insisted that local enterprises with no foreign shareholdings agree to a variety of contractual restrictions on the use of licensed technology for export sales (see Table 3-1). By contrast, the multinational parent of foreign subsidiaries and affiliates typically imposed fewer such contractual restrictions and relied instead on their greater managerial control to restrict the subsequent use of their technology.

For a few multinationals, using India as an export platform also became a first step toward gaining access to the Indian market. Burroughs, for example, tried unsuccessfully to enter the Indian computer market through a wholly owned subsidiary in 1972; yet by 1977 it had established in the Santa Cruz Export Zone an equal partnership joint venture with Tata, organized to export computer software and printers both to Eastern Bloc countries and to other Burroughs affiliates outside India.[69] Finally, in 1984 Burroughs gained access to the Indian market, but only after dilution of its shareholdings to 40 percent, in compliance with FERA. (Since Tata simultaneously diluted its shareholdings, Burroughs retained managerial control.) Similarly, Xerox in 1981 established a wholly owned subsidiary solely for export, after the government had rebuffed its proposal to establish an equal partnership joint venture with Modi, to produce for both Indian and export markets.[70] In 1984 Xerox did gain access to the Indian market by establishing a separate, minority foreign-owned joint venture with Modi, in which Xerox retained managerial control. But as a government-imposed condition for entry, the new joint venture agreed to export 30 percent of its production. In the case of Xerox and Burroughs (as well as other multinationals), exporting from India brought better treatment in subsequent negotiations with government regulators who controlled access to the Indian market.

Many multinationals agreed to enter the Indian market through minority foreign-owned affiliates because of relative changes in the international and Indian markets for electronics and electrical equipment. Before the 1980s multinationals in this industry had little incentive to confront the regulatory system, given the small size of the Indian market. Rather, they concentrated their attention outside of India, on faster growing segments of the world market. During the 1980s, however, growth in this larger world market slowed considerably, just as Indian demand for electrical equipment showed promise of increasing by some 40 percent per year into the 1990s. In fact, by 1984 India represented one of the few growth markets in the world, and the only large market free of competition from IBM. By the 1990s, if projections held, India would rank among the world's ten largest computer markets.[71] Given these changes, American electronics manufacturers rushed to India where, between 1981 and 1985, they accounted for nearly one-half of all American direct investments and one-quarter of all American technology licenses (see Table 4-1).

69. For further details on these negotiations, see Grieco, *Between Dependency and Autonomy*, pp. 84–88.

70. Data from interviews held in 1985 with senior managers in Modi-Xerox (India), Rank-Xerox (U.K.), and Xerox (U.S.), reported in Sanjeev K. Mehra, "Entry Strategies of Foreign Computer and Electronics Companies in India: 1977–86" (unpublished paper, Harvard Business School, March 14, 1986); also see *Financial Times* (U.K.), January 15, 1985, p. 3.

71. India (Republic), Department of Electronics, *Annual Report: 1982* (New Delhi: Manager of Publications, 1983), p. 119, and *Annual Report: 1983* (New Delhi: Manager of Publications, 1984), p. 61.

Faced with growing competition from foreign direct investors and foreign technology suppliers, Burroughs, Xerox, and other multinationals reluctantly agreed to compromise their initial demands for majority ownership; instead, they settled for minority foreign-owned affiliates, thus joining a larger trend: By the late 1970s—for the first time in Indian history—minority affiliates represented the principal means by which multinationals gained direct access to the Indian market, having supplanted majority subsidiaries. And this reliance of multinationals on minority affiliates has continued to the present.

Indeed, during this decade, encouraged by government policies, multinationals have entered India with fresh enthusiasm. While the Indian government has retained the FERA ceiling on foreign shareholdings, in the 1980s it also began to dismantle other components of the regulatory regime that affected the electronics industry.[72] In particular, the government simplified import licensing and drastically reduced most import duties; it did away with capacity licensing altogether and fixed minimum (rather than maximum) production volumes to encourage efficiency; it extended these liberalizations to those multinationals that respected FERA guidelines. Finally, the government directed SOEs to increase their expenditures for computers and other electronics equipment. Even though the government began its reforms by singling out the electrical equipment industry as a model for future policy changes in other industries, these first changes nevertheless exemplified a larger, more inclusive process: During the 1980s government policy as a whole has operated to increase foreign access to the Indian market. This result contrasts sharply with the trend during the previous fifteen years. Compared with other countries, however, India continues to keep its home market remarkably closed to multinationals.

DISLODGING MULTINATIONALS: STAGE THREE

Multinationals, as a rule, have never enjoyed unlimited access to the Indian market. Instead, quotas and tariffs have restrained their imports, while capital controls restricted their ownership of local enterprises. Moreover, such strict regulation of foreign trade and investment has remained in place for nearly four decades of political independence, well into the 1980s. That regulation—along with improved access to finance and technology—has allowed India to reach

---

72. Department of Electronics, *Annual. Report: 1982* and *Annual Report: 1983*.

the third and final stage in a national drama designed to dislodge multinationals from one domestic market after another. Those multinationals, of course, have tenaciously fought to retain their privileged positions, aided by periodic government liberalizations. But these liberalizations have failed to dispel the popular Indian belief that foreign domination over local markets imposed such high material and psychic costs that domestic control is well worth subsidizing. For many Indians who share this belief, economic nationalism remains the single most powerful political cry.

Among the first to support economic nationalism, Indian industrialists demanded a sharp reduction in India's dependence on imports, and an outright negation of exports. Recognizing that import restrictions could serve as powerful investment incentives for multinationals, these industrialists also called for government regulations on inflows of foreign equity which, they argued, were typically "accompanied by political influence or interference of foreign vested interests."[73] Majority foreign-owned subsidiaries represented the enemy, since multinationals could channel through such subsidiaries just those financial, technological, marketing, and managerial skills that might steal the protected Indian market away from less well-endowed local enterprises. Indeed, after two decades after independence, by 1966 multinationals already controlled more than 50 percent of several Indian markets, thus confirming the original fears of India's business elite.

Among those industrialists, J. R. D. Tata and G. D. Birla headed India's two largest business houses, those local institutional innovations which allowed a few entrepreneurs to manage the operations of an ever-expanding number of diversified business concerns. By combining buyers, suppliers, and potential competitors within a single conglomerate, Tata, Birla, and other business houses sought to develop and utilize economies of scale in management, production, marketing, and technology. While exploiting these scale economies, business houses also achieved in the Indian marketplace a high level of independence from foreigners. This eventually led them to substitute for foreign enterprises operating in India, a replacement that became highly visible whenever Indian houses acquired majority equity in— and eventually exerted managerial control over—former colonial British enterprises. In fact, market access through acquisition had begun long before independence, but it showed itself clearly only

73. "Bombay Plan," para. 82, in *Young Indian*, Special Independence Number (1972), p. D60.

during the years after 1947, when Indian business houses formally replaced British managing agencies as the dominant producers in most financial and industrial markets. That pattern of substitution reappeared during the 1970s, now with multinationals as the victims. By the early 1980s Indian business houses and other local enterprises controlled over one-half of nearly every Indian market.

Of course, as we have noted repeatedly, business houses and other local enterprises were not always, or unanimously, hostile to foreign enterprise during independent India's first four decades. In cooperation, Tata led the way among business houses, by establishing joint ventures with foreign partners; by 1973 Tata and seven other business houses accounted for one-sixth of all such ventures in India. For multinationals, close relations with business houses not only tapped into existing distribution channels and managerial expertise but also mobilized political organizations with the requisite skills to secure government licenses. In exchange, Tata and the others gained access to foreign capital and technology, as well as occasional entry to export markets. Such differences in endowments and capabilities, rationally linked, yielded several mutually advantageous agreements between business houses and multinationals.

Joint ventures with multinationals, along with technology licensing and other commercial transactions, served to reinforce a second important, if not unambiguous or unanimous, political demand: freedom from government interference in agreements privately negotiated. In India, such interference often reached epidemic proportions. The "license, permit, quota Raj"—as critics referred to the country's licensing system, reflecting its colonial legacy—long pervaded the Indian market. Overall, India's system operated like a zero-sum game, rewarding a few at the expense of many. Yet it often served to ameliorate hostilities between business houses and government regulators, especially when central ministries and parliamentary committees charged government regulators to direct business houses into targeted industries. Proposals to enter those industries simply fared better through the bureaucratic labyrinth than did other licensing applications. The government also charged regulators to conserve—and, more recently, to contribute to—the country's scarce foreign exchange. So, government regulators readily approved joint ventures abroad that increased exports of Indian-made capital goods, or that defended existing export markets from local competition. To accomplish these objectives, government regulators had little choice but to turn to Indian business houses, since only they could integrate horizontally and vertically the managerial and technological, financial and marketing resources necessary to convert the government's dispersal of licenses into production.

For their part, Indian business houses followed a rational calculus designed to craft mutually advantageous agreements with government regulators. After the 1969 passage of new monopolies legislation (the MRTP Act), for example, business houses concentrated most of their new domestic investments in industries accorded high priority by government, in which they often produced (perhaps illegally) in excess of licensed capacity. Business houses also exported to their own joint ventures abroad capital goods manufactured in India by affiliated suppliers and, when competition threatened existing markets overseas, replaced export earnings with repatriated dividends. By crafting mutually advantageous agreements between private industry and the state, moreover, business houses proved themselves adept as political organizations. Their "industrial embassies" in New Delhi monitored changes in government regulations and often submitted multiple applications when regulators opened industries for expansion. Subsequently, these "embassies" managed the massive two-way flow of information between licensing applicants and government regulators, frequently with the help of former civil servants. Then, they mobilized support among buyers and suppliers, as well as within the central and State governments. Consequently, enterprises that shared membership in a business house reaped the political equivalent of economies of scale and dominated business-government negotiations in India.

Local industrial conglomerates—even when members benefited individually from India's regulatory system—also stood to gain *collectively* from a climate of greater freedom for private enterprise. So, business houses occasionally joined together in pursuit of their shared interests, especially in industry associations, which exerted political pressures in favor of price decontrol and other common interests. In turn, these industry associations created regional and national business chambers, gaining with each move additional points of access to government policymaking. Political contributions also created and sustained "special" relationships with India's nationalist leaders and, later, with sympathetic politicians. Through all of these means, then, business houses reaped the political equivalent of economies of scale. Yet, collective action in pursuit of any grander interest, shared across large and diverse groups, remained quite rare—although in 1959 Tata did work to establish (and subsequently to finance) India's first political party advocating free-market principles. Only a few other business houses joined with Tata, however, and Birla remained conspicuously absent. Nevertheless, as Birla and other business houses established ever-growing numbers of joint ventures abroad, they increasingly advocated freedom from host (and home) government interference in the marketplace—also a favorite principle of foreign multinationals operating in India.

Meanwhile, for both multinationals and Indian business houses, state-owned enterprises seriously threatened their continued access to and expansion in the local market. Indian SOEs secured scarce government licenses and then proceeded to integrate their operations horizontally and vertically. Government-run railroads accelerated the demand for coal and steel, which in turn intensified demand upstream for more coal, iron ore, and rail transport, as well as demand downstream for capital goods and technical services. Government investments in each of these industries grew, as did the public sector's share of national production. The state concentrated these investments in a few SOEs, linked together vertically as buyers and suppliers, to pursue many of the same scale economies already enjoyed by Indian business houses and multinationals.

So long as these SOEs did not threaten private enterprise, state capitalism enjoyed wide support among India's powerful industrialists, who (as early as the Bombay Plan of 1944) called upon the state to enter and expand in markets unattractive to private enterprise. But as SOEs expanded, they achieved scale economies that won them increased independence in the marketplace—and they began to substitute for both business houses and multinationals operating in India. That substitution first became evident in the financial sector, with the early nationalization of the state's principal foreign competitor, and the later elimination of Indian business houses from the market (through a hostile takeover of the country's fourteen largest commercial banks). By means of subsequent nationalizations and with new investments in other industries, the state gradually emerged as a formidable competitor—a viable alternative to private enterprise in the home market.

In actual operation, however, state capitalism often worked to reduce hostilities between private enterprises and government agencies. Outside of the financial sector, the state rarely entered markets by means of a hostile takeover of private enterprise. In fact, most other nationalizations, from shipping to textiles, were welcomed by private owners then experiencing financial problems. Alternatively, nationalization followed the expiration of contracts with multinationals (as in petroleum)—or, rather than nationalize existing producers, the state simply established new production capacity. Occasionally, the state even established joint ventures with private partners (usually multinationals), thus adding new support for state capitalism.

Just as state enterprises and business houses were not consistently hostile to multinationals, so government regulators also varied their policies in response to changes in their environment. Indeed, those same government regulators who later implemented FERA had earlier encouraged the entry and expansion of multinationals in the Indian market, with policies dictated by a different rational calculus, born in the wake of the country's first foreign exchange crisis (beginning in 1957). For a decade afterward government regulators approved the licensing applications of multinationals at rates that rivaled the success enjoyed by state enterprises. (Both were surpassed by a few Indian business houses.) Once in possession of scarce government licenses—and using their generous financial, technological, marketing, and managerial resources—multinationals dominated most markets they entered, at least through the 1960s.

Subsequently, however, their position in the Indian market quickly eroded. Simply, monopolies legislation (the MRTP Act, 1969) and capital controls (FERA, 1973) combined to restrict the entry and expansion of multinationals in India. Almost simultaneously, Indian business houses and SOEs expanded and diversified their sources of technology to include new suppliers abroad and R&D investments at home; and both types of organizations relied on the state for new infusions of capital to finance such growth. Then, with technological and other barriers to entry disappearing, multinationals began to lose their market position, which had been based on control of product and process innovations as well as on other special resources.

Still, multinationals continued to turn adversity into opportunity. In exchange for an existing multinational's expanded exports or increased production in priority industries, government regulators acceded to demands by more than a hundred foreign enterprises that they retain majority shareholdings in their Indian operations. And those multinationals that did dilute their shareholdings to 40 percent or less (to meet the requirements of the law) also retained access to a protected market. Even when they operated in markets where government regulators proved unlikely to approve capacity expansions, multinationals, by remaining in India, entertained the added possibility of simply sidestepping the licensing system altogether by producing (usually surreptitiously) in excess of licensed capacity. Thus, although FERA created innumerable causes for conflict between multinationals (seeking majority ownership) and government regulators (seeking to limit that ownership), the implementation of this legislation served to generate many new opportunities for managers in business and government to forge mutually advantageous agreements.

Nevertheless, during the 1980s multinationals found it necessary to accept government demands embodied in FERA for equity dilution, since exit instead of dilution appeared unattractive in view of India's tight restrictions on imports. Meanwhile, ever-growing competition among multinationals in the same industry assured that the Indian market would be served from within, especially since the Indian potential for growth often exceeded opportunities elsewhere in the world. Of course, at the moment when India began to open these new markets to multinationals, alternative sources of foreign technology, especially American and Japanese, began to show themselves in greater numbers. As a result, prospects that any new foreign entrants into the Indian market could secure majority equity ownership diminished even further—until such chances appeared to be well below those that multinationals could expect to find in Brazil, as well as in other newly industrializing countries comparable to India.

CHAPTER FIVE

India in Comparative Perspective

Four decades after political independence, Indian nationalists had succeeded in reducing their country's reliance on foreign finance and technology, and in dislodging multinationals from domestic markets. Their success, however, did not come easily or quickly. Indeed, before 1973 multinationals exercised considerable bargaining power in their relations with local enterprises and the state. As a result, majority foreign ownership, technology bundled with foreign equity, markets unencumbered by competition—briefly, the full range of conditions typically preferred by multinationals—became the most likely outcomes of bargaining. So likely, in fact, were these outcomes in India that they seemed equivalent to the operations of multinationals in Brazil and elsewhere—countries that already had led a new generation of dependency theorists to express profound pessimism concerning the prospects for local institutions to alter fundamentally the creation and distribution of the proceeds from economic development. And so certain were these dependency theorists of the broader implications of their findings that one of their number, Peter Evans, included India in that "distinctive and critical subset of third world countries" to which "the Brazilian model of dependent development should apply."[1]

Although those bargained outcomes in India which predated 1973 may have supported the claims of Evans and other dependency theorists, subsequent Indian changes certainly did not, as local enterprises and the state improved their bargaining power relative to multina-

---

1. Peter Evans, *Dependent Development: The Alliance of Multinationals, State, and Local Capital in Brazil* (Princeton: Princeton University Press, 1979), p. 297.

tionals. By 1973, and into the 1980s, majority Indian ownership, technology free of foreign equity, local control over national markets—in short, the full range of bargaining outcomes increasingly sought by local enterprises and the state—became more probable in industry after industry. Such national improvements had long been predicted by bargaining theorists, beginning in natural resources and (in India, at least) extending to technology-intensive manufacturing. Here, in particular, India's success at dislodging multinationals transformed that country into a model to be emulated by other newly industrializing countries: "As they attain the bargaining capabilities currently enjoyed by India," Joseph Grieco concludes in his study of that country's computer industry, "they increasingly will be able to view India's bargaining successes as a realistic standard to which they can aspire."[2]

But to the present time few countries have, like India, achieved success in bargaining. Certainly not Brazil, which has not been able to dislodge many multinationals, although theorists from both the bargaining and dependency schools have asserted that nation's similarity to India.[3] Brazil and India do, of course, have much in common, including an aggressive pursuit of import-substitution strategies, which—according to Stephan Haggard and other critics of received theory—should lead to common patterns of foreign investment. Yet, rather than finding, as Haggard does in his comparison of Brazil and South Korea, that "import-substitution itself created a *comparatively* high level of dependence on foreign investment,"[4] in this chapter we see instead that (on this and other dimensions) India proved to have as much (or more) in common with export-oriented Korea as with import-substituting Brazil. What Korea and India did *not* share were comparable rates of growth. Such nation-to-nation comparisons have long dominated the ongoing political debate in India over national economic performance.[5] Currently, at the extremes of that debate stand two spokesmen—Pranab Bardhan and Isher Ahluwalia—both

2. Joseph M. Grieco, *Between Dependency and Autonomy: India's Experience with the International Computer Industry* (Berkeley: University of California Press, 1984), p. 7.

3. Indeed, Grieco (ibid., pp. 158–63) tries to demonstrate the parallel evolution of bargaining relations in the two countries' computer industries, and Evans (*Dependent Development*, pp. 291–98) repeatedly includes India in his discussion of the wider application of the Brazilian model of dependent development.

4. Stephan Haggard, "Foreign Direct Investment and the Question of Dependency," chap. 8 in "Pathways from the Periphery," unpublished manuscript, Center for International Affairs, Harvard University, 1988, p. 6, emphasis in original.

5. Comparisons between India and Korea have even crept into analyses undertaken by members of Prime Minister Rajiv Gandhi's cabinet. See, e.g., the series of articles written for the *Times of India* (August 4–6, 1986) by Energy Minister Vasant Sathe comparing the performance of Indian and Korean steel mills.

of whom habitually cite the example of South Korea to support their opposing arguments regarding causes and cures for India's slow growth.[6] The continuing burden caused by such poor economic performance, meanwhile, suggests that India's bargaining "successes"—and all prevailing theory—need to be seriously qualified.

Brazil, though boasting fewer "successes" over multinationals, nevertheless managed to engineer development with dependence. By contrast, in India a much slower economic growth represented the price paid for reduced dependence—a result that called into question a prevailing faith in the economic efficacy of bargaining, a belief held by most theorists. Moreover, though India's bargaining successes multiplied after 1973, multinationals still continued to share in mutually advantageous outcomes: They successfully acted to retain managerial control (if not equity ownership) over their Indian operations, and they constantly found ways to control both the use of existing technology and the introduction of new products and processes. Thus, bargaining did not necessarily reward one party at the expense of another, as received theory would again have led us to believe. Instead, multinationals, the state, and local enterprises remained locked in an "uneasy triangle," where they continued to bargain over access to finance, technology, and markets.

BARGAINING IN INDIA'S UNEASY TRIANGLE

Indian business . . . did not embrace foreign capital blindly. In the uneasy triangle formed by the government and the two wings of the private sector, foreign capital could count on being isolated whenever it attempted to retain or create a monopoly position for itself to the total exclusion of Indian interests.[7]

This conclusion, although written by Michael Kidron more than two decades ago, became after 1973 an ever more accurate portrayal of relations in India, as private business groups and several agents of the

6. Comparisons of India and Korea support much of Bardhan's conclusion that the role of the state in economic development must be reinforced and not dismantled; see Pranab Bardhan, *The Political Economy of Development in India* (Oxford: Basil Blackwell, 1984), esp. pp. 71–74. By contrast, comparisons of India and Korea support much of Ahluwalia's conclusion that the private sector must be given freer reign to develop; see Isher Judge Ahluwalia, *Industrial Growth in India: Stagnation since the Mid-Sixties* (Delhi: Oxford University Press, 1985), esp. pp. 126, 135, 163–65, 171.

7. Michael Kidron, *Foreign Investments in India* (London: Oxford University Press, 1965), p. 181.

state—industrial enterprises, financial institutions, regulatory agencies—successfully isolated (as Kidron hypothesized) and often dislodged multinationals from domestic industries. To achieve that unusual success, India's institutional innovations followed three sequential stages. First, Indians found alternative means to mobilize domestic and foreign capital, thereby gaining financial independence from, and managerial autonomy over, foreign enterprises. This, in turn, allowed domestic institutions to secure at home and abroad, during their second step, requisite technologies free of foreign capital. As a result, third, local enterprises and the state acquired control over product markets that previously had been dominated by multinationals and other foreigners. By following this sequence, Indian business houses and Indian government institutions during forty years of political independence succeeded in dislodging multinationals from industry after industry.

Still, even after 1973 local enterprises and the state very seldom controlled unilaterally access to finance, technology, and markets. (The same could be said for multinationals over the entire period.) Instead, a high level of interdependence—admittedly marked by an equally high potential for conflict—characterized India's uneasy triangle, as each party sought to advance its relative position through the rational calculus of bargaining. Typically, such bargaining succeeded in splitting up profits, parceling out government permits, allocating state finance, licensing foreign technology. In addition to producing these private gains, bargaining also allocated different property rights broadly to multinationals, the state, and local enterprises. The creation and distribution of these collective benefits, as well as of private gains, ultimately depended on the relative bargaining power of parties to the uneasy triangle. Those parties, in the process of bargaining, traded different endowments and capabilities, pursued shared interests, and exploited scale economies.

Within that triangle, local business groups and other such private enterprises have improved the range of plausible outcomes available to them and increased the probability of securing the outcome they preferred—that is, by definition, they have improved their bargaining power. Yet, such improvement has attracted little attention in existing research—which otherwise has minimized the importance of relations between local business groups and multinationals, and especially between local business groups and the state.[8] Yet, as I will dem-

---

8. In the most extreme example of this generalization, Charles Kindleberger does not even mention local enterprises in his discussion of the "bilateral monopoly" that pre-

onstrate, both sets of relations help explain the variation in multinational dominance I observe over time, across industries, and among countries. Nevertheless, despite the importance of all these relations, the existing literature has focused disproportionately on only one set: bilateral relations between multinationals and the state. Here, I shall begin with this familiar leg of the triangle and then move on to synthesize the findings that flow from the three preceding chapters (themselves arranged to reflect the three distinct stages of activity pursued by local business groups and the state in their efforts to dislodge multinationals from Indian industry).

Multinationals and the State

After the British left India in 1947, the state managed over the next forty years to increase its bargaining power relative to multinationals. The state's success, however, came only slowly. During the first decade of political independence few multinationals ventured into India, given the turbulence of partition and the new government's vacillation over the merits of foreign investment. In 1957, however, that vacillation ended, for a decade at least, when the country's first foreign exchange crisis threatened to reduce those imports of foreign technology necessary for the government to pursue its new policy of rapid industrialization. Rather than scale back its ambitious Second Five-Year Plan (1956–61) and further limit technology imports, Nehru's government decided to fund many of those imports of new plant and equipment, plus the licensing of patents and other less tangible technology, through the equity investments of multinationals. In exchange for the technology and finance they brought into the country, multinationals then considering investments in India demanded that government regulators permit them to own a majority of the equity invested in their Indian subsidiaries and thereby to exercise unchallenged managerial control. This, in turn, allowed multinationals to claim, through profits and other remuneration, a significant share of the private gains created, to the exclusion of Indian investors.

The government agreed to the conditions sought by multinationals—indeed, regulators often insisted that both foreign subsidiaries and local enterprises cover their import costs with new infusions of foreign direct investment. As an additional inducement to multina-

---

sumably exists between multinationals and the state; see Charles P. Kindleberger and Bruce Herrick, *Economic Development*, 3d ed. (New York: McGraw-Hill, 1977), pp. 320ff.

tionals, the state also granted them the same protection from foreign and domestic competition accorded local enterprises: Regulators imposed quantitative restrictions on imports and issued few permits for domestic production in the now-protected (and growing) Indian market. In fact, between 1956 and 1966 the government accepted applications for production licenses from multinationals at a rate that matched its acceptance of applications from SOEs and exceeded the rate achieved by all but a few Indian business houses. In such an accommodating environment, foreign investment accelerated: Just ten years after the 1957 crisis, multinationals controlled one-fifth of India's corporate assets, up from one-tenth at the time of the crisis. By bundling foreign equity with foreign technology, multinationals during the 1960s enjoyed a degree of bargaining power unrivaled in the history of independent India.

Subsequently, however, their bargaining power fell off dramatically. With the passage of amendments to the Foreign Exchange Regulation Act (FERA), in 1973, government regulators began to renegotiate foreign shareholdings in existing Indian subsidiaries and to limit foreign equity in new investments. Regulators now insisted that multinationals employ "sophisticated technology," export "significant proportions" of output, or operate in "high-priority industries" if they hoped to retain more than 40 percent of the equity holdings in their Indian subsidiaries. Even those multinationals that did qualify to retain majority shareholdings often had to reduce the proportion of total equity they held. So, during the 1970s and 1980s multinationals turned in unprecedented numbers to the Indian equity market to dilute their existing shareholdings. Thus, negotiations over equity dilution began to reverse the existing distribution of dividends and other private benefits resulting from foreign investment, and these changes served to dramatize the obsolescence of earlier deals.

That obsolescence reflected changed perceptions of risk—which, in turn, resulted from the exceptional profitability of foreign investment in India. Both government and business recognized that multinationals had little choice except to negotiate with regulators over equity dilution if they hoped to maintain their existing stream of high Indian earnings. Given India's tight restrictions on imports, one alternative—to exit—appeared especially unattractive. So barely a handful of multinationals chose to leave India rather than risk a diminution in equity ownership and (as they assumed) in managerial control. Instead, most multinationals preferred to stay and pay whatever cost. Subsequently, only a few retained majority ownership, since growing competition among foreign investors assured that some other multinational would enter lucrative Indian markets with direct investments in minority affiliates. That competition increased when changes in the international market (such as a general slowdown in sales) limited multinationals' options elsewhere. International competition also accelerated technology licensing, increasingly free of foreign equity, to state-owned enterprises and Indian business houses—local institutional innovations, which then threatened to enter markets already served by multinationals. The growth of these institutional alternatives and of competition among multinationals markedly changed perceptions of risk—and acted together to diminish the bargaining power of those multinationals seeking to retain majority equity in their Indian subsidiaries.

Still, most multinationals in their bargaining with the state proved able to secure mutually advantageous agreements. Simply, they constrained the bargaining range of government regulators by supplying technology not easily replaced. Also, they threatened to scare away other multinationals and (less frequently) to cut India off from those export markets multinationals already controlled. Indian regulators, in order to increase foreign exchange earnings and to attract new investment in priority industries—as they had been charged to do—often found that they urgently required cooperation from multinationals. So, in exchange for modifications in the internal operations of multinationals—more local R&D, increased exports, expanded investments in high-technology industries—government regulators acceded to the demands of a few multinationals that insisted on retaining majority shareholdings in their Indian subsidiaries, even when these multinationals reduced their existing shareholdings by greatly increasing the size of their total equity base, through local offerings of stock.

For those multinationals not granted exemptions, government regulators further agreed that the required equity dilution could be accomplished through a wider distribution of Indian shares (rather than through mergers with local enterprises). They also agreed that foreign debt could be partially substituted for foreign equity, in order to ensure multinationals of a continued stream of earnings after dilution. As a result of this process, multinationals typically expanded and diversified their Indian operations and retained unchallenged managerial control (even though foreign holdings often remained at less than 40 percent). As in any positive-sum transfer, each party to the negotiation secured an outcome it favored—multinationals retained managerial control and sometimes (but less frequently) majority equity in affiliates allowed to grow in the still-protected Indian market, while regulators reduced foreign ownership in the economy and actually managed to reshape the internal operations of multinationals. In the bargaining process, then, neither multinationals nor regulators proved able to dictate conditions to the other.

Bargaining between multinationals and SOEs similarly illustrated the continued pursuit of mutually advantageous agreements, even as the state again increased its bargaining power relative to multinationals. At first, the state proceeded independently to exploit its own access to public finance and exclusive markets (for example, railroads) requiring readily available technology. In fact, as late as 1966 Tata and Birla each licensed more foreign technology than did all state-owned industrial enterprises combined. Eventually, however, the internal resources of the state proved to be inadequate for entry into those industries characterized by high technological barriers to entry. To secure new product and process innovations, state enterprises imported substantial quantities of new plant and equipment, signed multiple licenses with foreign suppliers of less tangible technology, and employed very large numbers of foreign technicians.

Although most of these suppliers were multinationals, into the 1980s nearly one-tenth continued to represent foreign SOEs based in the Soviet Union and other Eastern Bloc countries. This diversification of technology suppliers greatly aided the unbundling of foreign technology from foreign capital, as did growing state expenditures for local R&D. In fact, joint ventures with new foreign investors remained quite rare, as did nationalizations of existing foreign enterprises. Except in mining and the financial sector, where nationalizations became more common, the government actually limited its takeover of foreign investments to cases where earlier joint-venture contracts had expired. Thus, the state neither redistributed the private benefits created by existing foreign investment nor shared in the benefits otherwise created by new joint ventures with multinationals.

Rather, by means of technology licensing, both multinationals and state enterprises shared in the private gains created by trading different endowments and capabilities. In exchange for supplying the state with foreign technology unbundled from foreign equity, multinationals extracted a high price: Beginning in the late 1960s and continuing into the 1980s, SOEs paid higher royalties and technical fees (as a percentage of sales) than did private enterprise, and they employed larger numbers of expensive foreign technicians. Moreover, during the 1970s and 1980s the state's dependence on both bundled and unbundled foreign technology grew, while its R&D expenditures exceeded those of private enterprise—even as technology licensing and joint ventures among private enterprise fell off. Thus, by granting multinationals indirect access to markets otherwise closed to them, the state secured (admittedly at a high price) the technology necessary first to corner markets untapped by private enterprise and then to invade markets previously dominated by foreign investors and Indian business houses. Indeed, such bargaining between the state and Indian business houses formed the second leg of the uneasy triangle.

The State and Indian Business Houses

Even before the state managed to increase its bargaining power relative to multinationals, it had extended its control over the operations of Indian business houses. But this did not happen immediately; before 1947 and during the first decade of independence, political leaders and prominent industrialists actively shared a set of interests concerned with the distribution of property rights in the national economy. Tata and Birla promoted import restrictions and foreign capital controls in the celebrated Bombay Plan of 1944, and Nehru's government eventually concurred with the adoption of these nationalistic policies. Tata and Birla also endorsed private ownership of property, without regard to the nationality of the owner, and later the government incorporated this interest into India's new constitution as a "fundamental right." Nehru's government also sought to increase its ownership of assets and its control over markets. Tata and Birla initially supported this state capitalism. Indeed, they had obvious incentives for advocating policies that promoted local ownership of private enterprises, complemented by a strong public sector—especially when the state agreed to operate in risky, capital-intensive industries.

During the first ten years of independence, despite a simultaneous pursuit of private and state capitalism, under the umbrella of economic nationalism little conflict ensued. While the state was enacting most of the regulatory programs that it subsequently employed to control private enterprise, it left Indian business houses and the remainder of the private sector alone. During that decade the state largely confined its entrepreneurial activities to legislated monopolies—notably, railroads and other infrastructure services of tremendous importance to private enterprise. Elsewhere in the economy, state-owned industrial enterprises and financial institutions remained virtually nonexistent. By contrast, the business houses owned by Tata, Birla, and a few other industrialists continued to exploit scale economies in the mobilization of the nation's scarce capital, limited technology, and untapped managerial talent. These resources they then distributed across a sizable and still-growing number of diversified companies, often integrated horizontally and vertically. As a result, for at least ten years these few business houses, largely unchallenged by the state, dominated the national economy.

Beginning in the second decade of independence and continuing subsequently, however, the state mounted its own challenge to the hegemony of Indian business houses. Thus, the potential conflict underlying India's simultaneous pursuit of private and state capitalism, initially hidden under a facade of nationalistic economic policies, now erupted in public. Indeed, such conflict proved endemic to the national system for allocating licenses to enter the market and for allocating capital to exploit those licenses as well. Economic planning rewarded a very few enterprises at the expense of all others, since licenses and capital remained limited over any plan period. Here, state enterprises emerged as principal beneficiaries. In marked contrast to private firms, SOEs seldom had their applications for increased production capacity and capital investments rejected by government regulators. As a result, from one-sixth of all corporate assets in 1962, the state's ownership of productive assets shot up to one-half by 1982. The state concentrated these assets in a very few SOEs and thereby tried to exploit scale economies in the mobilization and distribution of scarce national resources.

To control the remaining capital, the state nationalized the country's debt market and much of its equity market—and thereby redistributed the gains of Indian business houses (and others) who earlier had controlled those markets. Then, to allocate that capital, state financial institutions rewarded only a few enterprises, at the expense of many other applicants. Such zero-sum distributions also characterized the government's allocation of scarce production permits and of limited import quotas to a few private enterprises. Indeed, government licensing and state financing became highly interrelated: State debt and equity flowed readily to those few enterprises that received government licenses to expand. With its emergence as the preeminent regulator of national production during the 1950s and as a major financier and formidable entrepreneur during the 1960s, the state markedly increased its bargaining power relative to Indian business houses.

Of course, business houses still exercised much power in their negotiations with government regulators and state financiers. Defending their market shares, they continued to exploit economies of scale as an advantage in the mobilization and distribution of resources, which allowed them to produce (often illegally) in excess of licensed capacity after government regulators had rejected their applications for expansion. Indian business houses also exploited the political equivalent of scale economies: Their "industrial embassies" in New Delhi lobbied in and out of India's bureaucratic labyrinth to secure government approval for licensing applications and to block applications from their competitors. So successful was Tata's "embassy," for example, that government regulators consistently approved the licensing applications of its affiliated companies at rates that rivaled the success enjoyed by state enterprises. By contrast, Birla remained far less successful, but because its "industrial embassy" inundated government regulators with applications, it repeatedly secured more licenses than any other business house. Meanwhile, for smaller enterprises unaffiliated with business houses, the costs of comparable lobbying simply proved prohibitive. Also, these smaller enterprises remained less likely to join together in industry associations or to contribute to political campaigns that might provide legitimacy and muscle to their collective concerns. In these ways business houses continued to grow rapidly by securing licenses that translated into private gains.

Just as Indian business houses depended on the state both for licenses to gain access to the Indian market and for financing to exploit those licenses, so government regulators and state financiers depended on Indian business houses to achieve certain objectives that Parliament had decreed. Charged with reducing imports by increasing domestic production, government regulators distributed licenses to Tata, Birla, and other business houses with all the resources necessary to convert these licenses into production. Later, when increasing foreign exchange earnings became an additional charge, government regulators readily approved applications from Birla and a few other houses that sought to export Indian equipment to joint ventures abroad. Back at home, these same business houses concentrated most of their new investments in just those industries accorded high priority by the Indian government—and thereby satisfied an objective common to both government regulators and state financiers, who readily approved these applications for licenses and capital even while implementing restrictive anti-trust legislation (the Monopolies and Restrictive Trade Practices, or MRTP, Act) during the 1970s. In addition, the government charged state financiers with optimizing return and minimizing the risk to their portfolio of investments; this they accomplished by purchasing shares in the country's largest enterprises, most often controlled by business houses, and by limiting their shareholdings in smaller (typically more risky and less profitable) companies. State financiers and government regulators thus became highly interdependent with Indian business houses, and their interdependence actually increased over time, as the state and local enterprises tried to link means to ends as efficiently as possible in mutually advantageous agreements.

These agreements typically created and distributed private gains among a few business houses and government agencies. By contrast, any generation of collective benefits proved to be quite rare. Tata, for example, helped to establish, and subsequently to finance, India's first political party devoted exclusively to the curtailment (if not yet the elimination) of that country's established regulatory regime—the traditional "license, permit, quota Raj"—a termed coined by that party to characterize a pervasive colonial legacy. While Tata competed in industries (steel, for example) targeted early by state enterprises, Birla did not. And unlike Tata, Birla seldom supported political alternatives to the ruling Congress Party, remaining instead that party's largest campaign contributor. Like any free rider, Birla preferred to benefit from price decontrol and other policies advocated by Tata, but without incurring the wrath of the Congress Party. Even Tata never carried opposition to an extreme, since the Congress Party continued to represent the largest single recipient of Tata's campaign contributions. By channeling political contributions, business houses hoped to improve their chances of securing government licenses and other largess. Thus, for them, the pursuit of such private gains often stood at odds with the pursuit of collective benefits.

In the absence of any effective opposition to state capitalism, however, the state managed to increase its bargaining power, often at the expense of Indian business houses. During the 1970s, following passage of the MRTP Act, government regulators made it more difficult for business houses to expand into consumer products and other industries not accorded high priority. State financiers also threatened to convert debt into equity and ownership into control. Even though they seldom translated these threats into action, state financiers did insist on appointing company directors in proportion to an ever-growing equity ownership (and nearly complete control over debt) in private enterprise. Only seldom, however, did the state actually nationalize healthy private enterprises; instead, it typically invested in new plant and equipment, as it followed a pattern of horizontal expansion and vertical integration.

Early government investments in railroads accelerated the demand upstream for more coal, rail transport, and iron ore, as well as demand downstream for capital goods and technical services. With such diversification, the state's share of national production grew and overall imports fell. In several industries (mining, petroleum, steel) the state owned the country's largest producers, while in others (machinery) it had at least established a major presence. Further downstream, in consumer goods (pharmaceuticals, textiles), SOEs became increasingly active, and the state emerged as an alternative to, and at times a formidable competitor of, both multinationals and Indian business houses. In response, Kidron's "two wings of the private sector" sought to improve their position in the economy by actively trading their different endowments and capabilities; in short, they formed a powerful third leg of India's uneasy triangle.

Indian Business Houses and Multinationals

Just as the state acted to increase its bargaining power relative to multinationals, so too did Indian business houses. In fact, their gains occurred much earlier. Even before independence, business houses spearheaded the Indianization of colonial, principally British enterprises, which typically operated in textiles and other industries where Indian enterprises had long exercised technological advantages. By exploiting economies of scale in the mobilization of finance in India's otherwise weak capital markets, business houses slowly acquired equity ownership in these enterprises. Then, to convert equity ownership into managerial control, business houses once again exploited scale economies, this time in the utilization of scarce managerial talent, called upon through family connections or other strong social ties. Thus, before independence, Indian business houses began to substitute for foreign enterprises in industries with low technological barriers to entry, thereby claiming the profits and other private gains previously enjoyed by foreigners.

Outside these particular industries, however, such substitution proceeded slowly. Indeed, beginning in 1956 both business and government began to recognize that indigenous technologies would inevitably be incapable of satisfying India's ambitious plans for industrialization. So over the next decade government regulators more readily approved applications for market entry and expansion that included foreign technology, which soon flowed into the country. In exchange for the foreign products and processes they supplied, most multinationals did not demand that equity ownership be attached. Instead, they typically insisted that local enterprises pay royalties and other technical fees, abide by the several restrictions of licensing contracts, and rely on technology suppliers for related imports. Indian business houses readily agreed, and the government concurred: Between 1956 and 1966 these local conglomerates tied foreign technology to nearly two-fifths of the government licenses they secured to establish and expand industrial capacity. Thus, through technology licensing, both multinationals and local enterprises shared in the private gains created by trading different endowments and capabilities.

Several multinationals did insist that foreign technology come bundled with foreign equity and that they take—with the addition of dividends—a greater share of the private benefits created by foreign investment. In effect, the foreign exchange crisis of 1957 enhanced their ability to bundle equity with technology, as did the government's response to that crisis. Since India, after 1957, had few other ways to pay for technology, regulators granted scarce production permits more readily to those local enterprises that financed technology imports through foreign direct investment. Initially, Tata and a few other business houses emerged as likely joint-venture partners. In exchange for technology and some foreign capital, they offered both local marketing expertise and effective political organizations capable of securing government licenses and state financing. Thus, local enterprises and multinationals continued to share in the private benefits created by joint ventures.

More often, however, multinational investors rejected joint ventures with local partners as a means for gaining access to the Indian market; instead, they retained unchallenged managerial control over their Indian operations. In fact, through the 1960s multinationals operating in India channeled most of their equity into majority foreign-owned subsidiaries, where they typically owned upward of 75 percent of the equity. Then, by closely guarding their various financial, technological, marketing, and managerial advantages—and by readily securing scarce government permits—these foreign subsidiaries dominated most industries they entered. In 1966, for example, one or two multinationals together controlled more than 80 percent of the market for rubber and pharmaceuticals, more than 50 percent of the market for electrical equipment and food products, and more than 40 percent of the market for industrial chemicals and nonelectrical machinery. Thus, a decade after the 1957 crisis, multinationals supplying both finance and technology, often supplemented by marketing and managerial skills, reached the pinnacle of their bargaining power relative to Indian business houses.

By the late 1960s, however, the position of multinationals had begun to erode, partially as a result of pressure from Indian business houses. Here, Birla stood out, as it insisted that foreign technology come unbundled from foreign equity. To secure this unbundled technology, Indian business houses—like state enterprises—diversified their foreign suppliers and thereby exploited the growing competition among those multinationals seeking (albeit limited) access to the Indian market. Next, to pay for this unbundled technology, Birla and others increasingly turned to state financial institutions for the requisite foreign exchange. To such requests, state financiers readily acquiesced, and by doing so, they further enhanced the ability of Indian business houses to enter markets otherwise dominated by multinationals. Government regulators helped also when, by the late 1960s, they stood ready to approve applications from business houses that wished to establish and expand production capacity—now in the absence of all foreign financing of technology imports. To influence these decisions, business houses lobbied though their "industrial embassies" and industry associations and then actively funded the political campaigns of sympathetic politicians. Effective lobbying and campaign financing, preferential access to state permits and capital, and increased competition among multinationals together granted Indian business houses greater leverage in their negotiations with multinationals.

The bargaining power of Indian business houses reached new heights during the 1970s, thanks again to the state, when monopolies (MRTP) legislation and foreign equity regulations (FERA) combined to inhibit the entry and expansion of multinationals in India. FERA also led regulators to insist with greater frequency that foreign technology must enter India with less foreign equity attached, and that technology remittances should be reduced. Now, as technology licensing became more difficult, Tata led the way among Indian business houses seeking to develop local alternatives to foreign technology; these houses were aided by generous disbursements of government tax incentives and by their own achievement of scale economies. As a result, beginning in the late 1970s Indian enterprises spent more on local R&D (as a percentage of sales) than on foreign technology. With these R&D expenditures, Indian business houses readily adapted foreign technology to local conditions and, at times, produced important innovations. Next, confident about their own technological resources, these local conglomerates began to retire existing technology licenses and joint-venture contracts, and to curb future tie-ups with multinationals. As a result, foreign collaboration in Indian industry fell off dramatically during the 1970s.

With these new resources, Indian business houses also moved to invade those markets previously dominated by multinationals. By 1982 Indian houses actually controlled a majority of the country's largest producers in several key industries—ranging from food and tobacco to transport equipment and chemicals—industries previously off-limits to business houses because of technological and marketing barriers to entry. For multinationals, widespread production in excess of licensed capacity still failed to reverse the erosion in their market share, down from one-half of most markets in 1966 to less than one-quarter by 1982. In fact, through an active procurement of technology at home and abroad, this time assisted by government regulators and state financiers, Indian business houses had made themselves potent substitutes for multinationals.

Still, multinationals did not become powerless in their negotiations with Indian business houses. Once Birla and other large houses began to retire technology licenses and joint ventures, multinationals turned to other local licensees and joint-venture partners. In particular, several smaller Indian houses, now sensing grand opportunities, began to make increased use of foreign technology and (less frequently) foreign capital. Outside of these industrial conglomerates, the rate of foreign collaboration increased even more rapidly, as independent entrepreneurs sought to vault from the ranks of small-scale industry. During the late 1960s and continuing subsequently, enterprises unaffiliated with any business house imported most of the foreign technology entering India—in marked contrast to earlier years, when business houses had cornered most of the imports. And unlike business houses, these unaffiliated enterprises continued to rely on multinationals to finance the majority of their technology imports into the 1970s. By 1980, however, unaffiliated companies had reduced their reliance on both foreign financing and foreign technology and had joined hands with Indian business houses. Although the number of technology licenses and joint ventures did pick up again during the decade, the proportion of Indian investment decisions dependent upon foreign collaboration simply did not approach the levels characteristic of the 1960s. Their increasing ability to unbundle technology from foreign finance and then to reduce their reliance on foreign technology represented the increased bargaining power of Indian business houses and other local enterprises in their negotiations with multinationals.

For their part, multinationals remained largely capable of preventing further obsolescence in the bargains they struck, primarily because they could define more narrowly those contractual provisions which guided Indian usage of their technology. Then, to integrate their operations globally, multinationals began to tie (albeit limited) Indian imports closely to the use of that technology and thereby constrain the sourcing alternatives of local licensees. Moreover, multinationals typically sold Indian enterprises only that technology which was already experiencing rapid obsolescence abroad, and they kept out of negotiations all newer technologies, for future use as a bargaining chit. In addition, majority foreign-owned subsidiaries increased their local expenditures (as a percentage of sales) on R&D and then made other changes in their internal operations designed to secure exemptions from unpalatable government regulations. In these moves, a few multinationals proved so successful that they ranked among the country's largest conglomerates, even though foreign competitors greatly accelerated their licensing of technology to Indian enterprises.

Occasionally, these few multinational investors and several foreign suppliers of technology bolstered their position through domestic political alliances. Tata's high level of technological and financial interdependence with multinationals—in contrast to Birla—contributed to its support of India's only political party opposed to government restrictions on agreements privately negotiated. Even among supporters of the ruling Congress Party, Birla and other business houses that had established joint ventures abroad did increasingly support a policy of freedom from host (and home) government interference in the marketplace—long advocated by foreign multinationals in India. Indeed, Indian trade and investment overseas, while modest, exercised a growing influence on the politics of foreign investment in India.

Within India, multinationals remained singularly unsuccessful in forging domestic political alliances. Operating through foreign subsidiaries and a few joint ventures—typically unaffiliated with Indian business houses—multinationals simply could not tap the "industrial embassies" and political networks that so often guaranteed preferential access to government licenses and state financing. Only a few multinationals established their own local organizations to guide license applications through India's bureaucratic labyrinth; for most multinationals, however, industry associations became their principal means of lobbying government regulators. But Indian business houses actually prohibited multinationals from joining local industry associations; they insisted instead that foreign competitors in an industry segregate into separate, parallel business organizations. Of course, joint ventures with SOEs offered another means for acquiring access to government licenses and state finance—but again multinationals, with limited financial and technological collaboration, usually did not enter these partnerships. As a result, multinationals in India could not count on forming a triple alliance with local enterprises and the state to bolster their bargaining power. In Brazil, on the other hand, just such a cooperative arrangement did prevail, according to

Peter Evans. This national difference (and what it tells us about local institutions) helps to explain why India, over time, became far more successful than Brazil at dislodging multinationals from local industries.

INDIA AND BRAZIL REVISITED

Despite their obvious differences, India and Brazil have much in common.[9] Each nation represents a large underdeveloped domestic market and plentiful underutilized resources, both natural and human. Among newly industrializing countries, India and Brazil boast two of the four largest manufacturing sectors—industrialization achieved largely without the mixed blessings of either a common border (as in the case of Mexico) or a strong military alliance (as in the case of South Korea) with the United States.[10] Unlike Mexico, both India and Brazil imported most of the petroleum they needed to industrialize. And for far longer than South Korea, both India and Brazil maintained a policy of import substitution—which, according to Stephan Haggard, should lead India and Brazil to host comparable levels of foreign investment, levels that far exceed those attributed to Korea.

With these commonalities in mind, Evans includes both India and Brazil among those "crucial cases" which "illustrate the conditions, both institutional and contextual, that make dependent development possible."[11] To define those conditions, he explores the relative success of multinationals, the state, and local enterprises in gaining access to the finance, technology, and markets controlled by others. In this study, I expand the inquiry by comparing the separate experiences of India and Brazil as they industrialized. Both the generality and the uniqueness of the Indian case may now be distinguished.

Finance

For much of their national economic histories, private industrial conglomerates in both Brazil and India have monopolized the chief local sources of debt and equity. By the early 1970s Brazil had spawned fifty-five *grupos multibilionarios* that—like India's seventy-

9. We examined several of these differences in Chapter 1, esp. in the discussion of Table 1-1.

10. International Bank for Reconstruction and Development, *World Development Report: 1986* (Washington, D.C., 1986), Table 3, pp 152–53.

11. Evans, *Dependent Development*, p 51.

three business houses—controlled most large companies in the private sector through shared ownership and interlocking directorates. In Brazil, the earliest *grupos* were predominantly locally owned—founded before World War I as institutional innovations to poorly developed markets for capital and other resources. Only during and after that war did foreign *grupos* begin to appear, sometimes through the acquisition of existing Brazilian firms, but more frequently through new investments. So successful were these foreign *grupos* that, in 1973, they controlled over one-fifth of the Brazil's hundred largest companies, nearly twice the number controlled by locally owned conglomerates. Indeed, *grupos* formed by multinationals and newer foreign entrants controlled more of Brazil's largest companies than did local industrialists, according to Figure 5-1.

As we see from this figure, in 1973 multinationals operating in India controlled roughly one-quarter of that country's hundred largest corporations, a share comparable to foreign holdings in Brazil. But unlike foreign enterprises in Brazil, no multinational in India expanded its operations by acquiring existing Indian companies; and only a few multinationals diversified their operations sufficiently to be classified as business houses. Rather, most business houses were controlled by Indian industrialists, who operated nearly two-fifths of the country's hundred largest corporations in 1973—three times the share operated back home during that year by Brazilian-owned *grupos*. Again, in contrast to these *grupos*, only a few Indian business houses actively entered into joint ventures with multinationals, and their numbers began to fall off as early as the mid-1960s. After that time the small number of new joint ventures typically involved Indian enterprises unaffiliated with the largest industrial conglomerates—again, in contrast to Brazil, where *grupos* initiated most joint ventures with multinationals. In 1973, according to Figure 5-1, these private Indian "independents" together with business houses controlled over one-half of the country's hundred largest corporations, jointly forming a strong, local leg in the uneasy triangle, one notably absent in Brazil.

The Brazilian government, and not local business groups, owned a plurality of the country's largest corporations—forty-seven of the top hundred in 1973 (see Figure 5-1). In that year Brazilian SOEs accounted for roughly two-fifths of the nation's corporate assets,[12] spread over a large number of firms (indeed, the exact number remains indeterminant, but it ranged as high as six hundred in the early 1970s[13]). In India, SOEs controlled a comparable proportion of that

12. Ibid., Table 5.1, p. 221.
13. T. J. Trebat, *Brazil's State-Owned Enterprises* (Cambridge: Cambridge University

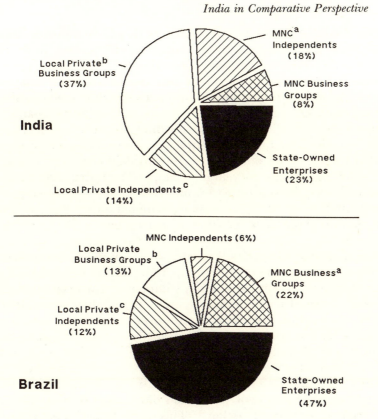

Figure 5-1. Ownership of the hundred largest enterprises: India and Brazil, 1973

SOURCES: Indian Institute of Public Opinion, "The I.I.P.O. Directory of the Hundred Largest Companies in India, 1973–74," *Monthly Commentary on Indian Economic Conditions* 17, no. 4 (April 1974): *Supplement*, pp. X–XVI; India (Republic), Ministry of Industrial Development, Internal Trade and Company Affairs, *Report of the Industrial Licensing Policy Inquiry Committee*, P. Dutt, Chairman (New Delhi: Manager of Publications, 1969), *Appendix II*, pp. 1–114; Peter Evans, *Department Development: The Alliance of Multinational, State and Local Capital in Brazil* (Princeton: Princeton University Press, 1979), p. 150.

Note: Ranking based on assets.

[a]MNC = multinational corporations.

[b]*Grupos multibilionarios* in Brazil; "Business houses" in India.

[c]"Newcomers" unaffiliated with existing *grupos*; "large independents" unaffiliated with existing "houses."

Press, 1983), pp. 37, 59, 121, 126; "State in the Market," *The Economist* (London) December 30, 1978.

nation's corporate assets (see Figure 2-1), which the state concentrated in far fewer SOEs—twenty-six (versus forty-seven in Brazil) of the country's hundred largest corporations in 1973. These few large Indian SOEs seldom entered into joint ventures with multinationals, or with local business groups. This contrasts with Brazilian SOEs— which often entered into joint ventures and tripartite financial arrangements (so-called "tri-pe") with multinationals and a few local *grupos*."[14] To these financial tie-ups, Brazilian SOEs (and local *grupos*) added ever-growing borrowings from foreign commercial banks, a source of foreign currency largely untapped by Indian enterprises. In both countries the central government owned most of the largest ten, or twenty-five, or fifty corporations; national ownership guaranteed the state a preeminent position as entrepreneur in the industrial economy.[15]

Again, in both countries the state became a major shareholder in, and lender to, private enterprise. In India the state exercised nearly complete control over the country's numerous financial institutions, following several nationalizations and generous new investment. In Brazil, by contrast, the state's control over that nation's capital markets was far less complete—the Brazilian government owned barely two-fifths of all assets in the financial sector in 1973.[16] Nevertheless, Brazil's federal government disbursed to private enterprise more funds (including the government's own foreign borrowings) through its National Development Bank than did India's three largest state financial corporations together.[17] This single Brazilian bank (like India's multitude of state financial institutions) invested large proportions of its equity and debt in *grupos multibilionarios* (shares comparable to those received by Indian houses), with the remainder going largely to SOEs. Yet, in India the nationalization of the country's financial markets still left Indian business houses and state enterprises with a degree of financial independence from foreign suppliers of technology unknown to their counterparts in Brazil.

Technology

India's financial independence both reflected and contributed to a greater national success in unbundling foreign technology from for-

---

14. Evans, *Dependent Development*, pp. 228–49.
15. For an explicit comparison of SOEs in India and Brazil, see Ravi Ramamurthi, *State-Owned enterprises in High Technology Industries: Studies in India and Brazil* (New York: Praeger, 1987), esp. p. 29, Table 1.2.
16. See Evans, *Dependent Development*, Table 5.1, p. 221.
17. Brian David Levy, "Industrial Economics of Entrepreneurship and Dependent

eign equity and foreign debt. As capital and technology came untied, the number of joint ventures, like that of foreign subsidiaries in India, declined, beginning in the late 1960s. By contrast, at that time foreign technology bundled with foreign capital continued to flood Brazil, as multinationals increased their equity investments in joint ventures and subsidiaries, and as foreign banks (otherwise absent from India) continued to lend foreign exchange for technology imports (see Table 1-1). In both countries, the diversification of, and resultant competition among, foreign suppliers of technology further accelerated the unbundling of foreign technology from foreign equity.[18] In their drive to diversify suppliers as widely as possible, Indian SOEs even licensed technology and secured foreign loans from the Soviet Union and other Eastern Bloc states, another option unavailable to local enterprises in Brazil. Finally, the mixing of local and foreign innovations and adaptations further hastened the unbundling of foreign capital and technology in both India and Brazil.

Local expenditures on R&D also contributed to the reduction of new technology licenses, as well as to the retirement of existing licenses. As a result, beginning in the late 1970s local private and state-owned enterprises in India spent nearly two times as much on local R&D (as a percentage of sales) as on foreign royalties and technology remittances. Moreover, through successful adaptation of foreign technology and the development of local innovations, Indian business houses also spearheaded a larger and more significant trend: the reverse flow of technology out of India, principally to other developing countries. Compared to their Brazilian counterparts, Indian enterprises moved abroad in greater numbers, and they became more widely distributed geographically. In fact, by the late 1970s there were more manufacturing plants established abroad by Indians than by Brazilians and all other Latin Americans combined[19]—yet another sign of India's growing technological independence from multinationals.

Indian business houses and SOEs did not, however, monopolize local expenditures for R&D. To the contrary: beginning in the late 1960s and accelerating during the early 1980s, majority foreign-owned subsidiaries in India at least matched the (albeit limited)

Development" (Ph.D. diss., Department of Economics, Harvard University, 1983), Table 4.5, p. 93.

18. For examples drawn from India, Brazil, and other newly industrializing countries, see Grieco, *Between Dependency and Autonomy*, pp. 156–68.

19. Louis T. Wells, Jr., *Third World Multinationals* (Cambridge: MIT Press, 1983), Table 1.2, p. 10; also see Sanjaya Lall et al., *The New Multinationals: The Spread of Third World Enterprises* (New York: Wiley, 1983), pp. 21–87, 220–49.

R&D expenditures of local enterprises (as a percentage of sales), and they often outspent these wholly Indian-owned firms and minority foreign-owned joint ventures. By contrast, wholly Brazilian-owned firms claimed to do local R&D as frequently as did majority subsidiaries (with less than 90 percent foreign shareholdings) and more frequently than did wholly foreign-owned subsidiaries.[20] Even within the same industry, such local expenditures by multinationals on R&D varied widely between Brazil and India (and always remained below R&D expenditures in home countries). In the chemical industry, for example, U.S. multinationals in 1972 spent just eight-tenths of 1 percent on local R&D in Brazil.[21] In the Indian chemical industry, by comparison, all majority foreign-owned subsidiaries during 1978–81 spent a little more (roughly 1 percent of their sales) on local R&D. Within pharmaceuticals, these expenditures increased again (by another one-half of 1 percent) and actually exceeded foreign payments by multinationals for technology licenses. Thus, as India's trade policies and foreign exchange regulations limited inflows of foreign technology, multinationals and Indian enterprises alike turned increasingly to local expenditures, which offered them an alternate means of guaranteeing access to the substantial Indian market.

Markets

As a general rule, multinationals never have enjoyed unrestricted access to either the Indian or Brazilian market. Instead, quotas in India and tariffs in Brazil served to limit imports, while capital controls have restricted ownership of local enterprises, especially in India. U.S. multinationals, for example, reported in 1977 and again in 1982 that the Indian government expressly limited foreign shareholdings in more than one-half of their Indian affiliates. Of course, countless other multinationals modified their investment proposals—either at the time of entry or before seeking government permission to expand—rather than run the risk of rejection by Indian regulators. Clearly, India's restrictions on foreign ownership have been extreme, even when measured against other developing countries, as we do in Figure 5-2.

In contrast to other countries, Brazil seldom has regulated equity investments by U.S. multinationals. In fact, few newly industrializing countries were so open as Brazil to foreign ownership. As a result,

20. Evans, *Dependent Development*, pp. 176–77.
21. Ibid., *Dependent Development*, Table 4.5, p. 178.

Figure 5-2. Government regulation of foreign ownership: India, Brazil, and Korea 1977, 1982

SOURCES: U.S. Department of Commerce, Bureau of Economic Analysis, *U.S. Direct Investment Abroad: 1982 Benchmark Survey Data* (Washington, D.C.: Government Printing Office, December 1985), p. 140 and *U.S. Direct Investment Abroad, 1977* (April 1981), p. 171.
aAll economically less developed countries.

several multinationals served that market through wholly foreign-owned subsidiaries, an impossibility in India after the amendment of FERA (1973). In the absence of total ownership, multinationals operating in Brazil nevertheless held majority shares. By contrast, most multinationals that remained in India after 1973 operated through minority foreign-owned affiliates. India and Brazil thus represented opposite extremes in their regulation of direct foreign investment in domestic markets.

As a result of such regulations, and of the increased technological and financial resources available to Indian enterprises, multinationals dominated fewer local industries in India than they did in Brazil. To confirm this fact, let us review the distribution of market shares among the three hundred largest enterprises in each country. In the early 1970s (as noted in Chapter 1), multinationals manufactured more than 50 percent of the products sold in several Brazilian industries, from transport equipment to machinery, from chemicals to pharmaceuticals. And in all these industries, multinationals over the next decade continued to control more than one-half of the Brazilian market, even as Brazilian enterprises slowly increased their own shares. Indian enterprises, by contrast, conceded to multinationals far fewer local industries—namely, rubber and pharmaceuticals—as early as 1971, and by 1981 they conceded nothing, as the shares held by foreigners in one Indian market after another typically fell well below 50 percent. Thus, no single Indian industry was relegated to foreign producers—in marked contrast to several Brazilian industries, as we see in Figure 5-3.

Indian business houses and large independent companies posed the most formidable challenge to multinationals operating in these

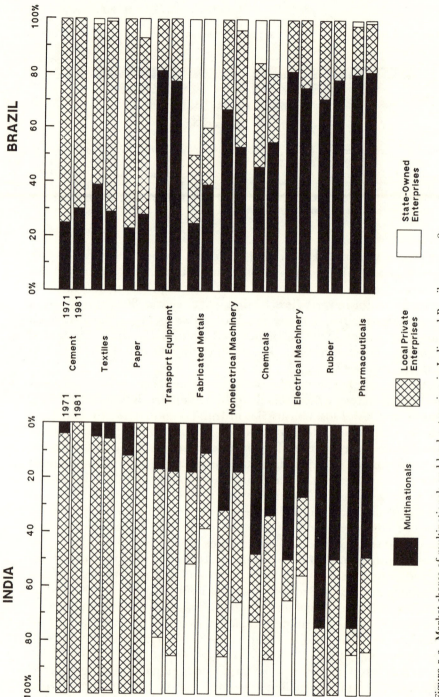

Figure 5-3. Market shares of multinationals and local enterprises in India and Brazil, 1971, 1981
SOURCES: Same as for Figure 1-1.
Note: 1971 and 1981 in India; 1970 and 1980 in Brazil. Data are for the 300 largest nonfinancial companies ranked by sales in each country.

domestic industries—again, a striking contrast to the Brazilian situation. Textiles provide a useful illustration of key differences between the private sectors of the two nations: By 1971, and subsequently, business houses monopolized the Indian textile market, and they soon began exporting local technology to growing numbers of Indian joint ventures abroad. In Brazil, by contrast, both local *grupos* and independents as late as 1981 continued to share nearly one-third of the home market with foreign producers, who themselves managed to retain much of their position by erecting formidable marketing barriers to entry. In fact, private Brazilian enterprises generally continued to limit their market dominance to the more technologically mature industries—cement and paper, in addition to textiles—industries long ago monopolized by the Indians.

Outside of such industries, in markets with still higher marketing and (especially) technological barriers, these Brazilian *grupos* proved even less successful in challenging the dominance of multinationals in possession of requisite product and process innovations. Here, pharmaceuticals seems representative: In 1971 foreign subsidiaries nearly monopolized domestic markets in both countries (see Figure 5-3). A decade later, while multinationals were still successful in defending their Brazilian monopoly, their Indian share had been severely slashed, as business houses and large independent companies tripled their own market shares. These private Indian enterprises then replicated their assault on multinationals in electrical machinery, rubber, and chemicals—industries in which they doubled their market share during the 1970s, to control (in the case of rubber and chemicals) roughly one-half of the local market. The Brazilians, by contrast, seldom matched these Indian successes, even though they often started in 1971 with roughly comparable positions in the home market. So, in rubber and pharmaceuticals—as in transport equipment earlier—the market share held by private Indian enterprises was actually twice that held by their Brazilian counterparts. Overall, then, Indian business houses and large independent companies successfully dislodged multinationals from those same industries which in Brazil continued to be dominated by foreigners.

State enterprises enjoyed similar successes in India, as they expanded their presence in a much wider range of industries than in Brazil (see Figure 5-3). During the late 1970s, for example, Indian SOEs improved their already impressive market position in electrical machinery, largely at the expense of multinationals, and they doubled their share in nonelectrical machinery—two industries dominated in Brazil by multinationals unencumbered by state competition. Only in fabricated metals (notably, iron and steel) did state enterprises in both countries come close to dominating the home market. Even here, however, Brazilian SOEs lost market share to multinationals during the late 1970s, while Indian SOEs gained share at the expense of both foreigners and Indian business houses. Like these business houses, Indian state enterprises improved their probability of entering new markets and of expanding existing production by overcoming the financial and technological limitations that otherwise restricted the market access of Brazilian SOEs. Still, the total production of state enterprises and business houses in India failed to keep pace with the combined output of local enterprises and multinationals in Brazil. For our present purpose, the national comparison must be judged by standards of performance.

Economic Performance

In 1960 manufacturers in India and Brazil contributed roughly equal output to their national economies. In fact, as we see from Figure 5-4, these manufacturers produced final goods and services of nearly comparable value (measured in constant U.S. dollars). During the following decade, however, manufactured output in Brazil grew twice as fast as did Indian production, and this rapid growth continued through the 1970s. In one bellwether industry, steel, Brazilian production grew over these ten years from rough comparability with Indian output to exceed that output by 50 percent in 1974.[22] In both countries, manufacturers of consumer durables utilized much of that steel, although Brazil produced twice as many passenger cars in 1974 and three times as many refrigerators. Even in textiles—an industry in which Indian manufacturers historically excelled—Brazilian production of synthetic fibers was five times larger. (Only in cotton fabrics, where production remained less technology intensive, did Indian manufacturers retain their long-term lead.) With production rising across many industrial sectors, Brazil doubled India's output of manufactured goods by 1980, as shown in Figure 5-4.

By 1980, as we can also see from this figure, Brazil's GDP—smaller than India's GDP as late as 1970—had jumped to nearly one-and-a-half times the size of India's national income. Manufacturers in Brazil spearheaded this growth and thereby contributed over one-quarter of the total output of goods and services in the economy, the

22. These and the following production statistics may be found in ibid., Table 6.4, p. 298.

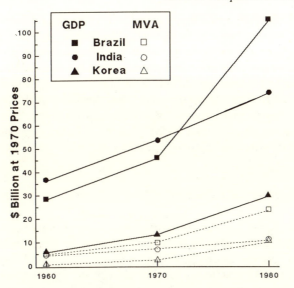

Figure 5-4. Industrialization in India, Brazil, and Korea, 1960, 1970, 1980

SOURCE: World Bank, *World Tables*, 3d ed. (Baltimore: Johns Hopkins University Press for the World Bank, 1983), 1:22–23, 84–85, 102–3.

Note: GDP = gross domestic product; MVA = manufacturing value-added.

largest share of any sector. By contrast, India into the 1980s remained primarily an agricultural economy, with manufacturers never producing more than one-sixth of the country's national income. The largest of these Indian manufacturers were SOEs: In 1980, the central government exclusively owned the country's ten largest corporations, and twenty-three of the largest twenty-five. By contrast, a combination of state enterprises and multinationals provided the largest share of Brazilian GDP. Indeed, in 1980 the largest corporations in Brazil—each with sales exceeding U.S. $1 billion—included four state enterprises and two multinationals.[23] The latter (Ford and General Motors) contributed both domestic sales and exports to Brazilian growth.

In fact, the performance of multinationals in Brazil (and elsewhere) has prompted Isher Ahluwalia and other critics of India's economic

23. "The 500 Largest Corporations Outside the U.S.," *Fortune*, August 10, 1981, pp. 205–24.

policies to endorse some relaxation of Indian restrictions on foreign direct investment—the very policies that had helped to improve that country's bargaining position with multinationals.[24] Defenders of these restrictive policies have contended, on the other hand, that limitations on foreign investment need not constrain any nation's economic performance. As an example, they look to South Korea, where, as Pranab Bardhan observes, "the state," as in India, "is actively and pervasively interventionist."[25] At present, Korea has replaced Brazil as the model for Indian development.

INDIA AND KOREA COMPARED

Like India, South Korea during the 1970s and 1980s severely limited foreign ownership of local enterprises. U.S. multinationals, for example, reported in 1977 and again in 1982 that the Korean government specifically restricted foreign shareholdings in more than one-quarter of their affiliates in Korea (see Figure 5-2), while countless other multinationals modified their investment proposals in order to enter that country. In fact, Korea's limitations on foreign ownership remained among the most restrictive encountered in developing countries; they were surpassed only by those of India and very few other nations. So, during the 1970s and after, the limited number of multinationals that did enter India and Korea typically operated through minority foreign-owned affiliates.[26] Fresh inflows of multinational investments in India and Korea also remained relatively small—and never exceeded one-twentieth of the foreign direct investment entering Brazil during the 1970s (see Table 1-1).

Yet, in the absence of significant investment by multinationals, the South Korean economy simply exploded between 1960 and 1980 while the Indian economy languished. In fact, Korea moved from producing barely 10 percent of India's real manufactured output in 1960 (see Figure 5-4) to nearly equalling all Indian manufacturing by 1980. Twenty years earlier, in 1960, manufacturing had represented an even smaller percentage of GDP in Korea than it had in India, while agriculture dominated both economies. But spectacular growth

24. Ahluwalia, *Industrial Growth in India*, esp. pp. 155–57.
25. Bardhan, *Political Economy of Development in India*, p. 71.
26. For data on Korea, see Larry Westphal et al., "Foreign Factors in Korea's Industrialization," in Changsoo Lee, ed., *Modernization of Korea and the Impact of the West* (Los Angeles: East Asian Studies Center, University of Southern California, 1981), pp. 204–5.

rates in Korean manufacturing over the next two decades—rates that greatly exceeded the extremely rapid growth in other sectors—soon propelled Korean manufacturing to a commanding position in an economy that already approached one-half the size of India's. In both countries, certainly, a few SOEs and local business groups spear-headed an unusual growth in manufacturing, but with phenomenal success in Korea!

State-Owned Enterprises

Although economic growth rates in India and South Korea diverged sharply after 1960, their institutional structures did not; in both economies the state emerged as a major entrepreneur. From its Japanese colonizers, Korea inherited several important state enter-prises, which greatly expanded operations during the 1960s.[27] By contrast, the British left India with few government corporations, and even after a decade of independence the state's entrepreneurial activities remained quite limited. During the 1960s, however, Indian state investments grew dramatically, until by 1972 SOEs in India contributed roughly the same share to the GDP as did SOEs in Korea (15 percent and 13 percent, respectively, of nonagricultural GDP).[28] By that year the state in both countries owned the five largest corporations, as well as a majority of the top twenty. Furthermore, the industrial origins of state production in the two countries appeared by 1972 to be "strikingly similar," to quote Leroy Jones, the leading analyst of SOEs in Korea.[29]

Especially noteworthy was the state's dominance over the financial sector. In both India and South Korea the nationalization of commercial banks, the establishment of other government financial institutions, and the regulation of private investments in financial services together guaranteed to the state control over access to domestic sources of debt.[30] This control took on added significance in India,

27. For a history of SOEs in Korea, see Leroy P. Jones, *Public Enterprise and Economic Development: The Korean Case* (Seoul: Korean Development Institute, 1975).

28. Leroy P. Jones and Edward S. Mason, "Role of Economic Factors in Determining the Size and Structure of the Public-Enterprise Sector in Less-Developed Countries with Mixed Economies," in Leroy P. Jones, ed., *Public Enterprise in Developing Countries* (Cambridge: Cambridge University Press, 1982), p. 21.

29. Quoted in Leroy Jones and Il Sakong, *Government, Business, and Entrepreneurship in Economic Development: The Korean Case* (Cambridge: Harvard University Press for the Harvard Council on East Asian Studies, 1980), p. 151. For further evidence, see Jones and Mason, "Economic Factors in Public Enterprise," pp. 21–22.

30. David C. Cole and Yung Chul Park, *Financial Development in Korea, 1945–1978*

where the government eschewed foreign commercial debt and failed to stimulate export earnings, relying instead on foreign aid for much of the country's foreign exchange. In Korea foreign aid payments, overseas commercial borrowings, and export earnings positioned the state as an intermediary between local enterprises and foreign lenders,[31] just as regulations on foreign equity inflows in both countries served to limit the financial options available to local enterprises. Consequently, in Korea, as in India, the state emerged during the 1960s and 1970s as the preeminent financier of national industrialization.

During the early 1980s, however, the similarities that Jones identifies had actually begun to dissipate. By then, the ten largest South Korean corporations all represented the private sector; they were not—as in India—enterprises of the state.[32] Indeed, among Korea's largest corporations, the state had actually sacrificed its ownership of two (Korean Oil, and Pohang Iron and Steel), which since had become "privatized." Here, sales of government shareholdings in Korean SOEs and a gradual diminution of government control over their management both contrasted sharply with the horizontal expansion and vertical integration taking place among Indian SOEs, which increasingly entered the same markets supplied by private enterprise in Korea. Finally, these contradictory trends emerged with special clarity in the financial markets: As the Indian government was completing its nationalization of that country's remaining commercial banks in 1980, the Korean government was just beginning to sell its shareholdings in that nation's five largest commercial banks and to encourage private expansion into other financial services. More specifically, in Korea local business groups proved to be the principal beneficiaries of these policy changes.[33]

(Cambridge: Harvard University Press for the Harvard Council on East Asian Studies, 1983).

31. Stephan Haggard and Tun-jen Cheng, "State and Foreign Capital in the East Asian NICs," in Frederic C. Deyo, ed., *The Political Economy of the New Asian Industrialism* (Ithaca: Cornell University Press, 1987), p. 112.

32. See, e.g., "The 500 Largest Corporations Outside the U.S.," pp. 180–205.

33. Indeed, as the Korean government "privatized" the country's five largest commercial banks and the national oil company *chaebol* bought most of the equity shares offered. See Seok Ki Kim, "Business Concentration and Government Policy: A Study of the Phenomenon of Business Groups in Korea, 1945–85" (DBA diss., Graduate School of Business Administration, Harvard University, 1987,) pp. 278–79, 286.

Local Business Groups

Just as state-owned enterprises in India and South Korea had much in common during the early 1970s, so too did local business groups. By 1972 Korea had spawned forty-six *chaebol*, which—like India's seventy-three business houses—controlled an ever-expanding number of diversified companies through shared managerial and financial resources, often reinforced by family ties.[34] Moreover, Indian business houses and Korean *chaebol* often grew in the same way, through the acquisition of former colonial (British or Japanese) enterprises. And after independence both national groups depended heavily on negotiations that yielded zero-sum transfers from the state, bargaining outcomes common to both countries. These included the selective allocation of import licenses and quotas for machinery and raw materials, plus the selective allocation of domestic credit and foreign exchange (including foreign aid). Here, success determined growth: Through 1984, for example, the ten largest Korean *chaebol* received nearly one-third of total outstanding domestic bank loans and payment guarantees, while the two largest (Samsung and Hyundai) together received nearly one-eighth.[35] These Korean figures are similar to those already reported for Indian business houses. In both India and Korea, local business groups, combining their own resources with government financing and aided by government import licenses, eventually gained control of roughly comparable shares of their national industrial economies. During the 1970s, according to Figure 5-5, in each nation the four largest business groups either controlled nearly one-seventh of total corporate assets (India) or contributed nearly one-seventh of total value added to the resources consumed in manufacturing (Korea). Thus, both national economies depended heavily on local business groups.

During the 1960s in India that dependence was even greater, when (in 1964) the top four business houses controlled nearly one-fifth of that country's corporate assets (and the largest seventy-three con-

34. For an early history of Korean *chaebol*, see Jones and Sakong, *Government, Business, and Entrepreneurship*, pp. 258–85; for an update, see Kim, "Business Concentration and Government Policy."

35. Data supplied by the Korean Ministry of Finance and reported in Kim, "Business Concentration and Government Policy," pp. 259–60. Note that the share of domestic credit secured by Korean *chaebol* far exceeded their value-added contribution to Korea's GNP; see the data supplied by Korea's Management Efficiency Institute and reported in ibid., pp. 2–3.

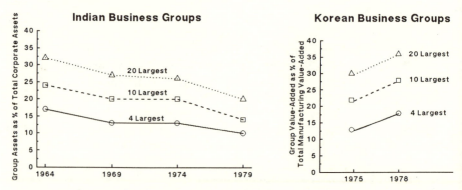

Figure 5-5. The concentration of "economic power" in India and Korea, 1964–1979
SOURCES: For India, 1964 data from India (Republic), Ministry of Finance, *Report of the Monopolies Inquiry Commission* (New Delhi: Manager of Publications, 1965), 1:119–22; 1969 and 1974 data same as for Figure 4-5, at Table 8.12; 1979 data same as for Figure 4-7 at pp. 18–25.
For South Korea, 1975 data from Leroy P. Jones and Il Sakong, *Government, Business, and Entrepreneurship in Economic Development: The Korean Case* (Cambridge: Harvard University Press for the Harvard Council on East Asian Studies, 1980), p. 268, Table 58; 1978 data from Il Sakong, "Kyang Jae Sung Jang Kwa Kyung Jae Jip Jung" (Economic growth and concentration of economic power), *Han Kook Kae Bal Yun Ku* (Korean Development Review), March 1980, pp. 2–13, as reported in Leroy P. Jones, "Jae-Bal and the Concentration of Economic Power in Korean Development: Issues, Evidence and Alternatives" (manuscript prepared under the auspices of the World Bank/UNDP Fifth Five-Year Plan Consultation Program for the Republic of Korea's Economic Planning Board and for the Korea Development Institute, Boston University, December 1980), p. 16, Table 2.

trolled nearly one-half[36]). By contrast, in South Korea, the twenty-three *chaebol* operating in 1961 remained relatively small. The largest of these, Samsung, comprised only thirteen companies, each dwarfed by Korean SOEs, whereas Tata, Samsung's counterpart in India, controlled at that time more than fifty companies, including the country's two largest. During the late 1970s, however, these positions simply reversed, as we can see from Figure 5-5: Korean *chaebol* controlled an even larger share of their national economy (during 1978) than did business houses in India (during 1979). So, by 1985 *chaebol* controlled nine of the ten largest corporations in Korea (the remaining large steel company was a recently privatized SOE),[37] while in India the state still owned all ten top enterprises, as it had done since the early 1970s.

Many of these Indian SOEs dominated industries that, during the

36. India (Government), Ministry of Finance, *Report of the Monopolies Inquiry Commission*, Vol. 1 (New Delhi: Manager of Publications, 1965), p. 121.
37. "The 500 Largest Corporations Outside the U.S.," pp. 180–205.

1970s, the South Korean government opened to only a few *chaebol*. More specifically, in heavy (electrical and nonelectrical) machinery, electronics, petrochemicals, and transport equipment (automobiles, locomotives, shipbuilding), the Korean government erected import restrictions while it dispersed licenses and cheap loans sparingly to the *chaebol* that then enjoyed either monopoly or dominant oligopoly status. As a result, by 1985 Korean *chaebol* concentrated fully 90 percent of their manufacturing assets in these heavy industries, up from 70 percent in 1972, when the government first targeted these industries.[38] During that same period, however, Indian SOEs monopolized domestic shipbuilding, maintained strong oligopolies in the production of heavy machinery of all types, and expanded aggressively into automobiles and electronics. The few Indian business houses that entered these industries secured government licenses and state financing to establish production capacities that may have satisfied plan targets but seldom achieved economies of scale in production for the protected home market. In Korea, by contrast, achieving scale economies increasingly became crucial to the government's export drive, as did improved access to foreign technology and overseas distribution channels, which were often controlled by multinationals.

Multinationals

Facing import quotas and capital controls as common impediments, multinationals have not enjoyed unrestricted access to resources and markets in either India or South Korea. Still, the large size of the protected Indian market, plus India's plentiful natural resources, together create a constant attraction to foreign investors, especially those interested in manufacturing. Korea provides a less attractive prize, however; and through the 1950s and 1960s it acquired less foreign capital, especially when opportunities for easy import substitution dwindled rapidly, in a small national market with limited resources. (In fact, before 1962, independent Korea attracted *no* foreign direct investment.[39]) Even after Korea departed from a sole reliance on import substitution and shifted in 1965 to an export-led industrialization strategy, multinationals responded slowly. Initial government incentives favored those sectors that employed mature technology, inexpensive labor, and little product differentiation, sec-

38. Data supplied by individual *chaebol* and reported in Kim, "Business Concentration and Government Policy," Table 4.14, p. 187, and Table 5.21, p. 267.
39. Westphal et al., "Foreign Factors in Korea's Industrialization," p. 203.

tors in which multinationals enjoyed few advantages. And in 1973 the government passed new regulations on foreign investment far stricter than those in the past—and, as noted above, far more stringent than those in all but a few other developing countries. Not until the mid- to late 1970s, therefore, did foreign direct investors discover South Korea—just when they began, coincidentally, to disinvest from India, during the implementation there of even stiffer foreign equity controls under FERA (see Table 1-1).

Under FERA regulations the Indian government sought to encourage multinationals to increase exports—the goals, as well, of Korea's minimum export requirements. The latter attained a greater success, however, in part because of special advantages—including government incentives—gained from using Korea as an export platform. Of the 857 foreign-owned projects in operation during 1978, for example, the Korean government insisted that more than one-half export at least 50 percent of their production.[40] By contrast, only one-quarter of these 857 projects were fully exempted from the government's minimum export requirements. As a result, during 1978 multinationals shipped over 18 percent of Korea's exports (up from 6 percent in 1971).[41] Here, Korea's principal (government-targeted) export sectors—electronics, and textiles and apparel—accounted for nearly four-fifths of multinationals' exports, and in 1978 they consumed nearly 30 percent of the total stock of foreign direct investment in Korea.[42] Another 30 percent of this investment produced chemicals, especially intermediate products (such as synthetic fibers and resins) targeted by government either for use in other exports or for bulk sales overseas.[43] As in India, chemicals and electronics represented the only sectors of the Korean economy in which multinationals continued to insist that foreign equity remain both tightly bundled with foreign technology and (in Korea, at least) integrated with downstream marketing.

Increasingly, however, technology licensing, local R&D, and alliances with downstream buyers obviated foreign direct investment in India and South Korea. Yet, in exploiting these options, the Koreans moved much faster than did the Indians. During 1977 and 1978, for

40. Ibid., p. 217.
41. For 1978 data, see Haggard and Cheng, "State and Foreign Capital," Table 1, p. 93; for 1971 data, see Westphal et al., "Foreign Factors in Korea's Industrialization," Table 6, p. 218.
42. Westphal et al., "Foreign Factors in Korea's Industrialization," pp. 218–19.
43. Haggard and Cheng, "State and Foreign Capital," pp. 95–97; also see Westphal et al., "Foreign Factors in Korea's Industrialization," pp. 204, 207.

example, combined royalty payments for foreign technology licensed in Korea exceeded India's total payments for foreign technology during the same period—and also exceeded the cumulative total in Korea for the preceding fifteen years.[44] With increased export earnings and foreign borrowings otherwise unavailable to India, Korea easily afforded these new licenses. Indeed, Koreans signed as many new technology agreements as did Indians during 1978,[45] even though Korea represented an economy only one-third as large as India's. Soon thereafter, enterprises in Korea combined technology licensing with increased expenditures on local R&D. In electronics alone, for example, local R&D in Korea consumed more than 3 percent of sales in 1983, twice the investment in 1979.[46] (In India, a comparable figure for 1981 was approximately 1 percent.[47]) Finally, in Korea buyers in export markets have supplied product designs and quality controls while specifying their orders and making plant inspections—critical sources of information unavailable to India's insulated manufacturers.[48] Korea's outward-looking policies involving finance, technology, and markets thus provided its industry with a competitive edge in world markets.

Economic Performance

Before South Korea began to look outside for help, that nation's economic performance mirrored India's achievements. During the 1950s, for example, the manufacturing sectors in both economies grew roughly 6 percent annually (in real terms) and contributed just one-seventh of each country's GDP (see Figure 5-4). Moreover, exports remained inconsequential to both economies, although, as late as 1965, India exported nine times more merchandise (as a percentage of its larger GDP) than did Korea (see Table 1-1). Thus, the early stages of import substitution in both India and Korea seemed to produce roughly comparable—if somewhat lackluster—results.

44. For Korean data, see Westphal et al., "Foreign Factors in Korea's Industrialization," p. 210; for Indian data, see Indian Investment Center, *Indian Economy at a Glance* (New Delhi, January 1984).

45. For Korean data, see Haggard and Cheng, "State and Foreign Capital," p. 124; for Indian data, see Figures 2-9 and 3-3.

46. Donald O'Connor, "Case Study of an Emerging Industry: Electronics in Korea," unpublished report prepared for the International Bank for Reconstruction and Development (March 26, 1986), p. 17.

47. Reserve Bank of India, *Foreign Collaboration in Indian Industry: Fourth Survey Report, 1985* (Bombay, 1985), pp. 81, 109, 136, 160, 178.

48. Westphal et al., "Foreign Factors in Korea's Industrialization," pp. 210–17.

However, soon after Korea adopted more outward-looking policies, such similarities in economic performance began to disappear. During the 1960s Korean manufacturing grew more than three times faster than did Indian industry, and it contributed an ever larger share of Korea's rapidly growing GDP (see Figure 5-4). Korean exports of manufactured goods also grew rapidly: By 1970 they amounted to nearly one-tenth of that country's GDP, compared with one-thirtieth of India's GDP. Citing such statistics, Isher Ahluwalia and other critics of India's economic performance began to look to Korean government policy as an attractive alternative, one that would bolster their claim that India must revise its economic strategy.[49]

Yet, several years after South Korea had implemented its version of expansionist policies, its overall strategy as well as the resulting industrial organization still looked about the same as India's. Indeed, these similarities (unlike the increasing disparity in performance) figured prominently in Bardhan's rebuttal of Ahluwalia,[50] which made clear some common policies: in both nations trade restrictions and capital controls continued to limit the access of multinationals to the domestic market. And the state remained the critical regulator, financier, and entrepreneur in an economy made up of a very few large public and private producers. Yet with little competition in the home market, heavy reliance on state production and resource allocation, and exceptionally low levels of foreign investment, Korea managed to engineer an economic miracle—while India, with basically the same policies, drew heavy criticism from Ahluwalia and others, who blamed those policies for lackluster national growth.[51] So what could account for the differences in performance?

By far the most important economic factor contributing to South Korea's remarkable industrial performance was its powerful export drive (cited by Ahluwalia as a model for Indian development[52]). By 1980 manufactured exports contributed more than one-quarter of Korea's GDP—nearly thirty times their share of the Indian economy (see Table 1-1). In export markets Korean *chaebol* encountered competition, which was otherwise less apparent in the domestic market—and virtually unknown to Indian enterprises. Such competition forced the Korean government to emphasize economies of scale in production, especially during its allocation of scarce licenses and capital. To achieve these same economies, Indian business houses typ-

49. Ahluwalia, *Industrial Growth in India*, pp. 163–64.
50. Bardhan, *Political Economy of Development in India*, pp. 71–74.
51. Ahluwalia, *Industrial Growth in India*, pp. 145–72.
52. Ibid., pp. 126, 163–64.

ically had to produce illegally in excess of licensed capacity, or to implement licenses and invest capital that could more profitably have been left underutilized. Finally, competition in export markets drove Korean *chaebol* to exploit every possible source of product and process technologies. Imports of machinery and other manufactured goods proliferated in Korea, as did technology licenses with potential foreign competitors and downstream alliances with overseas buyers—all paid for with export earnings and foreign borrowing.

Yet, as the costs of foreign technology shot up in South Korea, so did expenditures on local R&D. By contrast, in India business houses and SOEs with more limited financial resources and far less pressure from foreign competitors failed to exploit these locally generated technological alternatives with equal intensity. Put simply, every recent policy change in Korea—the privatization of SOEs, the relaxation of trade and foreign investment restrictions, and other such liberalizations lauded by Ahluwalia[53]—must be regarded as being of merely secondary importance to the incentives associated with exporting in explaining that nation's phenomenal growth.

Even after isolating its significance, the discipline of world market forces cannot alone account for complex national differences in economic performance. Equally relevant here, and perhaps even more complex, is wide variation across nations in the process of bargaining among the parties of the uneasy triangle. In Korea the state could dramatically shift from an inward- to an outward-looking development strategy because, in the words of Bardhan, "the framework of economic policymaking and implementation" had been "largely insulate[d]" from the multifarious "demands of the political process."[54] As a result, the state could—and did—favor a few local business groups at the expense of possible new entrants, and without fearing political repercussions. (Even in Brazil, Bardhan notes, "insulated parts of the state apparatus" became "extremely important in the implementation of growth-oriented policies."[55])

In India, after forty years of independence, the political situation remains unique, as Bardhan makes clear: "In a polyglot and vastly more heterogenous and fragmented society like that of India," the insulation of economic management has been "difficult to achieve and maintain alongside an open polity."[56] In fact, by tightly linking

---

53. Ibid., pp. 115–16, 159–60.
54. Bardhan, *Political Economy of Development in India*, p. 72.
55. Ibid., n. 12, p. 72.
56. Ibid., p. 73.

politics with economics, Bardhan convincingly refutes a recent argument by Lloyd and Susanne Rudolph: In India, they assert, "politics seems not to matter as much for economic performance as [we] would like to think."[57] My analysis suggests quite the contrary: for economic policy results from a process that is open—perhaps all too open—to the multiple, cross-cutting interests that so far have paralyzed the state and kept it from taking any *decisive* action that would change the basic rules of the Indian economic game. By themselves, those rules have drastically restricted national economic growth. For example, any proposal to improve relations between the state and Indian business houses based on the model of South Korea seems destined to produce negative political responses in India. In other words, the process of intense bargaining so characteristic of India's uneasy triangle actually has served to diminish prospects for fundamental reform of the nation's economic policies.

Without such basic political and economic reforms, however, every vision of an improved Indian economy remains dim, as that nation continues to incur exceedingly high costs for its development strategy. Among economic costs, excruciatingly slow growth, scarce supplies, high prices, and poor quality all remain endemic within a vast country plagued by widespread inefficiencies. Perhaps those inefficiencies could be justified if they also served to enhance social equity. But in India they do not. Rather, the same government policies that promote inefficiencies actually exacerbate inequities. For not only have these policies failed to "reduce the concentration of economic power in private hands"—as the MRTP Act of 1969 promised to do— but government regulation and state financing have also contributed to an increased concentration of private assets in a small number of Indian business houses. Certainly, the growth of these local conglomerates has often occurred at the expense of multinationals, much to the delight of Indian nationalists; and just so surely, their growth has not impeded the present domination of the "commanding heights" of national economic life by SOEs, to the equal delight of Indian socialists. Yet the legendary inefficiencies of most Indian state enterprises must finally bring into serious question their social value, just as a near exclusion of multinationals must raise doubts about national policies of technological choice, which so often have led Indian enterprises to reinvent the wheel, or to do without improvements. Studying India closely, we find almost no evidence of the traditional

---

57. Lloyd I. Rudolph and Susanne Hoeber Rudolph, *In Pursuit of Lakshmi: The Political Economy of the Indian State* (Chicago: University of Chicago Press, 1987), p. 224.

tradeoff between increased equity and improved efficiency. Rather, as India succeeded in dislodging multinationals, *both* equity and efficiency have been sacrificed—at extreme social cost.

THEORY REASSESSED

In terms of received theory, then, India remains a case as yet unexplained. Indeed, that country's failure to convert its bargaining successes into sustained economic growth runs contrary to the hopes and aspirations—if not the hypotheses—of all those dependency theorists who anxiously correlate reductions in foreign reliance with increases in local accumulation.[58] Yet, as another test of the dependency thesis, when compared with largely self-reliant India, dependent Brazil fares much better on most economic indicators. So, too, does Korea, perhaps because of its combination of self-reliance with a greater dependence (compared with India) on foreign finance, technology, and markets. Moreover, in the face of India's slow growth, the negotiated shifting of benefits from multinationals to their hosts—much heralded by bargaining theorists, who cite India as a model for other countries[59]—must actually be discounted to reflect a clear decline in the relative magnitude of those benefits. In short, the Indian case fails to corroborate the economic efficacy of negotiations among multinationals, the state, and local enterprises in developing countries—an efficacy touted by both bargaining and dependency theorists. For both schools of thought, India presents an unsolved puzzle.

The Dependency School

For a younger generation of dependency theorists, the Indian case proves especially enigmatic. When applied to India, their habitual pessimism about the likelihood of local enterprises and the state dislodging multinationals from domestic industries seems misplaced. In fact, contrary to many popular predictions (by Gereffi and Newfarmer, as well as Bennett and Sharpe[60]), the balance of bargaining

58. See, for example, Evans, *Dependent Development*, p. 276.
59. See, for example, Grieco, *Between Dependency and Autonomy*, pp. 3, 7.
60. Douglas C. Bennett and Kenneth E. Sharpe, "Agenda Setting and Bargaining Power: The Mexican State versus the International Automobile Industry," *World Politics* 32 (October 1979):86; Gary Gereffi, *The Pharmaceutical Industry and Dependence in the Third World* (Princeton: Princeton University Press, 1983), pp. 16–61; Gary Gereffi and Richard S. Newfarmer, "International Oligopoly and Uneven Development: Some Lessons from Industrial Case Studies," in Newfarmer, ed., *Profits, Progress and Poverty:*

power did *not* shift over time toward multinationals, even when (as these theorists have agreed) those multinationals were well established locally. Instead, Indian government institutions and Indian private enterprises (on the whole) overcame many of those economic and political constraints viewed by dependency theorists as insurmountable. Specifically, Indian institutions isolated foreigners politically and then eschewed integration globally; they also surmounted technological barriers by exploiting alternative sources at home and abroad—aided by the Soviet Union and by multinational competitors. Thus, the Indian case qualifies (and possibly refutes) a proposition central to the analysis of dependency.

Rather than force the "incremental . . . changes in multinational strategy" which Evans observed in Brazil, local enterprises and the state in India actually dislodged multinationals from national industries.[61] Even so, Evans does classify India among those "crucial cases" that "define the limits of dependent development."[62] In India, those limits—at least when measured by the distribution of bargaining power—seem far less certain than previously had been assumed. Moreover, the underlying causal model used to determine those limits in the past now must be called into question: Rather than being accepted as the primary *cause* of government policy and corporate strategy, dependency must be viewed instead as an *effect* of both policy and strategy. In truth, India simply became less dependent than Brazil on multinationals precisely *because* Indian business and the Indian government both followed sequentially a three-stage process to secure finance, technology, and markets. Here again, the Indian case forces a reassessment of all received theory, and especially of such critical analytical conventions as "dependency" and "dependent development."

Equally, the Indian case forces us to reassess the accepted logic of collective action that makes dependent development possible. Clearly, in India multinationals, the state, and local enterprises did *not* cooperate to form a triple alliance, although just such a cooperative arrangement did prevail, according to Peter Evans, in Brazil: "Over and above their differences," he writes, "is the[ir] consensus that all members of the alliance will benefit from the accumulation of industrial capital."[63] In India, however, such shared interests, rationally pur-

---

Case Studies of International Industries in Latin America (Notre Dame: University of Notre Dame Press, 1985), p. 432.

61. Evans, *Dependent Development*, p. 276.
62. Ibid., p. 51.
63. Ibid., pp. 11–12.

sued, did not result in collective action. Instead, as we have already seen, a variety of disincentives—free-rider problems, cross-cutting objectives, and the like—prevented all but a few highly interdependent, large conglomerates (such as Tata and Birla) from acting collectively. Moreover, even those business houses and unaffiliated companies that grew rapidly as a result of foreign financial and technological collaboration had little incentive to support the dismantling of a regulatory regime designed to erect barriers to the entry of future competitors—who might later employ foreign collaboration.

The original logic here was first set forth by Mancur Olson and applied to India more recently by Pranab Bardhan: "The inevitably crowded agenda and the weight of the pre-existing list of complex understandings in large lobbying coalitions make any negotiation on changing the basic rules of the game excruciatingly slow, and the incentives for plodding along . . . well-worn grooves . . . are too strong."[64] These general problems naturally grew more acute in a country of India's vast size and bewildering complexity of interests. As a result, multinationals in India could not count on forming a triple alliance with local enterprises and the state to bolster their bargaining power. Instead, as Kidron observed more than two decades ago, "foreign capital could count on being isolated whenever it attempted to retain or create a monopoly position for itself."[65] His conclusion later found support in the growing literature on bargaining.

The Bargaining School

Bargaining theorists have long questioned the claim that multinationals dominated the triple alliance, and more recently they have invoked the Indian case to uphold a proposition largely supported by my own research: Local enterprises and the state, on the whole, have increased their bargaining power over multinationals. That conclusion applies not only to natural resource industries, as Vernon and Moran have argued, but also to the manufacturing sector, as Grieco and this book have shown.[66] In industry after industry, existing con-

---

64. Bardhan, *Political Economy of Development in India*, p. 69; to support his conclusion Bardhan cites Mancur Olson, *The Rise and Decline of Nations: Economic Growth, Stagflation and Social Rigidities* (New Haven: Yale University Press, 1982).

65. Kidron, *Foreign Investments in India*, p. 181.

66. Raymond Vernon, *Sovereignty at Bay: The Multinational Spread of U.S. Enterprises* (New York: Basic Books, 1971); Theodore H. Moran, *Multinational Corporations and the Politics of Dependence: Copper in Chile* (Princeton: Princeton University Press, 1974); Grieco, *Between Dependency and Autonomy*.

tracts held by multinationals fall victim to a process known as the "obsolescing bargain" when local institutional innovations—private business groups, state industrial enterprises, public financial institutions, government regulatory agencies—can either substitute for multinationals or, at the very least, entice competing multinationals to vie for profitable opportunities in growing markets. Here, the Indian case seems to reaffirm a proposition central to the analysis of bargaining.

But only in part. Indeed, bargaining theorists have underestimated the phenomenal resilience of multinationals in the face of threats posed by both the state and local enterprises. Yet, this book—not to mention the literature on dependency—contains example after example of multinationals (including several from the same Indian computer industry studied by Grieco) that successfully acted to reverse the obsolescence of earlier bargains and then to minimize the possibilities of such obsolescence in the future. These multinationals traded local equity ownership for foreign managerial control, or they traded technology free of foreign equity for higher licensing fees and stricter contractual provisions—in other words, multinationals negotiated agreements that were advantageous both for themselves and for local institutions. These positive-sum agreements were not, of course, the only possible outcomes. To the contrary: India's "license-permit-quota Raj" typically yielded zero-sum distributions of government largess, rewarding a few firms at the expense of many. Faced with such unfavorable odds, most multinationals in India nevertheless succeeded in retaining a significant share of bargaining power, even as the state and local enterprises also advanced their own positions.

In turn, the relative bargaining power of these parties determined the creation and distribution of profits (and other private gains) to those specifically negotiating, as well as property rights (and similar collective benefits) to others *not* privy to the actual negotiations. Yet bargaining theorists have been reluctant to examine these additional benefits, despite the fact that economic nationalism, along with private and state capitalism, established broad rules that both govern the creation of property rights and determine which distributions of property (and other private gains) are permissible.[67] Just such rules

---

67. The failure of Vernon, Moran, and other bargaining theorists to examine property rights and similar rules appears in earlier criticisms of their work. See, for example, Bennett and Sharpe, "Agenda Setting and Bargaining Power," pp. 58–59; James A. Caporaso, "Introduction: Dependence and Dependency in the Global System," and "Dependence, Dependency, and Power in the Global System: A Structural and Behavioral Analysis," *International Organization* 32 (Winter 1978):1–12, 13–43.

have long been the concern of dependency theorists[68], and of negotiation analysts as well.[69] These latter analysts employ a more formal
logic to dissect and understand the processes and outcomes of bargaining. Yet, in the received literature on bargaining in developing
countries, these analysts have received surprisingly little attention, a
fact reflected in the failure of such literature to make its basic assumptions explicit and its definitions of bargaining power less tautological.[70]

Here, the work of Thomas Schelling and Howard Raiffa, David
Lax and James Sebenius, all negotiation analysts, demonstrates that
bargaining entails not only trading different endowments and capabilities for private gain but also sharing common interests in pursuit
of collective benefits.[71] In addition, by exploiting scale economies,
bargaining parties achieve both sets of outcomes. Among collective
benefits, property rights figure prominently. Among property rights,
rules that restrict foreign trade and investment have satisfied a widely
shared and long-standing belief in economic nationalism—the conviction that domestic ownership of assets, development of technology,
and control over markets convey both material and psychic benefits.[72]
In nationalistic terms, all these benefits are worth subsidizing at po-

---

68. Caporaso ("Introduction," p. 4) and, later, Gereffi (*Pharmaceutical Industry and
Dependence*, pp. 73–74), distinguish the "bargaining power" to control the outcomes of
distinct events from the "structural power" to govern the broad rules that shape
bargaining.

69. David A. Lax and James K. Sebenius, *The Manager as Negotiator: Bargaining for
Cooperative and Competitive Gain* (New York: Free Press, 1986), esp. pp. 6–11, 88–94,
106–7, 111–12.

70. According to both dependency and bargaining theorists, when multinationals
exercise power over the state and local enterprises, they can obtain an extremely good
deal from bargaining with these institutions; and these institutions, in turn, demonstrate power when they can extract an extremely good deal from their bargaining with
multinationals. So power appears inherent in the bargaining process. Yet, from such
analysis, how can we tell which party is the more powerful: multinationals or local
institutions?
Theorists of both persuasions answer that power is demonstrated when any party
obtains a good outcome from another. But defined this way, bargaining power, as
Thomas Schelling reminds us, "mean[s] only that negotiations are won by those who
win"; see his *Strategy of Conflict* (Cambridge: Harvard University Press, 1960), p. 22.
Indeed, as a result of using this tautological conception, the differences between power
and negotiated outcomes remain unclear in much existing literature.

71. In addition to the works cited in nn. 67 and 68, see Howard Raiffa, *The Art and
Science of Negotiation* (Cambridge: Belknap Press of Harvard University Press, 1982).

72. For a discussion of economic nationalism as a "collective benefit" or "public
good," see Harry G. Johnson, "A Theoretical Model of Economic Nationalism in New
and Developing States," *Political Science Quarterly* 80 (June 1965):172–77; for a similar
treatment, see Robert E. Baldwin, *The Political Economy of U.S. Import Policy* (Cambridge:
MIT Press, 1985), esp pp. 6–32.

tential public expense, measured in terms of higher prices, reduced quality, and supply scarcity. And, as we have noted above, such nationalistic economic policies have galvanized political coalitions in India far more readily than have policies promoting state or private capitalism. Yet, the politics of the policy process has too often been ignored.

One Possible Critique

After decrying the absence of any theory adequate to explain the policy process, Stephan Haggard introduces his own, which rightly reasserts the priority of politics in determining those state actions that shape a nation's dependence on foreigners.[73] In India, at least, such determinants long maintained their historical importance, which could be traced back to the origins of the national movement for political independence. At that time a powerful coalition of industrialists and political leaders joined in urging sharp reductions in the young country's reliance on foreign finance, technology, and markets. Over the first forty years of political independence only severe foreign exchange crises forced deviations from this national policy. The first such deviation occurred after the 1957 crisis; before the next major crisis, in 1966, however, that deviation had been fully reversed. Similarly, the national pattern in the 1970s and 1980s showed alternative periods of deviation and reversal. Still, except for periods of extreme foreign exchange crisis, the original coalition in India strongly supported the goal of self-reliance; it did not encourage dependence.

Of course, from time to time, some cracks in that coalition did appear—but only when unusual conditions prevailed. The first breach occurred when state enterprises encroached on Indian business houses. Then, beginning in the 1950s Tata and a few others sought common cause with supporters of private enterprise, including foreigners, but with only limited success. When, on the other hand, large business houses like Tata, with their superior assets, threatened smaller enterprises, these lesser upstarts also sought common cause with foreigners—and thus, beginning in the 1960s, they initiated a second crack in the dominant coalition. Here, independent companies and smaller business houses pressed for policy liberaliza-

73. Haggard, "Foreign Direct Investment and the Question of Dependency," and "The Newly Industrializing Countries in the International System," *World Politics* 38 (1986):343–70.

tions so that they might employ foreign technology and (less frequently) foreign capital to leapfrog over the larger, more conventional houses, which resisted these tie-ups. Limited to specific industries, these liberalizations seldom lasted very long, since new entrants typically reversed position quickly, to begin seeking renewed restrictions on potential competitors. Finally, during the 1970s and 1980s a third fissure in the dominant coalition emerged as Indian business houses gradually increased their trade and investment overseas. There, Indians encountered many of the same restrictions that foreigners faced in India, restrictions Indians now sought to modify abroad and, occasionally, at home (following a pattern well documented by Helen Milner in her examination of more industrialized countries[74]). Despite these three deviations, however, Indian enterprises and the Indian state largely managed to sustain the "political will"[75]—forged during India's original struggle for independence—necessary to dislodge multinationals from India's domestic industries.

To promote those industries and the goal of self-reliance, India adopted a strategy of import substitution devoid of export promotion, following a course consistent with Haggard's "theory of public policy." According to that theory, such strategic choices will ultimately determine the degree of any country's relative dependence on multinationals. To illustrate, Haggard compares Brazil and South Korea (among other countries) and goes on to declare: "The prolonged pursuit of ISI [import-substituting industrialization] was accompanied by a secular *increase* [emphasis in original] in aggregate dependence on foreign savings" in Brazil, while "the transition to export-led growth in Korea . . . was accompanied by a secular *decline* [again, emphasis in original] in [that] dependence." As a result, Haggard then concludes: "Import substitution itself created a *comparatively* [his emphasis] high level of dependence on foreign direct investment."[76] Associated with that investment, he argues (citing dependency theorists), are a variety of resources and skills, which "enhance the bargaining power of import-substituting [multinational] firms over time."[77]

---

74. Helen Milner, "Resisting the Protectionist Temptation: Industry and the Making of Trade Policy in France and the United States during the 1970s," *International Organization* 41 (Autumn 1987):637–65, and *Resisting the Protectionist Temptation: Industry Politics and Trade Policy in France and the U.S. in the 1920s and the 1970s* (Princeton: Princeton University Press, 1988).

75. The notion of political will has figured prominently in earlier studies of dependency; see, for example, Newfarmer, "An Introduction to the Issues," in Newfarmer, ed., *Profits, Poverty and Progress*, p. 6.

76. Haggard, "Foreign Direct Investment," p. 4, 6, 7.

77. Ibid., p. 64.

Thus, according to this line of reasoning, a strategy of import sub-stitution should ultimately limit the success of local enterprises and the state in developing countries as they seek to dislodge multination-als from the host market.

When Brazil is compared with South Korea, Haggard's conclusion may hold, but not when India is added to the comparison. Indeed, India pursued import substitution (unadulterated by the slightest hint of export-led growth) far longer than did Brazil, yet Indian depen-dence on foreign savings did not increase, contrary to his prediction. Instead, it declined, and that decline served, in turn, to reduce India's dependence on foreign direct investment—which soon fell far below the growing levels of investment in both import-substituting Brazil and export-oriented Korea (again, contrary to prediction). Of course, Haggard notes, countries following similar development strategies do vary in their reliance on multinationals, depending in part upon their foreign investment policies. These policies, in turn, reflect both local political alliances and local firm development.[78] Certainly, in theory, foreign investment policies based on disparate underlying causes should not negate the impact of any country's development strategy, but they do! For example, beginning in the mid-1970s Korea stood somewhere between Brazil and India in terms of restrictions on for-eign direct investment and, correspondingly, dependence on that in-vestment. Yet, at the two extremes on these continua (between most and least restrictive, and between most and least dependent), Brazil and India followed comparable import-substitution strategies. Thus, considered alongside Haggard's "theory of public policy," the results of the Indian case prove baffling.

My Alternative Explanation

To explain why two countries that adopted comparable develop-ment strategies—Brazil and India—finally achieved very different levels of success in dislodging multinationals, I have constructed an alternative model—one that also accounts for the important sim-ilarities between import-substituting India and export-oriented Korea. My own formulation (tracing the path of earlier theorists, and especially beholden to formal negotiation analysts) underscores the importance of bargaining—that rational calculus pursued by interde-pendent and potentially conflicting parties, who actively seek to create and distribute both private gains and collective benefits. Here, I can-

78. Ibid., p. 7.

not overemphasize the importance of local institutional innovations, a significance that has been evident to both bargaining and dependency theorists.

Most of this earlier commentary, however, has focused attention almost exclusively on state innovations—industrial enterprises, financial institutions, regulatory agencies—to the neglect of private innovations. Certainly, the public sector did play a major role. State financial institutions employed economies of scale successfully to mobilize and distribute the capital necessary for new investments in plant and equipment. In India (and South Korea) their success obviated much of the need to bargain with multinationals for access to finance, making joint ventures with state industrial enterprises rare. These enterprises, in turn, employed this capital (supplemented by occasional nationalizations) to expand horizontally and integrate vertically into markets coveted, if not already controlled, by foreigners. Access to these markets remained under the control of state regulatory agencies, as did permission to import or license technology from abroad. With growing control, the state in industry after industry gradually increased its bargaining power over multinationals—meaning that the state improved both the range of outcomes it could secure and the probability of securing the one outcome it preferred. Finally, using that enlarged bargaining power, the state through its several institutional innovations in India—as in Brazil and South Korea—acted to dislodge multinationals.

So did the forces representing private institutional innovations—most notably, local business groups. What now seems clear is that all existing literature simply fails to accord these local groups the attention they deserve, largely because so much of that literature relies primarily on the experiences of Brazil (and other countries) where *grupos* remained the vestigial wing, both in a private sector dominated by multinationals and in a national economy dominated by the state. But unlike Brazil, in India and Korea business houses and *chaebol* bargained successfully with state financial institutions and regulatory agencies for access to finance and technology, and ultimately for control over those domestic markets not reserved to the state. These successes bolstered the potency of such groups in their bargaining with multinationals until, in both countries, business houses and *chaebol* became as likely as state enterprises—indeed, became even more likely—to dislodge multinationals from the domestic market.

Note that this success was *not* dependent upon competition among multinationals or growth in the domestic market, two conditions considered necessary by bargaining theorists. Nor was their success dependent on low technological barriers to entry, as dependency theorists claim. Although these conditions could—and did—accelerate the demise of multinationals, even in their absence local business groups succeeded in controlling markets in India and Korea otherwise controlled by multinationals in Brazil. Domestic political alliances and global economic integration—two other conditions also cited by dependency theorists—could have posed far more important obstacles, but already we have seen how India's political history and development strategy negated their impact. (Even South Korea's historically greater dependence on foreign markets and military alliances did not grant multinationals a local presence comparable to their dominance in Brazil.) Finally, and contrary to Haggard's predictions: India's import-substitution strategy posed no real impediment to that country's effort to dislodge multinationals, just as Korea's export-led strategy offered no real bargaining advantages otherwise unrealized in India. In short, existing theory *cannot* explain why business houses in India and *chaebol* in Korea slowly overcame the same problems that proved crippling to Brazilian *grupos*. Even more important, it cannot explain why business houses finally dislodged multinationals from one Indian industry after another.

To explain variations observed over time, across industries, and among countries, I have proposed that Indian business houses—as well as state enterprises and other local firms—followed a three-stage sequence. First, by exploiting economies of scale to mobilize and distribute capital, Indian houses became financially independent and managerially autonomous. Earlier, Indian houses had bargained their market knowledge, distribution channels, and management skills in exchange for multinationals' finance and technology. But now, aided by state financial institutions, Indian houses initiated a second stage in their negotiations with multinationals, when they no longer had to secure foreign technology bundled with foreign equity. With foreign technology licenses replacing joint ventures and indigenous technology replacing foreign products and processes, Indian business houses—aided now by government regulatory agencies— entered a third stage in which they acquired control over markets previously dominated by multinationals and other foreigners. As their control spread from finance to technology and, finally, to markets, Indian business houses gradually increased their bargaining power over multinationals—improving at each stage the probability of securing their preferred outcome from a growing range of possibilities. Korean *chaebol*, I have shown, followed a similar pattern and—like the Indian business house—proved finally capable of dislodging multinationals from domestic industries.

Politics figured prominently in this causal sequence, as Indian business houses and multinationals both tried to secure private gains and collective benefits from the state, and as the state's several agents placed claims on these private institutions and on one another. Often, I have modeled these transactions as simple trades: Just as all enterprises in India depended on the state for permits and capital, so government regulators and public financiers depended on these enterprises to achieve a reduction in imports (or another objective that Parliament had designated). Members of Parliament, in turn, depended on these enterprises for campaign financing and jobs for constituents back home. These were exchanged for privileged access within the "license-permit-quota Raj." Here, Indian business houses enjoyed peculiar advantages, by exploiting the political equivalent of scale economies: Their "industrial embassies" lobbied for specific actions, which worked to establish property rights and other broad rules that helped to shape all subsequent bargaining. These collective benefits, they also sought (albeit less frequently) through industry associations and political parties, which together provided additional legitimacy and power in support of shared interests. (By contrast, in Brazil, the military regime that dominated politics for much of our period had fewer organic ties with *grupos*, while in Korea, *chaebol* enjoyed an even more privileged position than did Indian business houses.) With such political power, Indian business houses, like their counterparts in South Korea, worked to dislodge multinationals from the domestic market. And the Indians largely succeeded.

But the same political factors that gave rise to India's bargaining successes also caused a national economic demise. I believe (following Pranab Bardhan) that the process of hard bargaining in India has paralyzed the state and made local enterprises blind to the need for fundamental reforms in the nation's economic policies. (To the present, we have seen only short-lived sectoral reforms.) Such fundamental reforms will have to address the other cause of India's slow economic growth—the absence of any serious discipline based on market forces. That discipline need not replace local enterprises with multinationals, as it so often did in Brazil; instead, the discipline of the international market can also be harnessed by national enterprises, as South Korea amply demonstrates. But in the absence of such market discipline, and of any policy process suited to crafting such fundamental reforms, the "miracle" growth achieved by these other newly industrializing countries will continue to elude India.

Index

227

Library of Congress Cataloging-in-Publication Data

Encarnation, Dennis J.
   Dislodging multinationals : India's strategy in comparative perspective / Dennis
J. Encarnation.
      p.   cm. — (Cornell studies in political economy)
   Includes bibliographies and index.
   ISBN 0-8014-2315-5 (alk. paper)
      1. International business enterprises—Government policy—India.
   2. Investments, Foreign—Government policy—India.   3. Industry and state—
   India.   4. International business enterprises—Government policy—Brazil.   5.
   International business enterprises—Government policy—Korea (South)   I.
   Title.   II. Series.
HD2900.E53   1989
338.8'8854—dc 19   89-730

Cornell Studies in Political Economy

EDITED BY PETER J. KATZENSTEIN